The face of fashion

This book breaks new ground in the study of fashion and the body by establishing the relations between codes and systems of clothing and the conduct of everyday life. The author questions the trickle-down theory that fashion is dictated by elite designers and opinion leaders with evidence of a trickle-up effect from sub-cultures, mass consumer behaviour and the everyday bricolage of fashion items. The book addresses the neglected area of men's fashion as well as women's fashion within a broad examination of the role of fashion in gender identity.

The argument is developed through a number of key agencies and processes: consumerism and everyday fashion, the iconisation of the body through fashion models and photography, the use of cosmetics to 'make-up' the body, the nexus between fashion and gender and the changing fashions in underwear and swim-wear as maps of the revealed body. The topics are approached from an inter-disciplinary perspective that treats fashion systems as ethnographic traces of the cultural projection of the body.

Jennifer Craik is Senior Lecturer in Film and Media Studies and Deputy Director of the Institute for Cultural Policy Studies at Griffith University, Brisbane.

The face of fashion

Cultural studies in fashion

Jennifer Craik

London and New York

First published 1994
by Routledge
11 New Fetter Lane, London EC4P 4EE

Simultaneously published in the USA and Canada
by Routledge
29 West 35th Street, New York, NY 10001

Typeset in Times by LaserScript, Mitcham, Surrey
Printed and bound in Great Britain by
Biddles Ltd, Guildford and King's Lynn

British Library Cataloguing in Publication Data
A catalogue record for this book is available from the British Library.

Library of Congress Cataloging in Publication Data
Craik, Jennifer.
  The face of fashion: cultural studies in fashion/Jennifer Craik.
  p. cm.
  Includes bibliographical references and index.
  1. Costume – Social aspects. 2. Fashion. 3. Body, Human –
  Social aspects. I. Title.
  GT525.C73   1993
  391 – dc20   93-10546
                                                              CIP

ISBN 0–415–05261–0
     0–415–05262–9 (pbk)

Contents

Figures

Preface

Fashion is perplexing, intriguing, irritating and, above all, compulsive. Like it or not, fashion exerts a powerful hold over people – even those who eschew it. While reactions to fashion are ambivalent, there is no doubt that clothes matter. The old adage that clothes maketh the 'person' still counts, while the wrong look for a particular occasion can have disastrous consequences. But how are knowledges about appropriate dress codes acquired? How are everyday codes of dress constructed and modified by new styles? How do the ways we clothe the body contribute to the performance of the 'self' or person? Indeed, why does fashion matter so much, why does it matter at all?

The Face of Fashion tackles these issues. Above all, the book explores the relationships between high (elite designer) fashion and everyday fashion (clothing behaviour in general). By high fashion, I mean prevailing modes and styles, while everyday fashion refers to the lexicon of dress and techniques of selection, combination and embellishment. Such relationships are often complex, disjointed or oppositional. The interconnections between high fashion and everyday fashion are still only partially understood. This book analyses some of the relationships and tensions between those domains, while seeking to acknowledge the influence of everyday fashion on other forms of fashion.

But what is meant by the term 'fashion'? Histories of fashion and records of western clothing systems are usually centred around high fashion (*haute couture* or elite designer fashion) which become designated retrospectively as *the* norm of fashions of the moment. Hence, the mini-skirt stands for the swinging 1960s while tight-laced corsets epitomise the Victorian era.

Yet fashion behaviour is far less exclusive, more pervasive and more perverse than the world of high fashion can accommodate. Everyday fashion (dress codes, a sense of fashionability) does not simply 'trickle down' from the dictates of the self-proclaimed elite. At best, a particular mode may tap into everyday sensibilities and be popularised. Often, street fashion ignores designer innovations or belatedly takes up only certain elements.

Meanwhile, designers are constantly searching for new ideas, themes and motifs from historical dress, non-European dress, popular culture and sub-cultures. Like birds of prey, they rob the nests of other fashion systems in a process of appropriation and cannibalisation. These stylistic motifs are then reconstituted in a process of *bricolage*, the creation of new patterns and modes from the kaleidoscopic bits and pieces of cultural debris (see Poole 1973: 50–2).

So, why has the term 'fashion' been used as an exclusive description of western elite fashion? And why is 'fashion' distinguished from terms such as 'costume', 'uniform', 'folk' and 'ethnic' dress? Fashion is associated with the rise of mercantile capitalism in Europe at the end of the Middle Ages (e.g. Wilson 1985: 3; König 1973: 139). The economic formations of Europe established the conditions for rapidly changing cultural forms. Thus, the hallmark of fashion is said to be change: a continual and arbitrary succession of new styles and modes that render previous fashions obsolete. Fashion is conceived as an authoritarian process driven by a recognised elite core of designers dictating the fashion behaviour of the majority:

> Fashion is the imposition of a prevailing mode or shape. It is a largely arbitrary imposition and it precludes all other modes or shapes although, of course, variations on the basic theme are permitted.
>
> (McDowell 1984: 9)

For example, the western high-fashion system is constituted by a group of fashion dictators; a mass of passive imitators and consumers; rule-bound behaviour (with appropriate rewards for adherence and punishments for transgression); an equation of fashionable statements with qualities of 'success, importance, attractions and desirability' (McDowell 1984: 9); indulgent distinction from the majority; and the visible index of power and status. In other words,

> Clothes were a tool of oppression, a weapon wielded against the poor. They were used to drive home the lesson that the grand were not simply different, they were better, *because* they were rich. They wore on their backs the proof that they were superior intellectually, morally and socially.
>
> (McDowell 1984: 10)

In short, the western fashion system goes hand-in-hand with the exercise of power. But this is also true for other fashion systems. All fashion systems demonstrate the cultural politics of their milieu. The question posed by this book is whether fashion can be confined to the development of European fashion. Fashion histories frequently offer a teleological account of fashion as if it were an unfolding cultural map with a design or purpose (usually invoking modernity, civilisation or individuality). But is the history of European high fashion so seamless? Are competing and contradictory fashion histories waiting to be written?

The exercise of power cannot simply be associated with the unfolding development of modern consumer capitalism. Even western fashion is not just an annex to power relations in capitalist societies. Capitalism and cultural politics display different loci of power and fashion responds to them in various and changing ways. Hence the underlying theme of this book is that the term 'fashion' needs revision. Fashion should not be equated with modern European high fashion. Nor are fashion systems confined to a particular economic or cultural set of arrangements. Rather European high (elite designer) fashion is one specific variant of fashion. Although it may dominate popular consciousness about fashion, other fashion systems co-exist, compete and interact with it. These incorporate other elite designer systems, for example, European settler (post-colonial) cultures; as well as non-European cultures; and non-capitalist cultures. In short, the term fashion should be dissolved and reconstituted.

By displacing the European-dictator (ethnocentric or cultural superiority) model of fashion, the field of inquiry multiplies alarmingly, but it also makes the process more dynamic and sensitive to local variations. Above all, it allows fashion to be conceived as a cultural technology that is purpose-built for specific locations. This revised idea of fashion systems entails systematic and changing styles of dress, adornment and conduct; 'grammars' of fashion (bodies of rules and forms) that underpin codes of dress behaviour; consensual denotations of power, status and social location; and recognised codes of self-formation through the clothes and bodily adornment.

Thus, one of the central arguments of this book is that western fashion is not unique. This argument runs counter to that of many commentators who portray western fashion as a grand and peculiar practice. Indeed, one of the most noticeable characteristics of western fashion is the *investment* in it as unique and different. This investment is perpetuated by the elite (couture) design system (especially, though not exclusively, in Paris, New York, Milan, Tokyo and London) and the assumption that the creative brilliance of individual designers alone can capture the imagination of a given moment.

The Face of Fashion recasts the phenomenon of fashion. It distinguishes elite fashion from everyday fashion rather than assuming a particular derivation. While elite fashion is appropriately related to the cultural impulses of the era within economic and political conditions, systems of everyday fashion are more accurately compared with other fashion systems, including those in non-European and non-capitalist cultures.

Everyday fashion plays an important role in the lives of most people. Systems of fashion and cycles of popularity percolate through contemporary life. Styles, conventions, and dress codes can be identified in all groups, including sub-cultures, ethnic groups, alternative lifestyles, workplace and leisure cultures, and in all the mundane places and institutions of everyday life. While some parts of the everyday fashion system are directly attuned to elite fashion codes, most aspects have an indirect, oppositional or remote relationship with elite fashion. There is little in common between a secretary, homemaker or law-enforcement officer and a *habitué* of the seasonal Paris collections. To the latter, clothes are, indeed, 'the poster for one's act' but to the former, clothes are predominantly shaped by one's 'rank, profession or trade', characteristics which Wilson allocates to 'pre-industrial' clothing (Wilson 1985:242).

The Face of Fashion considers everyday fashion in an ethnographic way, drawing on parallels with studies of non-western dress and body decoration. Several themes are exemplified through studies of some key elements of every-day fashion – the play of exoticism in fashion; the formation of femininity and masculinity through body/clothes relations; the iconisation of fashion through fashion models and conventions of fashion photography; tensions between revela-tion and concealment in underwear and swimwear; technologies of cosmetics; and the contours of consumer fashion systems.

These are indicative rather than definitive studies, combining historical overviews, cultural and sociological interpretations, and readings of fashion phenomena. Because many areas of non-elite fashion have been researched only superficially, some of the topics addressed in this book have drawn on a variety of materials, including media and popular accounts. Although the number of detailed historical studies of particular topics is increasing, the selection of topics is often idiosyncratic and patchy. Hence, this book endeavours to piece together fashion histories and sift available material in order to map various fields of fashion practice as groundwork for the level of analysis outlined in Chapter 1. The readings offered here are starting-points for students of fashion to expand, revise and embellish.

In accordance with this approach, *The Face of Fashion* adopts an inter-disciplinary perspective, incorporating cultural studies, anthropology, sociology, art history and social history. The central concern of *The Face of Fashion* is how fashion systems are shaped by and, in turn, shape social conduct.

Acknowledgements

This book has been a long time in gestation and I am indebted to many people who have encouraged its production. Above all, thanks are due to Chris Rojek of Routledge who proposed the book. Not only did he have faith that the book would eventually materialise, but his enthusiasm and helpful comments facilitated the process of writing. The assistance of Anne Gee and Angie Doran in guiding the manuscript through the process of production has also been greatly appreciated. For partly funding the research, I am grateful to the Faculty of Humanities, Griffith University, especially Julie James Bailey, Judith Hoey, Greg Burns and Rhonda Henderson. The staff of the Australian National Gallery library and the Inter-Library Loan section of Griffith University Library have been extremely helpful in finding elusive material.

Rod Rhodes, Neil Carter, Judy Evans, Haleh Afshar and the administrative staff of the Department of Politics, University of York, generously provided facilities, assistance and enthusiasm during a period of leave, which enabled me to edit the manuscript. The research assistance of Frances Somers, Julie Morrison and Lisa Denomme has been invaluable, while Robyn Pratten, Olwen Schubert and Karen Yarrow have typed and prepared the manuscript with their usual efficiency and patience. Thanks also to Erinn Wanna for help with the index and to Heather Hill for help with proofreading.

The support of many colleagues over the long life of the project has been appreciated. They include Beverley Brown, Bernardo Ceriani, Bonnie English, Anne Freadman, John Frow, Denise Meredyth, Jeffrey Minson, Albert Moran, Lyndall Ryan, Lydia Staiano, Lesley Stern, Graham Turner and Gillian Whitlock. A number of colleagues agreed to read parts of the manuscript and offered invaluable advice of an improving nature. My sincere thanks to Tony Bennett, Glyn Davis, Margaret Gardner, Cathy Greenfield, Toby Miller, Francie Oppel, Gail Reekie, Peter Williams, and especially to John Wanna, Ian Hunter and David Saunders. The usual caveat applies.

Robyn Beeche kindly gave permission to reproduce her photograph, *Sonia*, for the cover; and Olwyn Schubert has generously provided photographs of her fashionable, far-flung forebears. I am also grateful to Photographic Services at Griffith University for reproducing the illustrations, and to all of those who have kindly given permission to reproduce illustrations. Although efforts have been made to contact all holders of copyright, where this has not been possible, they may contact the publishers.

Above all, I am indebted to John and Erinn Wanna, who have endured the process of production with encouragement, patience and – amazingly – good humour.

ILLUSTRATIONS

Picture credits are acknowledged as follows:

Illustrations 1.1, 1.2, 3.1, 3.2, 6.9, 6.10, 6.11, 6.12, 6.13, 8.1, 8.2, 8.3, 9.2, 9.3, 9.4, Olwen Schubert; 2.1, Wintergarden Centre, Brisbane; 2.2, Deepam Silk International, Bangalore; 2.3, R.V. Pandit, Bombay; 2.4, 6.1, 6.2, Board of Trustees, Victoria and Albert Museum, London; 2.5, Issey Miyake; 3.3, Orbis Books/ Little, Brown & Company, London; 3.4, 5.5, Australian Consolidated Press, Sydney; 4.1, Time Inc., New York; 5.1, 5.2, 5.3, Cintra Galleries, Brisbane; 5.4, Patrick Russell, *Vogue* Australia and Condé Nast Publications Pty Ltd; 6.3, Trustees of York Castle Museum; 6.4, Lincoln Underwear; 6.5, Wong Industries; 6.6, Lovable; 6.7, Myer Stores Limited, Melbourne; 6.8, Jil, France; 6.14, Ken Done, Sydney; 6.15, Andrew Rankin and *The Australian Magazine*, Sydney; 7.1, Proctor and Gamble; 7.2, Guerlain Perfume; 7.3, Yves Saint Laurent Perfume; 7.4, Austrabelle, Sydney; 8.4, Versace; 8.5, Van Gils, Melbourne; 8.6, Peter Hillary, Lacoste and Sportscraft; 9.1, Emporio Armani; 9.5, Country Road Australia; 9.6, Phillip Whelan and Joe Bloggs.

Chapter 1

The face of fashion
Technical bodies and technologies of self

FASHIONING BODY TECHNIQUES

> From a simple masquerade to the mask, from a 'role' (*personnage*) to a 'person' (*personne*), to a name, to an individual; from the latter to a being possessing metaphysical and moral value; from a moral consciousness to a scared being; from the latter to a fundamental form of thought and action – the course is complete.
>
> (Mauss 1985: 22)

Fashion is often thought of as a kind of mask disguising the 'true' nature of the body or person. It is seen as a superficial gloss. Yet, if we follow Mauss (1973, 1985) and Bourdieu (1986), we can regard the ways in which we clothe the body as an active process or technical means for constructing and presenting a bodily self. Western fashion (elite or high fashion) is a particular variant of this in which the designer plays the role of definer. The 'life' of the body is played out through the technical arrangement of clothes, adornment and gesture. This relationship was recognised by poet Blaise Cendars in his poem *The Simultaneous Dress*, written, in 1914, for artist and designer Sonia Delaunay:

> On her dress she wears a body.
> Woman's body is as bumpy as my skull
> Glorious if you are made flesh
> With Spirit.
> Couturiers have a foolish profession
> As foolish as phrenology
> My eyes are kilos weighing the sensuality of women.
> All things that swell advance in depth
> The stars hollow out the sky.
> Colours disrobe by contrast.
> 'On her dress she wears a body.'
>
> Under the heather's arm
> lurk shades of lunala and pistils

When the waters swirl down the back over sea-green
shoulder blades
And the double conch of the breasts passes beneath
the bridge of the rainbow

Belly
Discs
Sun
And the perpendicular cries of colour fall on the
thighs
Sword of Saint Michael
There are hands stretching out
The drapes conceal the trick – all the eyes, all the
flourishes and all the habits of the Bal Bullier
And on the hip
The poet's signature.

(Cohen 1975: 79)

Cendars's theme, that women wear their bodies through their clothes, is central to *The Face of Fashion*. Delaunay's approach to clothes was revolutionary. She combined her interest in the 1920s art movements of cubism, futurism and fauvism with a belief that women's clothes should suit their new lifestyles. Accordingly, Delaunay favoured simple practical lines of clothing which followed the shape of the female body (rather than dictating it). But she then took the surface of the fabric and the way in which it draped the body as a canvas on which she designed unique body paintings. In anticipation of Roland Barthes, she transformed the female body into maps of vectors, forces and dynamic movements. Her clothes were characterised by bold geometric patterns and colours that followed the bodily vectors, reminiscent of her canvases. This approach to clothing influenced subsequent trends in the fashion industry, although Delaunay's outspoken views about women's autonomy in their clothing were somewhat lost. Her designs do suggest new ways to look at the phenomenon of fashion.

The starting-point of this book is the dissolution and reconstitution of the term fashion. While acknowledging that not all clothing is fashion, all clothing systems have at least a distant relationship with fashion systems and stylistic conventions. For example, military, religious and legal clothing can be related to earlier dress codes where associations of tradition, authority, order, distinctiveness and hierarchy – even intimidation – are deliberately invoked. Moreover, such clothes do change over time – albeit slowly – with considerable thought going into the design of new regalia. The excessive western-style military uniforms adopted by many contemporary military regimes underline the fact that even these garments are directly infuenced by fashion.

A recent example has been the ordination of women, necessitating the creation of special clerical robes. In Australia, these red, flowing, yoked surplices featured a broad frontal panel decorated with a design chosen by each woman – a concession to women's interest in fashion, perhaps. While women have adopted this variation on traditional garb for church services, they are wearing other outfits (more like a corporate wardrobe) for their non-pulpit duties. In anticipation of this, the *Sydney Morning Herald Good Weekend Magazine* asked three leading designers to suggest appropriate outfits (Stead n.d.). Their designs combined style with practicality.

Adele Palmer described her mix-and-match array of pants, shirt, jacket and coat dress, in finely pinstriped black wool, as 'a fairly demure outlook with a certain reverent attitude'. Jill Fitzsimon proposed a longline jacket and 'modest but fashionable' length skirt in mid-grey wool teamed with a white 'draped neckline blouse' featuring 'a delicate random blue cross print – a chic alternative to the dog collar'. Linda Jackson's choice was 'an intense blue' wool or linen suit, consisting of a straight skirt and long-line single-breasted jacket buttoned to the neck. A matching white blouse featured a dog-collar neckline. She also designed a cyclamen pink smock for more formal occasions.

The designs attempted to balance the austerity of religious garb with the conventions of career dress, yet also incorporate elements of high fashion. Thus, all the designs featured a collar (variations on the dog collar) or incorporated a high neckline, 'modest' skirt or jacket length, and the insignia (a cross) of office (as jewellery or patterned the fabric). Each designer stressed the need to create identifiable and distinctive outfits which displayed a symbol of religious ministry. This example illustrates how the clothing of women clergy constitutes a technical means of fulfilling an occupational role by clothing the body to produce particular practical, social and gestural effects. The bricolage of fashion systems combined in these designs suggests that fashion systems interact and compete in the production of appropriate garb.

The viewpoint adopted here rejects the assumption that fashion is unique to the culture of capitalism. That argument draws on the work of Simmel (1973) and Veblen (1970) who explicitly linked the development of fashion to the emergence of discourses of individualism, class, civilisation and consumerism. Moreover, this concept of fashion is specifically European or western, and is differentiated from the clothing behaviour of other cultures. Simmel's views have grounded subsequent work. He argued that:

> This motive of foreignness, which fashion employs in its socialising endeavours, is restricted to higher civilisation, because novelty, which foreign origin guarantees in extreme form is often regarded by primitive races as an evil. This is certainly one of the reasons why primitive conditions of life favour a correspondingly infrequent change of fashions. The savage is afraid of strange appearances; the difficulties and dangers that beset his career cause him to scent danger in anything new which he does not understand and which he cannot consign to a familiar category. Civilisation, however, transforms this affection into its very opposite. Whatever is exceptional, bizarre, or conspicuous, or whatever departs from the customary norm, exercises a peculiar

charm upon the man of culture, entirely independent of its material justifi-
cation. The removal of the feeling of insecurity with reference to all things
new was accomplished by the progress of civilisation.

(Simmel 1973: 176)

Treating fashion as a marker of civilisation, with all its attendant attributes, is the
reason why fashion has been excluded from the repertoires of non-western
cultures. Other codes of clothing behaviour are relegated to the realm of costume
which, as 'pre-civilised' behaviour, is characterised in opposition to fashion, as
traditional, unchanging, fixed by social status, and group-oriented.

This theoretical framework, with its rigid distincion between traditional and
modern, has produced a remarkably inflexible and unchanging analysis of
fashion. Moreover, it fails to account for the circulation of changing clothing
codes and stylistic registers in non-European societies. The relation of bodies to
clothes is far deeper than the equation of fashion with the superficial products of
'consumer culture' allows. Clothing is neither simply functional nor symbolic in
the conventional senses.

Clothing does a good deal more than simply clad the body for warmth, modesty
or comfort. Codes of dress are technical devices which articulate the relationship
between a particular body and its lived milieu, the space occupied by bodies and
constituted by bodily actions. In other words, clothes construct a personal *habitus*.

'Habitus' refers to specialised techniques and ingrained knowledges which
enable people to negotiate the different departments of existence. Habitus includes
'the unconscious dispositions, the classification schemes, taken-for-granted
preferences which are evident in the individual's sense of the appropriateness and
validity of his [*sic*] taste for cultural goods and practices' as well as being
'inscribed on to the body' through body techniques and modes of self-
presentation (Featherstone 1987: 64).

The body, as a physical form, is trained to manifest particular postures,
movements and gestures. The body is a natural form that is culturally primed to
fit its occupancy of a chosen social group. Body trainings create certain possibilities (such as special skills, knowledges, physical disciplines), impose constraints
(such as not spitting, not slouching, not being naked) in the process of acquiring
a range of body habits that are expected and taken for granted in a particular
cultural milieu. They form part of a 'habitus' – simultaneously a set of habits and
a space inhabited, as a way of being in the world. Rules and codes are inhabited
through the prohibitions and transgressions. Bodies are worn through technologies of movement, restraint, gesture and projection.

Equally, the habitus occupied by the body imposes expectations, conventions
and skills as being essential for operating in specific technically organised
environments. Thus, bodies are 'made up' in both senses of the term –
constructed through the acquisition of body techniques, and known through the
ways in which they are made presentable in habituses or living environments.
Techniques of fashioning the body are a visible and primary denotative form of

acculturation, that is to say, we use the way we wear our bodies to present ourselves to our social environment, mapping out our codes of conduct through our fashion behaviour. Our habitus of clothing creates a 'face' which positively constructs an identity rather than disguising a 'natural' body or 'real' identity.

In this sense, fashion is a technology of *civility*, that is, sanctioned codes of conduct in the practices of self-formation and self-presentation. The body is trained to perform in socially acceptable ways by harnessing movement, gesture and demeanour until they become 'second nature'. Nonetheless, there is a tension between unstructured and untrained impulses (licence and freedom) and structured and disciplined codes of conduct (rule-bound, deliberate) in the dynamic creation of declarations of the limits of the habitus of the body.

A fashion system embodies the denotation of acceptable codes and conventions, sets limits to clothing behaviour, prescribes acceptable – and proscribes unacceptable – modes of clothing the body, and constantly revises the rules of the fashion game. Considered in this light, 'fashioning the body' is a feature of all cultures although the specific technologies of fashion vary between cultures.

RECONSTITUTING FASHION

The Face of Fashion rejects the argument that the term 'fashion' refers exclusively to clothing behaviour in capitalist economies, that is, where certain

Figure 1.1 The face of femininity: a consensus on clothes, hair and gesture among four Welsh girls circa 1915.

economic exchanges are invoked in the production, circulation and distribution of clothes. There are fashions and fashions. While western elite designer fashion constitutes *one* system, it is by no means exclusive nor does it determine all other systems. Just as fashion systems may be periodised from the late Middle Ages until the present (rather than assuming an unfolding teleology), so too contemporary fashion systems may be recast as an array of competing and inter-meshing systems cutting across western and non-western cultures.

Nonetheless, fashion under capitalism exhibits peculiar features such as planned obsolescence. Western European fashion is pivoted around the concept of 'newness, or nowness' (Fox-Genovese 1987: 11). Consequently, fashion is deemed to have no inherent meaning beyond serving as a means to an end; namely, the eternal perpetuation of the system of newness that depends on the desire to acquire each new mode. The consumer relation is specific to western capitalist fashion systems, but not necessarily to every system of fashion. Fashion systems can be and have been constructed around other forms of economic or symbolic exchange.

However, accounts of western fashion typically treat it as unique, by virtue of its economically driven consumption. In such accounts, fashion behaviour itself is of marginal importance, having no meaning beyond the reaffirmation of economic exchanges and their ideological reflections. Western peoples indulge in fashion according to their class position and social status. As a result, fashion is frequently explained as being a trivial or ephemeral phenomenon. When not being discussed as the trumpery of capitalist consumer culture, fashion is celebrated as the expression of artistic genius.

Analysts of fashion have recycled these themes especially within fashion histories (see Newton 1975; Perrot 1981) (e.g. Batterberry and Batterberry 1982; Cunnington and Cunnington 1981; de Marly 1980; Laver 1968, 1985; McDowell 1984; J. Robinson 1976, n.d.; Rothstein 1984; Yarwood 1982). Rather more insightful and imaginative studies have been offered by Hollander (1980) and Steele (1985a, 1988, 1991). The theme of creative genius is common to writings on individual designers, which tend to adopt a eulogistic mode (e.g. Art Gallery of New South Wales 1987; Charles-Roux 1989; Etherington-Smith 1983; Healy 1992; Miyake 1978; Penn 1988; Saint Laurent 1983; P. White 1973, 1986).

Complementing these studies are those from a psychological perspective (e.g. Bergler 1955; Flügel 1930; Soloman 1985), and sociological or anthropological analyses and histories (e.g. Brenninkmeyer 1965; Kidwell and Christman 1974; König 1973; Martyn 1976; Roach and Eicher 1965; Simmel 1973; Veblen 1970). In the past decade other analysts have adopted interdisciplinary frameworks and more critical points of view. In particular, they have turned their attention to issues of everyday fashion, popular culture, gender and consumerism. The most influential of these are Barthes (1984) and Wilson (1985). Recent studies have drawn on these works, including Ash and Wilson (1992); Evans and Thornton (1989); Finkelstein (1991); Gaines and Herzog (1990) and Garber (1992). These studies have shifted the terrain of inquiry away from elite fashion and aesthetics.

All these studies share the view that fashion is specific to capitalist economies, political practices and cultural formations. Despite variations in national, class and subcultural dress codes, Wilson (1985: 5), for example, argues that all these ways 'of dressing are inevitably determined by fashion'. In other words, everyday clothes are 'dim replicas' of fashion modes: 'they began life as fashion garments and not as some form of traditional dress'. This seems to be somewhat wishful thinking, overstating the influence of elite fashion and underestimating the purpose-built nature of specific technologies of self-formation.

One of the features of this definition is the emphasis on capitalist systems of production, distribution and consumption – and, in particular, on mass production. Yet, courtly and Paris fashion (designer-driven, client-oriented, exclusive one-offs) predated – and were subsequently remote from – mass markets. Indeed, Kidwell and Christman (1974: 14–17) point out that mass consumption in the sense of the demand for ready-to-wear clothes preceded the technical competence required for mass production (see Chapter 9). Many Paris designers were ambivalent about the lure of Hollywood (financial and promotional) (Keenan 1977: 82). Eventually they dismissed American fashion design which was explicitly geared towards 'the new suburban "lifestyle"' as mere dressmaking, not art. One commentator observed that 'the French might still dress for "Veblenesque leisure", but Americans enjoyed active leisure in the form of social events like backyard barbecue parties' (quoted by Steele 1991: 112).

Designers resisted the mass market until economic circumstances (and potential profits) persuaded them to initiate ready-to-wear lines and licensing arrangements. The latter in particular have been extraordinarily profitable. A casualty of licensing was Coco Chanel who signed away the rights to her perfumes (including Chanel No. 5) in the 1920s. When she realised her mistake, she attempted to regain rights but failed (Steele 1991: 46). By contrast, many designers support their loss-making couture fashion by licensing arrangements. Although this cross-subsidisation keeps the high machine industry going, clearly the majority of fashion activity occurs quite independently. Even so, elite designers typically sneer at everyday fashion systems.

As well as being unified by capitalism, western fashion is deemed to be imbued with the aesthetic expression of 'ideas, desires and beliefs circulating in society' (Wilson 1985: 9). The aesthetics of fashion are informed by the modernity of urbanism and consumerism (and subsequently by postmodernity). Fashion plays off the preoccupations, contradictions and taboos of western culture. Several other elements are also invoked in definitions of fashion: individuality, Judeo-Christian morality, gender identity and imperialism. According to Wilson (1985: 15), fashion is a flexible means of expressing the ambiguity of capitalism, identity and art, thereby becoming 'modernist irony'.

Accordingly, few commentators invest significant social meanings in western fashion. Instead fashion is seen to epitomise the ephemeral character of contemporary western societies – if not the modern malaise. Fashion has been especially attractive to postmodernists (e.g. Kroker and Kroker 1987; Faurschou

1987; Wark 1991) because its slipperiness – the ambivalence, polyvalence, semiotic smorgasbord and excess – fits into a world view of consumerism, pluralism and masquerade gone mad – the unfettered circulation of free-floating signs. The elements of fashion that leak out of dominant theories accord perfectly with a postmodern vision. Fashion is described as 'an early warning system of major cultural transformations' and a parody of hypermodern culture (Kroker and Kroker 1987: 16). Fashion is a visual commentary on the excess of post-modern culture providing 'aesthetic holograms' that 'introduce the *appearance* of radical novelty, while maintaining the *reality* of no substantial change':

> Fashion, therefore, is a conservative agent complicit in deflecting the eye from fractal subjectivity, cultural dyslexia, toxic bodies, and parallel processing as the social physics of the late twentieth-century experience.
>
> (Kroker and Kroker 1987: 45)

In an evaluation of fashion and postmodernism, Wilson (1992: 4) characterises a postmodernist explanation of fashion as a combination of fragmentation and identity in which dress either glues 'the false identity together on the surface' or lends 'a theatrical and play-acting aspect to the hallucinatory experience of the contemporary world' (Wilson 1992: 8). The pastiche of fashion design meshes with the pluralism of everyday dress codes (Wilson 1992: 6). Fashion is the perfect foil for a world of fragmented and incommensurate identities and personae, offering a dynamic procession of free-floating signs and symbolic exchanges:

> Postmodernism expresses at one level a horror at the destructive excess of Western consumerist society, yet, in aestheticising this horror, we somehow convert it into a pleasurable object of consumption.
>
> (Wilson 1992: 4)

For Wilson, the schizophrenic ambivalence of the 'portmanteau concept' of postmodernism is its very importance. It has opened up the space to 'rescue the study of dress from its lowly status, and has created – or at least *named* – a climate in which any cultural aesthetic object may be taken seriously' (Wilson 1992: 6). According to Wilson, postmodernism can account for dress as a 'powerful weapon of control and dominance' *and* 'its *simultaneously* subversive qualities' (Wilson 1992: 14).

Yet, as Featherstone has observed, postmodernist explanations explain nothing and merely feed the fashion cycle itself:

> Their cultural innovation proclaiming a *beyond* is really a *within*, a new move within the intellectual game which takes into account the new circumstances of production of cultural goods, which will itself in turn be greeted as eminently marketable by the cultural intermediaries.
>
> (Featherstone 1987: 69)

In all these accounts, body techniques and codes of fashion are held to be imposed by external forces over which individuals have little control. Even when such forces are visible, fashion continues to exert a powerful fascination. For example, women continue to buy and enjoy fashion magazines although they know about the falsity, exploitation and stereotyping of advertising and fashion features (see Chapter 3). One attempt to reconcile this intellectual critique with the hypnotic appeal of fashion has been the notion of female pleasure, namely that women's magazines, soap operas, romantic fiction and other images of femininity, and the like, offer particular pleasures for women readers and spectators. Rather than reinforcing 'patriarchal' relations, these texts are said to offer women fantasies, identities, and momentary escape from the contradictions and pain of everyday life. In proposing a particular 'feminine' system of pleasures, this account supports the project of disaggregating the phenomenon of 'fashion' into distinct systems.

Thus, fashion is conceived as a 'body technique' which displays markers of social conduct expressed and displayed through clothes. As such, techniques are not simply imposed from above (in a trickle-down process) but constitute acquired abilities of collective and individual practical reason. In a process of 'prestigious imitation', individuals borrow movements, actions, gestures and demeanours to fabricate an array of customised body techniques (Mauss 1973: 73–5). Rather than restricting fashion to the province of consumerist culture, fashion is a general technique of acculturation.

By regularising and codifying the display of the body and its comportment, fashion composes 'custom in the guise of departure from custom' (Sapir 1931: 140). According to Blumer (1968: 344), there are three features of fashion custom: uniformity through consensus on a prevailing mode and its association with propriety; an orderly and regulated way to monitor and mark the shifting sands of social life; and the distillation of 'common sensitivity and taste' by the sanctioning of new modes and the rejection of old ones. Thought of in this way, fashion operates as a conservative barometer of body–habitus relations.

McCracken (1990) extends this view in his consideration of fashion as a language. He concludes that fashion is less of a language than a limited set of pre-fabricated codes. In other words, it is a shorthand way of signalling place and identity as well as a way of performing social intercourse, both synchronically and diachronically. However, he shows that clothes are 'read' not as individual units composed into a whole, either in terms of the 'social type' evoked by an outfit (for example, housewife, hippie, businessman), or in terms of 'the look' as a whole. Where an outfit cannot be interpreted, people either take one item of clothing as being the most salient and classify that, or else produce an account which can reconcile the codes attached to different items of the outfit. McCracken concluded that clothing constitutes 'a peculiar kind of code' which is 'almost fully constrained' because it lacks rules of combination and selection:

> In short, the code has no generative capacity. Its users enjoy no combinatorial freedom . . . The code specified not only the components of the message, but also the messages themselves. These messages come, as it were, pre-fabricated.

Because the wearer does not have this combinatorial freedom, the interpreter of clothing examines an outfit not for a new message but for an old one fixed by convention.

(McCracken 1990: 66)

By thinking of these codes as techniques of body display, fashion behaviour can be considered in terms of predetermined gestural and expressive arrays. Fashion under capitalism has merely inflected fashion codes in a 'consumerist' manner. Thus, *The Face of Fashion* dissolves the rigid distinction between fashion and costume, between western and non-western fashion, and between high and everyday fashion in order to consider fashion systems as clothing, body and decorative techniques that are instrumental and pragmatic. They convey and compose pre-fabricated codes of self-hood as the basis of social intercourse.

FASHION AND HABITUS

Fashion constitutes the arrangement of clothes and the adornment of the body to display certain body techniques and to highlight relations between the body and its social habitus. The body is not a given, but actively constructed through how it is used and projected. Clothes are an index of codes of display, restraint, self-control, and affect-transformation (cf. Elias 1978: 187). As such, fashion behaviour varies with context. Accordingly, fashion has no absolute or essential meaning, rather the clothes–body complex operates in ways appropriate to a particular habitus or milieu.

Often, clothing behaviour is determined by pragmatic criteria and situations. Choosing the appropriate clothes for going to college, for studying, or for doing housework, gardening or yardwork, going grocery shopping, or going to the beach do not require much more than criteria of comfort. On the other hand, dressing for a job interview, a dinner party, for a wedding, or as a law enforcement officer, entail specific calculations about clothing behaviour and milieu. Thus, rather than seeking some essential explanation of fashion, we must look for more localised rationales.

At a general level, fashion is a technique of acculturation – a means by which individuals and groups learn to be visually at home with themselves in their culture. Given the local character of fashion milieux, acculturation is not a single-society process. Rather, fashion relates to particular codes of behaviour and rules of ceremony and place. It denotes and embodies conventions of conduct that contribute to the etiquette and manners of social encounters. Capitalism may change the production and consumption of fashion but not its play. Capitalism does not overdetermine fashion as a social practice.

The growth of consumer cultures has enhanced certain features of habitus associated with practices of consumption. But the place and significance of fashion as one aspect of habitus has changed little. Particular meanings vary historically and are culturally specific, since the rules, codes and language of the garments and how they should be worn are definite and limited in scope (cf. Barthes 1984). The development of fashion systems in Europe has been associated with the emergence of courtly etiquette and subsequent challenges to the power of the court with the expansion of civil society (Elias 1978, 1983) (see Chapters 8 and 9).

Although Elias's account presumes a teleological drift towards a civilising imperative, his characterisation of the emergence of the French system of etiquette is pertinent to understanding how the relations between bodies, clothes and habitus operate. Elias argued that etiquette associated with personal space (habitus) was a vital part of the development of civil society in eighteenth-century Europe (Elias 1978). In this connection, he describes the ritual of Louis XIV's levée (getting up ritual) in support of his argument (Elias 1983: 84–6). Household staff, courtiers, family members and others seeking favour visited the king during the process of his getting up and dressing. Not only did they make their appearance in a strict hierarchical order but each was entrusted with giving specific assistance to the king in his toilette. Despite being dressed in only a wig, the king would receive complete strangers with aplomb. Family members only entered once he was dressed. This elaborate ritual served to cement loyalties to the body of the king (through his toilette) and hence to his reign (relations of power emanated from this social hierarchy). His political regime was built on allegiance to the habitus of his body. The exercise of power was dependent on the acquisition by courtiers of body techniques in which power was invested, manifested and maintained.

In western, 'democratic' regimes, relations with institutions have largely replaced personal allegiances as the lynchpin of political power. Nonetheless, there are vestiges and allusions to politics and power through codes of dress and associated etiquette. The emergence of corporate wardrobes, 'femocrat' dressing (career feminists in the bureaucracy working on gender-related projects) (Yeatman 1990: 65), and corporate power dressing are recent examples of the use of clothes as effective political tools. Even academics have smartened up their dress codes as they are nudged out of the ivory tower and into liaisons with government, industry and other agencies. Clothes do, indeed, matter.

Elias's account of the queen's levée ritual illustrates another dimension of the form of European body-space relations, namely, a particular relationship between power and the naked body. From the standpoint of contemporary western morality, the scenario seems brazen, almost unthinkable:

> The maid of honour had the right to pass the queen her chemise. The lady in waiting helped her put on her petticoat and dress. But if a princess of the royal family happened to be present, she had the right to put the chemise on the queen. On one occasion the queen had just been completely undressed by her ladies. Her chambermaid was holding the chemise and had just presented it to the maid of honour when the Duchess of Orleans came in. The maid of honour gave it back to the chambermaid who was about to pass it to the duchess when

the higher-ranking Countess of Provence entered. The chemise now made its way back to the chambermaid, and the queen finally received it from the hands of the countess. She had to stand the whole time in a state of nature, watching the ladies complimenting each other with her chemise.

(Elias 1983: 86)

This ritual depended on the acceptance of the naked body. Nudity in the eighteenth century was not only not a problem but an irrelevance. Social hierarchy and modes of polite conduct took precedence over cladding the body. However, with the development of European civil society – the decline of the monarchy and rise of elected governments, the expansion of the economy, and blurring of class distinctions – such intimate cementing of political relations declined. Gradually, according to Elias, our culture developed a 'shame frontier' which problematised nudity and exposure of the body to all but intimate family members (Elias 1978: 167–8). Appropriate body behaviour consists of an array of acts of restraint. Modern European fashion has also been characterised by Judeo-Christian attitudes that problematise the relationship of the body to sexual desire. In order to manage attention to the body, and deflect inappropriate sexual desire, dressing presumes that a code of restraint, self-control and 'affect-transformation' is a habit.

Western cultures have erected a psychological barrier to nudity that underpins ideas about the body and its habitus. Bodies are regarded as a barrier separating the inner self from the outer world, a relationship articulated through clothes and modes of wearing them. Western fashion is represented as a 'civilising' process invoking a tension between the 'pre-civilised' codes of conduct (denoted by licence and freedom) and 'civilised' codes of conduct (which are rule-bound and constrained). In practical terms, this becomes a play between revelation and concealment of the body through clothes and adornment. In rhetorical terms, western fashion problematises the body, nudity and natural functions.

Trends and fashions in lingerie epitomise the tension between the body and its habitus. The shame frontier is especially elaborated for women. Public displays of nudity by western women are rarely sanctioned. Only under specific circumstances are these barriers to nudity lifted, for example, around medical examinations, some venues for swimming and bathing, stripshows, and certain communal bathing complexes. The shame frontier stems from the oppositions between mind/body and male/female within western philosophy. This conceptual framework also underpins western fashion systems and techniques of accounting for them. The development of psychoanalysis provided a means for understanding some of the gendered aspects of western fashion.

Some recent feminist work in literary and art criticism has applied aspects of psychoanalysis to the representation of women, cultural production and popular culture (e.g. Betterton 1987) (see Chapters 3 and 5). These accounts have argued that forms of looking in western culture can be explained through the psychoanalytic theory of the 'gaze'. The observer objectifies the subject of the gaze in the pursuit of scopophilic and voyeuristic pleasures. Consequently, the gaze is structured as if from a *normative* male point of view. In other words, the look is structured in such a way that women are represented and viewed as the object of male heterosexual desire. Such an account assumes that all acts of looking have their basis in psychoanalytic impulses that are coded by sex. In linking sexuality with the look as the dominant sense, these accounts ignore other ways of representing and of seeing which are not organised by normative heterosexual desire, including auto-eroticism, homo-eroticism, sensual pleasure and fantasy. A number of other theorists have sought to revise the psychoanalytic approach and to provide other accounts of representation and the look that can accommodate other points of view and gender relations (e.g. Ash and Wilson 1992; Evans and Thornton 1989; Gaines and Herzog 1990; Garber 1992; Steele 1991).

For example, Sawchuk (1987: 69) has warned against concentrating too much on the look and its scopophilic pleasures since 'clothing, the act of wearing fabric, is intimately linked to the skin, and the body, to our tactile senses'. If looking is only part of the process, then other facets of practices of interpretation, projection and fantasisation need to be explored. To do so, the orthodoxy of the male gaze as the basis of the look and in turn as the lynchpin of fashionable behaviour must be displaced.

Subsequent chapters explore numerous instances where the western cultural preoccupation with particular notions of femininity and masculinity have inflected fashion systems in idiosyncratic ways. For example, the relative neglect of men's fashion in many studies of fashion is a consequence of the peculiarity of western notions of gender. Whereas techniques of femininity are acquired and displayed through clothes, looks and gestures, codes of masculinity are inscribed through codes of action, especially through the codes of sport and competition. Accordingly, where men's fashion has been studied, it has been almost exclusively in connection with sports clothes and suiting. In general, the cultural attributes attached to the unclothed body and different arrangements of body–space relations and techniques of acculturation underpin other systems of fashion with localised effects.

The process of prestigious imitation described earlier means that the process by which fashions are popularised or lose favour are complex and interactive. In the language of fashion theory, fashion trickles up and down. While fashion is an aspirational device, there is no uni-directional set of influences that originate in fashion elites and flow down to other social strata. Rather, there are multiple fashion systems that compete and interact.

For example, western fashion designers make regular pronouncements of new styles, few of which are popularised. Designers expend enormous sums on publicity for new modes by trying to influence fashion editors, gain spreads in fashion magazines and newspapers, and seeking to persuade the tiny group of couture customers to buy the new look. At the same time, the design industry hopes to influence arbiters responsible for translating design fashion into high street fashion. There is a fine line between plagiarism and influence that characterises the clothes available in fashion boutiques and department stores. In fact, designer fashion has an indirect and volatile relationship with everyday fashion. As the high incidence of fashion 'failures' has shown, the promotion of a new style by a designer is a huge gamble that is frequently rejected by consumers (Blumer 1968: 343, 1969: 281). More frequently, a style is radically modified either by high street manufacturers or by consumers themselves. Thus, the process of fashion influence is more anarchic than is commonly acknowledged.

Trends

Moreover, the inspiration for seasonal collections frequently comes from a variety of sources. These include styles which actively oppose designer fashion such as extreme street fashion as found in subcultures; styles outside the western fashion systems such as ethnic or pre-industrial cultures; radical or innovative styles from art colleges; and re-vamped versions of previous fashion styles (such as the Flapper look or empire line) or historical costumes (such as the Marie Antoinette look). Blumer (1969: 280) noted the convergence in the designs offered to consumers by designers and buyers. Success in fashion depends on the ability to recognise and translate 'the incipient and inarticulate tastes which are taking shape in the fashion consuming public'. Thus, the process is less one of derivation from the elite than the sanctioning of trends in taste by the elite. In other words:

> The prestige of the elite does not control the direction of this incipient taste. We have here a case of the fashion mechanism transcending and embracing the prestige of the elite group rather than stemming from that prestige.
>
> (Blumer 1969: 280)

Designer fashion, then, does not inevitably influence high street fashion, and even less so, everyday wear. This process is a multifaceted one which entails complex patterns of influence, differentiation, repudiation and imitation.

Figure 1.2 East meets West: tourists in Shanghai circa 1922.

Ironically, while elite designer fashion has endeavoured to remain distinct from high street fashion, its success has depended on the popularisation of styles in non-elite groups. Examples of popularisation that have simultaneously under-mined yet bolstered elite fashion include the role of designers and fashion in Hollywood films; the 'Americanisation' of fashion design, production, distribu-tion and consumption; the emergence of designer systems outside Paris; the development of ready-to-wear lines; licensing arrangements; the appropriation of design motifs in high street fashion, subcultures, countercultures and trans-gressive cultures; home sewing; and counterfeiting.

The movement is a form of 'selective borrowing' (McCracken 1985: 45) or institutionalised plagiarism which may occur between social groups (up and down) or across various subcultures, and vary over time. While some fashion sub-systems seem to operate independently, as a bulwark against other systems or social groups, others compete or interact.

TECHNOLOGIES OF SELF

This chapter began with a poem about Sonia Delaunay and her revolutionary approach to fashion design. Her contribution to design was the incorporation of the shape and movements of the female body into the design of clothes them-selves. This created a direct relationship between clothes and the bodies they house and highlight. Delaunay's designs acknowledged that women were inextricably bound up with the spaces or milieux they occupied and inhabited. Another French designer, Coco Chanel, also articulated this relationship in her influential designs. Her approach was poignantly illustrated in an anecdote recorded by her biographer, Edmonde Charles-Roux. Devastated by the death of her lover, Captain Arthur 'Boy' Capel, in a motoring accident in 1919, Chanel expressed her grief through her choice of mourning habitude, by redecorating her bedroom. First, she had the room done totally in black – walls, ceiling, carpet, sheets – but after just one night, ordered that it be redone in pink. Charles-Roux interprets this whim of interior decor as Chanel's only way of expressing her feelings by displaying her emotions in colour:

> When she gave orders for her bedroom to be, first, 'dressed in black' and then 'done in pink', Gabrielle was using shoptalk. She presumably hoped her heart would be as docile as the strangers who made up her clientele, that it too would follow the fashion for pink, and that sorrow, once she had made her palace fresh, light, and luminous, would subside.
> In short, she was telling her pain what to wear. Oh, costume!
> (Charles-Roux 1989: 184)

This transformation, Charles-Roux suggests, was not trivial, but a literal trans-lation of Chanel's emotions into metaphors that could be registered in her physical surroundings. Charles-Roux cites Roland Barthes's claim that:

> As a substitute for the body, clothing, by its weight, partakes of man's basic dreams, heaven and cavern, sublime and sordid, flight and slumber; by its weight a garment becomes wing or shroud, enchantment or authority.
>
> (Barthes quoted by Charles-Roux 1989: 184)

In western culture, clothing and immediate surroundings are used to protect and project a sense of self in very literal ways. Bodies and clothes exist in a symbiotic relationship. The system of mourning clothes is a highly elaborated example of this (see L. Taylor 1983). Commentators have noted the strangely eerie quality of clothes in exhibitions on mannequins rather than living bodies (Wilson 1992: 15). For this reason, the curator of the Yves Saint Laurent travelling exhibition, Stephen di Pietri, sought out clothes from clients rather than museums. He observed that:

> When clothes have been on display for too long, the fabrics 'die'. A dress that's been on display for too long is different to a dress that's been too much worn. Somehow a dress is 'fed' the warmth of the body of the person who's been wearing it. But when you have a dress on a cold mannequin, under a light and with the dust falling on it, it loses something. No matter how much you clean it and refresh it, in a funny way it seems to lose its life.
>
> (Quoted by Symons 1987: 20)

He found that worn clothes had an 'energy' that was absent in samples. By the same token, clothes that were 'devoured' by spectators began to have their life sucked out of them. After the exhibition closed in Russia, de Pietri commented:

> The Russians were famished for fashion, style, design. They almost salivated at the silks, taffetas, velvets. They looked at the fabrics almost more than they looked at the dresses . . . By the time the exhibition closed, it was entirely devoid of atmosphere. The dresses were completely tired. They had been looked at and looked at and studied and studied until nothing was left.
>
> (Quoted by Symons 1987: 21)

In short, clothes are activated by the wearing of them just as bodies are actualised by the clothes they wear. In acknowledging this interdependence, fashion can be considered as an elaborated body technique through which a range of personal and social statements can be articulated. Fashion systems adapt to the requirements of distinct habituses. Fashion is purpose-built to secure certain effects. The following chapters explore aspects of the face of fashion – the formation of styles, and looks under particular circumstances. Through clothes we wear our bodies and fabricate our selves.

Chapter 2

Exotic impulses in techniques of fashion

FASHION AND EXOTICA

> Early [European] travellers and missionaries, blissfully blind to their own
> powdered wigs and tight laces, considered all other body techniques signs of
> barbary and savagery.
>
> (Brain 1979: 9)

The argument of Chapter 1 was that fashion is a body technique which articulates
certain aspects of the language, gestures and disciplines of the trained body in its
habitus. The keynote of body techniques is that they are unremarkable. Dress and
body techniques are 'tailor-made' for their environment. Yet, in this process,
fashion is the technique for establishing distinctiveness. Through different body
styles, one wearer is distinguished from another, one group from other wearers.
Fashion techniques are also the perfect device for playing on the rules of social
intercourse by visually displaying calculated transgressions (see McCracken 1990).

In this connection exoticism comes into its own. The term 'exoticism' can be
used in two ways. It can refer either to the enticing, fetishised quality of a fashion
or style, or to foreign or rare motifs in fashion. The incorporation of exotic motifs
in fashion (across all cultures) is an effective way of creating a *'frisson'* (a thrill
or quiver) within social conventions of etiquette. Because fashion systems are
built on the interrelationship and tension between exotic and familiar codes,
exotic looks are all the more effective as techniques of display.

Consequently, fashion systems plunder 'exotic' techniques and codes from
'other' looks and fashions (including traditional costumes, previous fashion looks,
subcultures, and other cultures which are regarded as 'exotic'). In western fashion,
the term 'exotic' is used to refer to elements of new fashion codes or 'new looks'
codified as profoundly 'different' from previous or contemporary fashion techniques. The ethnocentric underpinnings of western fashion (European or European-
derived) ensure that differences between codes of exoticism and mundanity are
played up. Exoticism is one such technique although 'exotic' impulses in fashion are
not confined to motifs from non-western cultures. Yet, as Brain (1979: 8) has pointed
out, 'Western practices of body decoration [can serve] as yardsticks by which we can
understand "exotic" – that is "different" – techniques.'

In this chapter, three forms of exoticism in fashion are considered. First, certain techniques of dress and decoration in non-western cultures (for example, the customs associated with the sari in India or the veil in some Islamic cultures; body decoration in Africa or Oceania). Second, adaptations of traditional dress combined with elements from western fashion systems in post-colonial cultures and displaced cultures in western societies (for example, adaptations of the sari or the veil). And third, 'exotic' elements in western fashion borrowed and adapted from other fashion systems (for example, the 'Indian' influences in the 'hippie' look; the toga and use of draped fabric more generally; 'peasant' motifs in high fashion).

While distinguishing these uses of the term, exotic elements in fashion are incorporated in deliberately ambiguous and trangressive ways. In particular, elements from diverse fashion systems are inter-mixed. Thus, this chapter considers the different forms of exoticism as particular body techniques which produce different marks of distinctiveness.

BODY TECHNIQUES IN NON-WESTERN CULTURES

[T]oday well-dressed ladies from Thailand, wearing what seem to the coarse Western eye to be their own timeless styles of clothing, will tell you that everybody is wearing brown this year, that those large leaf-patterns are out or that a sleeve with no border at the wrist is terribly old-fashioned.

(Newton 1975: 305)

As already noted, techniques of dress and decoration in non-western cultures are distinguished from fashion. They are regarded as traditional and unchanging reflections of social hierarchies, beliefs and customs. Non-western dress embodies meanings of spirituality, religiosity and fertility while also encoding power relations. Occasionally, dress is also acknowledged as an art form with aesthetic meanings. For western observers, the idea that non-western dress does not change is central to establishing its difference from western fashion, which is predicated on regular and arbitrary changes.

Symptomatically, the term fashion is rarely used in reference to non-western cultures. The two are defined in opposition to each other: western dress is fashion because it changes regularly, is superficial and mundane, and projects individual identity; non-western dress is costume because it is unchanging, encodes deep meanings, and projects group identity and membership. In either case, dress is taken out of its 'lived' resonances and theorised in structural or functionalist terms to account for beliefs located elsewhere.

As a consequence of this opposition, the similar operation of techniques of dress and decoration are generally overlooked. Yet, when they are treated as techniques, parallels emerge between western and non-western systems of dress. Although the amount and pace of changing fashions is less pronounced in cultures with less emphasis on economic exchange, changes do occur. Rarely, though, have *synchronic* studies of dress and decoration demonstrated cycles of change. The elements of a dress system at a particular moment are often generalised across a culture. In accordance with the way anthropology has conceptualised non-western cultures as timeless and unchanging, so too techniques of dress and decoration have been regarded in the west as fixed.

The argument of this chapter is that this approach does a disservice to non-western styles of dress and fails to acknowledge the subtleties of non-western fashion. Such an approach merely confirms the assumptions of European philosophy, specifically, the distinction between western cultures as civilised and other cultures as pre-civilised. Since western notions of civility rest on the internalisation of social disciplines and the distinction between public (outer self) and private (inner self), western fashion needs little explanation, other than as a sign of individual adornment (self-presentation), group identity and role playing. By contrast, non-western fashion is regarded as being determined by forces beyond individual control or understanding. Cultural processes are thought of as inevitable, unconscious or collective emanations. The ways in which cultural phenomena are explained reflects this philosophical divide.

The tendency to account for the difference of non-western cultures in terms of western systems of meaning arises from the observer's desire to discover 'orderliness'. This is a 'preoccupation of intellectuals rather than of the peoples they study' (Ron Brunton quoted by Andrew Strathern 1987: 14). This chapter takes up some work on non-western dress and decoration that points to elements of fashion codes and similarities with western fashion systems. It proposes an ethnographic approach which treats dress and decoration as specialised techniques of display and comportment rather than as mere reflections of general and impersonal social forces.

The most suggestive work in this regard concerns self-decoration among the Hagen people of the New Guinea highlands. Hageners are often cited for their use of 'exotic' body decoration and elaborate headdresses in ceremonies and rituals. Notably, the custom is most highly elaborated among male dancers. Yet, the difficulty of interpreting this form of body decoration was compounded by the fact that the Hageners themselves did not – or would not – consciously make sense of it themselves. The frustration was expressed by Andrew Strathern:

Decorations were obviously elaborate, painstakingly assembled, brightly coloured, and impressive, and central to dancing occasions. In general, it was obvious that many of the items employed were also wealth goods used in exchanges and that persons were displaying this idea of wealth on their own behalf or for others. But specific inquiries about the meaning of pieces of decoration were consistently met with the phrase 'it is just decoration'. We had to revise our approach and work from the context back to the items to see if clues would emerge, and in doing so we repeated many of our specific questions whenever they appeared relevant or useful in any way.

(A. Strathern 1987: 13)

Crushed velvet dress
with spaghetti straps
available from
DOTTI. Matching
bolero jacket
also available.
Earrings from
TAKA JEWEL BOX.

The "Siriul Titiul"
Dance Group from
Sai Bai Island in
Queensland's own
Torres Straits –
weekly guest
performers of
Kewarra Beach
Resort, Cairns.

Figure 2.1 'Tropical Pulse': exotic motifs in western fashion derivative of New
Guinea Highland dress.

Source: Wintergarden Centre, Brisbane, Spring/Summer catalogue, 1991.

Instead of trying to pin down the meanings of the decorations, Marilyn Strathern and Andrew Strathern (M. Strathern 1979; A. Strathern 1987) treated the decorations as a system of dress and as a set of body techniques. They built up patterns of usage and codes of wearing. This showed that there were a *range* of techniques of decorative behaviour, and variable relationships between decorative practices and the interactions composed by them. For example, decorative techniques did not always have the same meaning or relevance. In particular, the elaborate decorative techniques employed on ceremonial occasions differed significantly from decorative techniques in everyday life. While everyday techniques reconfirmed and reinvented dominant cultural underpinnings, those on special occasions (such as celebrations and confrontations) also prompted certain rituals and symbolic behaviour.

The Stratherns also investigated the dimensions of decorative techniques beyond these ritualistic investments. In doing so, they found that there were individual variations in decorative behaviour as well as changes in decorative techniques over time. In short, there were changing fashions in the details of the headdresses and make-up. At any one time, not only did dancers compete with other dancers, groups of dancers (identified by similar stylistic themes) competed with other groups.

Thus, although the Hagen dancers drew from established materials, stylistic patterns and decorative ornaments, each dancer (and group of dancers) developed unique variations and statements in the detail of their make-up and headdress. In the process, an eclectic array of materials was used in the process of decoration, including pig grease, charcoal, ochre, colourful bird feathers, spreadeagled wings and whole birds, bones and tusks, shells, woven fibre bands, flowers, possum fur, leaves and foliage. Dancers went to extreme lengths to secure the best materials to achieve spectacular effects, and varied their designs year after year. Not only did the decorative competition allude to ritualistic play, the Hageners enjoyed the process of decoration *per se*. It was essential to mix and match fundamental design principles and traditions in order to surprise other dancers and the spectators with spectacular 'looks'.

Other evidence confirms the fact that the rules of Hagener decoration were not unchanging or simply rooted to deeply held symbolic associations. New materials from western contact, such as empty meat and fish tins, paper labels, and combs, have been incorporated in the decorative techniques. Tin lids became especially popular because they shone like gold or silver and served as a mirror. It has been western observers who have often refused to accept change and the influence of the detritus of western contact. Describing a Highlander's wig, one western commentator dwelt on:

> the corrupting influence of an alien culture . . . Note the fragment of broken comb suspended from the finely decorated wig. This man is a dandy: he uses tiny pieces of yellow ground vine, seed pods and even a feather-adorned nose-stick to enhance his undeniably striking appearance.
>
> (Sinclair 1973: n.p.)

This reaction both acknowledges the individual stylishness of the dancer by using the western term for a modish man, while insisting on classifying his decorative behaviour as tradition that should not be sullied by signs of western 'civilisation'. In other words, some western observers have insisted on establishing different codes and meaning systems to account for what are really fashion and decorative systems in non-western cultures.

This becomes clear in Marilyn Strathern's comparison between western use of cosmetics and Hagen decoration. She argues that there is a cosmetic paradox in western culture. In beautifying the body, western techniques of cosmetics are seen as projecting an outer shell which disguises and hides the 'true' inner self. The act of beautification draws attention away from the individual as a person and thus detracts from individuality, and:

> Whether or not those who use cosmetics employ a holistic view of themselves, their critics are struggling with a contrast between body and soul, between physical appearance and individuality, between an outer shell and an inner identity. For this critical approach to cosmetics makes sense only if the act of beautification is taken as applying solely to the body. The skin, the outer surface, is in this context truly superficial, trivial in relation to personal identity. And cosmetics in the first place attend to the body's surface and its features.
>
> (M. Strathern 1979: 242)

By contrast, Hageners see a continuity between the body and the techniques for displaying selfhood and identity. Not only are they aware of the paradox but consciously exploit the fact that beautification 'can draw attention away from the person' and consciously strive for this effect:

> They emphasize that when as a group they dress themselves in feathers, paint and leaves, the first thing spectators should see is the decoration – so discovering the individual underneath becomes a pleasurable shock. They are not dressing up in costumes taking an animal or spirit form; they are not wearing masks, enacting myths or working out dramas. They are pretending to be no one but themselves, yet themselves decorated to the point of disguise. This idea is incorporated specifically into aesthetics: a dancer recognized at once has decorated himself poorly.
>
> (M. Strathern 1979: 243)

By decorating themselves as a group, the decorations of the person – not the individual – hold the attention of spectators. But the decorations must also drape the qualities and attributes of the individual, as well as of the group, on the body of the dancer. In other words, the body is disguised by decorations 'precisely because the self is one of their messages' (M. Strathern 1979: 243). As Ebin, another analyst of Hagen body decoration, has observed:

> the body is the field upon which people demonstrate their personal holdings of wealth and status. Sexual appeal and the appearance of strength are obviously

best achieved by enhancing what is already there, but the body can also serve as a display counter for valuables of a more material kind – objects from the owner's hoard of calculable wealth. Their added values are superimposed upon the self and in their social presentation the two are inextricably bound together.

(Ebin 1979: 66, 71)

Signs of wealth, strength and power conveyed by decorations must be realistic, credible and in accordance with the tangible assets and political position of each dancer and clan. A dancer who exaggerates his position is said to show shame on the skin: the outer self reveals the inadequacies of the inner self (M. Strathern 1979: 252). Thus, the Hageners use body decoration as a visible index of the inner self. In other words, Hagener practice and their interpretation of it demonstrate the general use of body techniques as the embodiment of identity and relationships between body and habitus. As Ebin has commented:

In Western society, too, we deck ourselves out in costly objects which we also deem to be beautiful or symbolic: our aesthetic and material values are synchronized. When we delight ourselves with objects which to us are beautiful but have little monetary value . . . we are likely to provoke little more than the amusement of our friends: pretty, yes, but peculiar. If coupled with a particular label, however, such objects become respectable.

(Ebin 1979: 74)

While the play of clothes, diversity of decoration and technical virtuosity are essential to high fashion, western body techniques also articulate fundamental characteristics of the person and habitus. For some, like Newton, 'our clothing provides a deadly means of communication as, silently, we inspect each other' (Newton 1975: 305). In a similar vein, Andrew Strathern has concluded that:

Dress and decoration contribute to the realisation of . . . social values and political processes . . . There is little doubt that the same basic aims of competition, declaration of status, and the construction of differences between the sexes *also* underlie modes of dress and adornment in contemporary Europe and America. To an observer from this part of the world however, the special advantage that New Guinea offers is simply that, in superficial appearances, the societies there are strikingly different from one's own. The experience should also, naturally, be true the other way around and I am reminded here of the Amerindian who asked why European people were in the habit of looking at themselves in the mirror first thing every morning; were they afraid they would die – that is, lose their souls – if they omitted this ritual?

(A. Strathern 1987: 10)

By drawing comparisons between the techniques themselves and their place in the practice of self-expression, diverse techniques of dress and decoration can be seen as purposeful and constructive.

Another illustration of the common threads of body techniques can be seen in the practice of tattooing. Usually, tattooing is regarded as body decoration rather than as a form of dress. But tattooing can also be thought of as a specific technique of dressing the body. Equally, dress constitutes a particular technique of tattooing. Some discussions of tattooing indicate the difficulty of disaggregating these terms. For example, in eighteenth-century Japan, tattooing was popularised as an alternative to clothing. This was the result of edicts designed to stop merchants wearing the 'fine silks, brocades, or gold or silver ornaments' of the nobility:

> One could, however, wear an expensive tattoo, displaying it only to trusted confidants. So while a rich merchant might wear a plain kimono, vividly embroidered with gold threads on the inside, the merchant's son might sport an equally expensive tattoo on his arm or thigh.
>
> (Richie 1973: 50)

Tattooing has been widely practised as a form of dress and decoration. Particular systems of tattooing elaborate culturally distinctive themes, patterns and techniques. Within a system, changing styles of tattoos have been observed, for example, among Polynesian cultures:

> Over the centuries the Marquesas designs seem to have fluctuated according to social changes, just as any fashion does, and to have varied from island to island. In 1595 the Spanish explorer Mendana described the fish and birds painted upon the body, the men sporting lizards on their faces and the women with patterns of birds and fish behind their ears. By 1772, according to J. R. Forster, the decoration had changed to geometric patterns – 'blotches, spirals, bars, chequers and lines'. In the early twentieth century old people still displayed these patterns, with the addition of rounded forms, circles and half-circles. Naturalistic representations, although highly stylized, were common – the most usual were fish, seaweed, birds and shells: after the first European presence, one ingenious tattooer devised a pattern for the legs based on a pair of boots.
>
> (Ebin 1979: 92–3)

This Polynesian example suggests that tattooing was a technique of fashion within cultural groups and among individuals. People sought out distinctive and unique designs created by tattooists who had the status of artists (not simply as craftspeople). Among New Zealand Maoris, tattooists were high status professionals whose work was sought after and recorded by preserving the tattooed skins of corpses as samples of their best work – rather like the retrospective exhibitions of western artists (Brain 1979: 60). Tattoos were personalised to the point where the facial tattoo was regarded as a personal signature. Thus, Maoris sealed land sales with the Europeans, not by a signature or cross, but by drawing (reproducing) the tattooed patterns on their faces (Brain 1979: 59).

The most elaborate tattooing skills were developed by the Japanese into a recognised art form (*irezumi*) (Richie 1973). The major artists offered tattoo designs through catalogues which were extremely popular (Richie 1973: 59). Designs were constantly updated and new ideas created, including the tattooed body 'suit':

> A completely tattooed man wore his decorations from his shoulders to his elbows, halfway down his thighs; his entire back and buttocks were covered; and only a section from his throat to the sternum to the navel, the genitals, and the insides of the thighs was left undecorated. With this suit a footman or a fireman could simply put on a loincloth and be considered well dressed by his peers.
>
> (Richie 1973: 59)

So revered were these 'dressed' bodies, that a private museum in Japan was established with the sole purpose of displaying tattooed skins (Brain 1979: 64). In other words, the tattooed skin was regarded as a form of 'clothing' and not merely as surface decoration. It was a technique that literally inscribed body–habitus relations. When missionaries tried to outlaw tattooing as a pagan practice, they forced people to wear clothes to cover their tattoos. In response, people simply reversed their dress habits. Instead of wearing the tattoo outside, as the visible 'cloak', they wore their tattoos underneath disguised by the line of the clothing and had new ones done in places that were covered by clothing, thereby creating a 'double' skin which reconciled conflicting systems of body decoration.

Although the popularity of tattoos has declined across most cultures, tattooing remains an exotic element in fashion. If anything, attempts to outlaw tattooing increased its exoticism because of its rarity and association with non-western codes of dress. In fact, tattooing has become associated with subcultural phenomena, such as certain criminal groups (especially in Japan); certain professions (sailors, prostitutes); particular sexual practices; and oppositional social groups (bikers, punks, 'new age' followers and hard rock musicians) (cf. Brain 1979: 159–64).

Tattooing is a form of 'dress' that provides both a badge of identity and a personal signature: an exotic statement within a fashion system. Indeed, the popularity of tattooing has been revived in western fashion since the 1980s. The development of non-permanent tattoos (transfers) and techniques to remove tattoos have alleviated some of the stigma attached to tattooing and enabled it to become a component of high fashion as a form of dress that is desirable because of its exotic associations. In sum, the history of tattooing shows similar patterns of usage, change and adaptation across cultures. There are strong parallels between Sillitoe's observations on the body decorations of New Guinea Highlanders and western patterns of body decoration and tattooing:

> Recent changes in self-decoration fashion, such as the adoption of new face designs painted in manufactured brightly coloured powder paints, suggest that straightforward once-only explanations for the origins of these practices are

distorting and inadequate. They indicate that this highly developed complex came about by a process of accretion, building up over generations, today's fashion changes only modifying aspects of previous tradition, not revolutionising it.

(Sillitoe 1988: 308)

The examples of Hagen body decoration and tattooing suggest that body techniques of dress and decoration in non-western cultures share many of the features associated with western fashion techniques – including change, individual variation, the demonstration of personal attributes, and specification of location within a reference group. In addition, different cultural forms of body techniques must be considered in terms of specific localised effects. Considered as techniques of display, dress and decoration are powerful ways to articulate aspects of the self, compose identities, and assert particular relationships with a wearer's habitus. As part of the dynamics of the formation of personhood, such techniques transcend cultural boundaries and historical periods. While 'exoticism' may be grist to the mill of western fashion, cultures deemed 'exotic' cannot be pigeonholed as beyond fashionable sensibility and thus beyond understanding.

MODIFICATIONS OF DRESS AND DECORATION IN NON-WESTERN CULTURES

In 1984, the Yves Saint Laurent exhibition was staged in Beijing, and was 'an enormous success'. The curator, Di Pietri, recalled:

Thousands and thousands of people came to see it. I don't know what they thought of all these things . . . They didn't have a historical perspective to understand how fashion changes or any background of European fashion, especially the younger people who were brought up during the cultural revolution. Still they poured in, quietly, respectfully and almost every person with a sketchbook and pencil.

A year after the exhibition they were in the Beijing streets in YSL copies, in everything from the Mondrian dress to the Ballet Russes.

(Quoted by Symons 1987: 19)

This quotation suggests not only that western fashion is comprehensible to non-western cultures, but that the latter appropriate and cannibalise elements for their own fashion systems. Thus, while western fashion may be represented in terms of imperialistic intentions to take over the world of clothes, and thereby extinguish other systems, many non-western cultures have shown remarkable resilience and ingenuity at retaining other dress codes, modifying indigenous codes, and developing their own versions of 'western' fashion.

The integrity of non-western techniques of dress and decoration was demonstrated in countless instances of colonisation. In conjunction with conventional techniques of persuasion and acculturation, dress codes were often treated as integral to the process of subjugation. Along with indigenous languages, local dress codes were suppressed as if the acquisition of a new visible identity worn on the body ensured the acquisition of a new 'modern' cultural identity. Clothes became a weapon in the struggle between colonisers and colonised. First, the colonisers used clothes to impose the authority of 'western' ways; later, local people used indigenous clothes to resist that imposition. Although the political currency of clothing codes is often mentioned in studies of colonisation, only a few have dwelt on the significance of these 'style wars'.

The relationship between dress codes and wider political processes was the subject of a study of Yoruba dress in five generations of an extended Nigerian family (Wass 1979). Wass identified a succession of compromises between western and Nigerian dress over the generations. Four garments signified indigenous and western clothing systems: the *iro* wrapper (female indigenous), the *sokoto* trousers (male indigenous), the dress (female western), and the shirt (male western) (Wass 1979: 345). These garments were selected, rejected and combined in changing patterns which Wass related to several political factors: the strength of western influences, new educational opportunities, the growth of nationalism, emerging patterns of class, and changing gender roles.

In the early days of colonisation, when there was little nationalist sentiment, western dress was more likely to be adopted by highly educated people in western-type occupations. Other Nigerians maintained indigenous clothing codes. At this time, it was rare to find mixtures of the two systems. Once nationalism became a strong political movement, more Nigerians adopted forms of indigenous clothing while others began to mix western with indigenous elements, for example, by adding indigenous necklaces, arm and ear jewellery to 'western' outfits; by wearing western footwear with indigenous clothes; or by carrying handbags with indigenous outfits. This strategy of mix-and-match suggests that while western dress codes were an integral technique for embodying the colonial perspective, Nigerian dress codes were modified in accordance with the articulation of an identity under colonisation.

After independence was granted, Nigeria experienced a bitter civil war between ethnic groups. This seemed to trigger another change in clothing styles, namely, a huge increase in the number of western-indigenous mixtures of clothes, as well as the emergence of a local adaptation of men's suits. Called the conductor's suit, this adapted garment 'evolved for men in roles identified with Western-type industrial development but who at the same time had gained a voice in decision-making which allowed them to express themselves as independent Nigerians' (Wass 1979: 344). The conductor's suit bridged the two regimes of identification. An equivalent adaptation for women was the use of the handbag and the popularity of traditionally braided hairstyles worn uncovered. In other words, Nigerian techniques of dress and decoration responded deftly to changing political circumstances, economic conditions and nationalist movements as part of the process of reformulating Nigerian identity and coming to terms with new conditions of existence.

The Nigerian experience has been repeated elsewhere. Mazrui (1970: 30) contrasted the different implications of edicts about clothing in numerous colonies, citing the examples of the French ban on the veil in Algeria, and the imposition of clothes on the Masai in Tanzania, with Kemal Ataturk's ban on the fez in Turkey, and the imposition of the Maoist suit during the Chinese revolution. He argues that the French and Masai bans were cases of cultural assertiveness to impose French and British culture on Algeria and Tanzania respectively; while Ataturk's ban and Mao's tunic were expressions of cultural defensiveness in their respective efforts to break away from the Ottoman empire and modernise Turkey in order to survive and compete with the west, and to impose a new kind of peasant communism.

Yet despite edicts and penalties to force the people of non-western colonies to wear western clothes and abandon exotic fashions, these were met with dogged resistance. Mazrui cited numerous instances where the wearing of non-western clothes was allied to political movements to resist colonisation and European-isation. Ghandi's choice of 'a *dhoti*, naked from the waist upwards, even when he was having an audience with British Royalty, was a striking case of cultural assertiveness' and reinforced 'the proud use of their traditional dress by Indians and Pakistanis although they had been familiar with Western civilisation for years' (Mazrui 1970: 27).

In Kenya, the Mau Mau rebellion involved 'ritualised objection to Western dress', thus reinforcing the symbolic action of Eliad Mathu, the first African in the Kenya Legislative Council, who:

> once tore his jacket off at a public meeting in a dramatic gesture of rejecting Western civilisation – if the price was the loss of land for the African. 'Take back your civilisation – and give back my land!'
>
> (Mazrui 1970: 27)

Similar processes have been observed elsewhere. During the rise of Cuban nationalism in the late nineteenth century, 'a highly elaborate system of fashion and representing it as the new order of things' developed as part of the process of forging an independent Cuba (Holland 1992: 153). Fashion became a means by which Cubans could wear their new identity. Through the space and body of fashion, and as modern consumers, they constructed themselves as national subjects.

In Algeria, the forcible unveiling of women during the Algerian war became a metaphor for the rape of Algerian society. Subsequently, the veil thus became the sign of unified Algerian identity and the focus of Algerian resistance. Veiled women were used as military camouflage to evade detention by the French, while, on other occasions:

> the Algerian woman sometimes *abandoned* the veil as an exercise in military masquerade. There were occasions when it was important that the feminine Algerian soldier should walk the streets looking as European as possible.
>
> (Mazrui 1970: 29)

In Islamic cultures, more generally, the veil has become a key element of moves to re-impose or strengthen Islamic states and undermine western influences. Although traditionally, the veil has religious connotations, the new veil is said to have more complex associations. According to MacLeod (1992), veiling meets the conflicting demands on contemporary middle-class women, caught between traditional expectations and actual living conditions. In a study of the new veiling in Cairo, MacLeod concluded that it was a practical technique of resolving the dilemma of travelling and working outside the home with the rhetoric of domesticity and femininity:

> Through the veil, these women express their distress with their double bind; they want to reinstate their position as valued centres of the family but without losing their new ability to leave the home.
>
> (MacLeod 1992: 551)

Rather than seeing the veil as a threat to their independence, women regarded it as an achievement of women who have successfully combined marriage, family harmony and outside employment. As such, the new veil is both an act of protest and of accommodation: 'Protest is firmly bound to accommodation in a resonant public symbol, creating an ambiguous resistance, an accommodating protest' (MacLeod 1992: 552–3). By adopting a traditional element of Muslim dress, women have reconstituted it within contemporary circumstances 'not as an indiscriminate recollection of all traditional values, but as a highly selective attempt to revitalise and emphasise some of the old ideals' (MacLeod 1992: 555). Thus the veil has become a body technique intricately linked to wider political and cultural struggles.

A recent study of female politicians in Korea shows how techniques of dress have been used as strategic tactics in gaining credibility and authority. Still a minority in the legislature, Korean women have developed a dual system of dress, drawing on elements of western and traditional dress, as a means of negotiating 'the traditional patriarchal' system (Soh 1992: 375). Depending on the occasion, they adopt one of three codes: the *hanbok* (traditional skirt and dress jacket), a western-style woman's business suit, or a western-style men's suit:

> The three styles may be reclassified as the feminine versus masculine style, depending on whether the lower outer garment is a skirt or a pair of trousers. The feminine style may then be subdivided into the more conservative *hanbok* versus progressive Western-style clothes.
>
> (Soh 1992: 377)

Despite the popular choice of western clothes in everyday life in Korea, some women politicians have preferred to wear the *hanbok* to assert traditional qualities and values of nationalism, gender and rural life. Some wear the *hanbok* for official occasions and western clothes at other times. Women associated with progressive politics and social movements generally choose western clothes which convey 'western' values and 'careerism'. In practice, they tend to adopt conservative versions of the suit because they appear to be 'respectful and unobtrusive'. They also minimise 'the display of feminine attraction':

> They tended to avoid wearing bright colours. Makeup was played down. One of them told me she had her shoulder-length hair cut shorter after she began her legislative career to look more dignified.
>
> (Soh 1992: 380)

One woman was daring enough to adopt cross-dressing, wearing a man's suit, necktie, mannish haircut and men's shoes. She regarded it as 'a kind of ritual robe' which facilitated her acceptance into the political system:

> her complete assimilation into the masculine style symbolized by her tailored men's clothes offers a significant illustration of the transforming power of symbols – in this case, the dress styles and other nonverbal behaviour – in creating favourable public images of gender-role identity and personhood for a woman candidate to win political office.
>
> (Soh 1992: 381)

This use of strategic dressing illustrates the significance of clothing in the deployment of power and prestige. Rather than simply being an opposition between traditional (authentic) and western (inauthentic) values and techniques, these examples suggest that a much more complex process is at work. Elements from different dress codes are strategically played off against one another in the process of forming other dress codes and body techniques. Fashion systems are important because of their accessiblity and visibility as commentaries on political exigencies as well as practical ways to negotiate the conflicting departments of existence.

Thus, non-western cultures engage in their own versions of fashion behaviour incorporating elements from western fashion to rework their own body techniques. In particular, there is an investment in maintaining the distinctness of non-western fashion systems because western fashion is often associated with undesirable social practices that other cultures may not wish to emulate. In Bengal, for example, distance from western fashion is maintained by *not* coining a Bengali word for the phenomenon:

> while Bengali words were coined for *modernity* and 'culture', there are no Bengali words to translate *fashion* and *style*. One can infer that the Bengalis wanted to be modern and cultured on their own terms, but to be fashionable or stylish was considered the negative byproduct of unbridled Westernisation. To this day, Bengalis use the English words *fashion* and *style* when a need arises to speak about such matters.
>
> (Nag 1991: 108)

The absence of an indigenous term and the employment of neologisms suggests that non-western cultures distinguish their behaviour as unique and different. Notwithstanding this linguistic reticence, contemporary Bengalis actively seek new patterns and styles of clothes, playing off elements of western fashion with modifications of Bengali dress and decoration. Contemporary Bengali dress codes strategically meet the challenges faced by a modernising culture. The variety of dress codes among Bengali and other Asian women living in different cultures (such as Britain) and exposed to an array of western fashion influences, suggests that fashion systems are more dynamic and responsive than is often presumed.

In her study of Bengali saris, Nag explores how the sari – previously associated with traditional customs – has been given a new lease of life as a fashionable garment. Its virtues are its dual resonances of tradition and modernity. Contemporary advertisements for saris in Bengali women's magazines use the imagery of tradition and nostalgia to entice women to buy the 'new' handwoven saris in order to recapture a mythical past (Nag 1991: 101). The popularity of the 'new' sari is related to the nationalist movement and rise of a new middle class. New economic circumstances have combined with new lifestyles (such as opportunities for working outside the home) and access to western culture (through films, media, popular culture, travel and consumer goods) to create a new fashion system.

While Nag confined her analysis to dress behaviour in Bengal, Khan (1992) has compared dress behaviour in India with that of Asian women in Britain, finding important similarities and differences. She found that older Indian women were more conservative in Britain and clung to traditional dress, while younger and more socially mobile women were caught between clothing systems and conflicting cultural demands. Recent modifications of the sari have reflected these changes:

> In fact the sari is the last, or the most recent of the unexpected changes that have overtaken Asian women's dress in the sub-continent and in Britain. For though, to Western eyes, the sari may have seemed a constant, in actual fact, it has been anything but that. The last decade has seen an extraordinary phenomenon – the arrival of commercial fashion, with all that implies.
>
> (Khan 1992: 62)

Indian designers have created modifications of the sari such as the *nouvelle saree* which:

> may replace the *pullu* with a length of dissimilar material, or decorate itself with environmentally conscious natural substances like bits of wood or bone, or create a turtle-neck for itself, or thread its *pullu* through a slit in a matching blazer. One designer suggested tucking the sari not into a petticoat but into *churidars* or tight trousers instead. Or why not reverse custom and have a fine organza sari over a heavily embroidered petticoat? And its *choli* or blouse might have holes nipped in it.
>
> (Khan 1992: 62)

These versions are sold as fashion, featuring new designs, fabrics and colours geared towards new consumer groups and their lifestyles. The advertising copy in magazines has a familiar ring to it:

The art of the handwoven sari of Bengal has blossomed like a lotus . . . whoever it is – a young girl, a teenager, a middle-aged woman, an older woman – will find something to her liking . . . everyone is coming up with new designs. The market is flooded with variety that was unimaginable even a few years ago. There is no end to the variety of colour . . . Pure silk shines with a royal dignity in silk Tangail saris. Within these varieties there are further distinctions in the form of bright and delicate colours for the young and the teenagers and colours suitable for older women – such as ivory or off-white with plain red border . . . *Jamdani* Dhakai [with intricate embroideries] tops it all. Like the Queen among saris, it commands respect from all others. If you are wearing one of these, then wear some heavy jewellery in the style of your granny's days. Never use a French perfume with it, but use some delicate-smelling *aatur* [an indigenous perfume associated with an atmosphere of classical music and dance on special formal occasions]. Every sari has its own personality and your accessories should go with that. This is the Word about today's fashion.

(Nag 1991: 105)

The traditional associations of the sari have been reworked. Now the sari is promoted as a necessity and advantage for today's modern woman. Whereas, in the recent past, Western clothes were *the* sign of modernisation for non-traditional women, the language of fashion now represents the sari as combining the 'dignified beauty' of tradition with the signs of fashion – through a wide choice of colour, design and fabric. An advertisement for a silk store in Bangalore pictures an elegant woman in a sari sipping a cocktail and reading a letter at an outdoor bar. The text reads:

Sunset, strangers and silks . . .
Sunset by the poolside. An evening with special friends. She waits. Looking alluring in a Benarasi black crepe georgette. With exquisite handwoven motifs in sunset shades. The world seems to stop. And stare. A message hurriedly scrawled asks 'Are you for real?'
(Advertisement for Deepam Silk International, *Glad Rags*, 11(6), 1990: 48)

While saris have gained a new lease of life as fashion items and as signs of the modern sensual Indian woman, fashion magazines also promote another traditional garment as being ideally suited to modern living. The *churidar-kurta*, a loose knee-length shirt worn over a pyjama, has been adopted by young women leading active lives outside the home. The advantage of the *kurta* over the sari is its practicality:

The reason offered is generally that the sari, with its hanging end part and comparatively intricate process of wrapping, obstructs one's freedom of movement, especially when one is not functioning within the privacy of one's home but has to struggle with the jostling crowds of the city.

(Nag 1991: 106)

Sunset by the poolside. An evening with special friends. She waits. Looking alluring. In a Benarasi black crêpe georgette. With exquisite handwoven motifs in sunset shades. The world seems to stop. And stare. A message hurriedly scrawled asks "Are you for real?"

DEEPAM

SILK INTERNATIONAL

M G Road ◆ Bangalore-560 001◆ Phone : 578560 567291

THE SILK STOP

HTA 9182

Figure 2.2 'Sunset, strangers and silks . . . ': the sari as commodity.

Source: Deepam Silks International, Bangalore, *Glad Rags*, 11 June 1990.

Figure 2.3 A fashionable version of Indian dress: 'Peach Mullmull "Gherdar" *Kurta* with "Jali Waistcoat"' by Vinita Pittie.

Source: *Glad Rags*, 11 June 1990.

Throughout India, the *kurta* has become popularised as the basis of the *shalwar* suit which can be found in the wardrobes of modern (middle-class and mobile) Indian women. The suit:

> is made up of three components: a variety of trouser (baggy *shalwar*, either wide or tight at the ankles; wide, straight-legged *pyjamas*; narrow *churidar*) with a tunic-like *kameez* (or shirt-like *kurta*), and co-ordinated *dupatta*, or stole worn with both ends hanging loose over the shoulders at the back.
>
> (Khan 1992: 62)

The outfit used to have religious connotations concerning Muslim values and codes of femininity. It was regarded as regionally specific and was mostly worn by teenagers. Now it is worn everywhere and in many forms: plain colours or with regional motifs; for day or evening wear. The suit has been glamorised. It acts as a transitional item of clothing spanning non-western and western fashion systems. It offers Indian women a choice of clothes to suit the practical requirements of different lifestyles and occasions. For example, while the sari may be preferred by women on special occasions, at home or leisure, the *kurta* is the choice of active students and working women. Both the sari and the *kurta* have been adapted for new conditions and endowed with new meanings. Of the two, the sari has greater symbolic investment. Because the new sari embodies stability in Bengali culture and emergent cultural patterns, it has become a force of new national culture (Nag 1991: 111). Nag also speculates as to whether the sari can contribute to 'a loosening of the hold of nationalist-modernism over femininity' (Nag 1991: 112).

While the sari may indicate the state of nationalist debate, the *kurta* and other adapted clothes reflect the desire of some Indian women to be westernised and cosmopolitan. Accordingly, Indian fashion magazines oscillate between promoting indigenous clothes and western fashion, often choosing to mix and match the two. The models in these magazines project a western 'look' and the text emphasises western fashion designers, models, singers and fads as the role models for local trends. The clothes combine western advertising rhetoric with subtly eastern referents. For example, a fashion feature entitled 'The New Medievalism' was introduced with the.following text:

> This season's new directions take a romantic turn for a look which begins with the rich evocative style of the Moghul 'Begums'. A soft muted palette accentuated with an extravagant use of fabric, Vinita Pittie's collection blazes with soulful splendour. The organic texture of Mullmull, the Angarkha form of organza, the crinkled ruffles and the unfurling drama of the Dupatta bring back the romance of an unforgettable period that was.
>
> ('The New Medievalism', *Glad Rags*, 11(6), 1990: 40)

Another article in the same magazine noted the influence of traditional Indian clothes on Parisian fashion. Citing the example of Romeo Gigli's 1990 summer collection, the magazine celebrated the style as:

pure Rajasthan with a dash of Goa . . . a masterly combination of East and West. Gigli scours the Orient for fabrics and ideas. He translates peasants' clothes into designer outfits that cost hundreds of dollars and sell in thousands in upmarket boutiques from London, Paris, Milan and New York.

('Out of India', *Glad Rags*, 11(6), 1990: 85)

Clearly, different fashion systems compete and interact in the production of these East–West fusions. Changing living and cultural circumstances, the influence of western ideas and consumer fashion, and the interchanges between India and ex-patriate Indian communities have forged a complex array of dress codes and body techniques. While the sari has remained the central element of these practices, its form and rules of usage have been modified.

These examples suggest that techniques of dress and decoration are crucial to assertions of identity and to reformations of identity. Both the westernisation of dress codes and renunciation or modification of western dress have been important strategies in colonialisation and nationalist struggles. In other words, tensions between fashion systems are part and parcel of cultural and political formations. Rather than being mutually exclusive, western and indigenous clothing systems are dynamic, changing and in competition for cultural allegiances.

EXOTIC MOTIFS IN WESTERN FASHION

Western cultures are obsessed with demonstrating their civilised ways – to show that they are different from, and superior to, other cultures, hence the emphasis on newness and nowness. But the technique of establishing signs of civility involves the assertion of distinctiveness against other forms of culture. Accordingly, western fashion systems relentlessly re-invent otherness, by references to the past (historical allusions), to non-and pre-industrial cultures (folk costume and ethnic looks), and to previous moments in fashion (cyclical re-vamping of the 'look' of earlier decades). The western fashion system poaches from other systems and cannibalises diverse influences in reconstituting new techniques of dress and decoration.

Yves Saint Laurent's 1976 peasant collection was a well-documented example of the process. The collection adapted elements of European peasant dress (milkmaids' tunics, embroidered folk blouses and gathered skirts, and touches of Cossack costume) and transformed them into glamorous couture. Although greeted with controversy, the collection proved to be highly successful, spawning diverse adaptations of the peasant theme in high street fashion. Saint Laurent's achievement was to marry 'the pop culture themes of the street to high fashion itself'. According to one critic, he 'crystallized a new image of femininity and coopted the growing ethnic consciousness and pastoral nostalgia for the guardians of multinational finance' (Fox-Genovese 1978: 59). Saint Laurent enabled the rich to 'play act' at being peasants while ordinary women felt an affinity with the humble origins of this new style. These contradictory messages

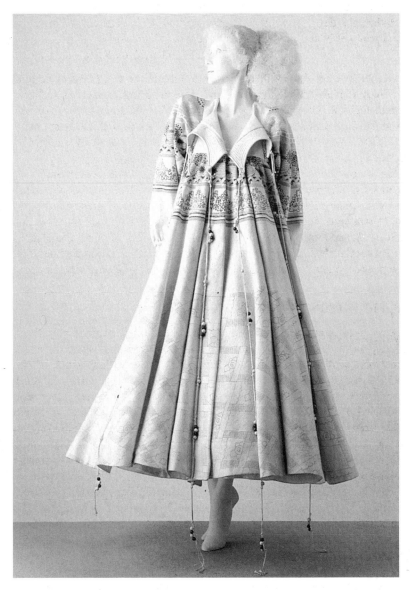

Figure 2.4 Ethnic influences in western fashion. Evening coat in screen-printed felt by Zandra Rhodes 1969.

Source: Reproduced by courtesy of the Board of Trustees of the Victoria & Albert Museum.

appealed simultaneously to the cultural preoccupations of the moment – political upheavals, the assertion of popular opinion through demonstrations, moral panics about mass culture, and the women's movement: 'The peasant look turned explicitly to women to embody – to display – those values which cannot be assimilated into the nitty-gritty of modern life and must therefore be left to culture' (Fox-Genovese 1978: 83).

The theme of the collection tapped a nerve among women that defied simple marketing logic. Despite retrospective explanations for its success, the peasant collection exemplified the volatility of the fashion industry. Exotic themes have become a leitmotif of new fashions through the incorporation of themes such as jungle or tropical imagery, 'exotic' peoples and cultures, elements of 'folk' and 'ethnic' costume, and recycled items from earlier fashions. Frequently, exotic motifs from tourist destinations or from post-colonial cultures form the basis of fashion derivations.

Indian fashion has been used in this chapter as an example of mutual appropriation. Modifications of Indian clothing under the impact of western culture have been discussed above. During the period of contact with western culture, India has made several vestimentary responses: in some cases, abandoning traditional clothes for western ones; sometimes maintaining traditional clothing codes; or else, modifying traditional and/or western clothes.

Khan (1992) suggests that even greater changes were prompted by the interest in the Indian 'ethnic' look in the 1960s and 1970s. At first, this involved adaptations of Indian clothes by the west and export of fashions to the west. Gradually, this western interest was taken up by culturally mobile Indians who wished to fuse their sense of ethnic identity with western fashion systems: 'Western flares triggered off a response in the East – long *kurtas* over co-ordinated, bell-bottomed trousers' (Khan 1992: 63–4). During the 1980s, more extravagant modifications of traditional Indian fashion were revitalised using local skills in fabric weaving and dyeing, silk, embroidery, and jewellery: 'The old, heavy, village jewellery, inches of lacquered bangles, decorative, "third-eye" *bindi* on the forehead reinforced the vivid and lively "ethnic" look' (Khan 1992: 64).

These modified fashions were popular both in the sub-continent and among certain groups of Asian women in western societies. Khan (1992: 68) attributes the changes to three factors. First, there was a 'creative fashion explosion' in India which produced 'vivid, imaginative clothes that explored and celebrated Indian roots'. Not only did this radically change clothing codes in India but impacted on ex-patriate Indians who revived a sense of pride in Indian culture through these desirable new looks. Second, a new generation of educated and articulate women were entering professions both in India and elsewhere. Their lifestyles required some accommodation between traditional and contemporary clothing systems. Third, the 1980s witnessed a new attitude to ethnicity and multiculturalism which celebrated a variety of non-western cultural forms. According to Khan:

It cannot be accidental that the first signs of local Asian designers and clothes boutiques became apparent [in Britain] soon afterwards. Nor can it be accidental that their clothes aimed for an East–West synthesis.

(Khan 1992: 68)

These new designs modified traditional garments and combined them with the logic of western fashion. They rapidly gained popularity:

At last, said the middle- and upper-class women who bought them, here were clothes that could take in both East and West, that didn't involve them in a choice between two different worlds, and that mirrored their own confidence in presenting themselves on their own terms as Westernised Asian women.

(Khan 1992: 70)

These fashions have proved to be a practical technique to suit dual cultural systems. They have been adopted by fashionable women in Asia, Asian women in the west, and by western women with a fascination with eastern culture. The interplay between these competing fashions systems, both at the level of design, clothing habits and economic exchange constitutes a microcosm of fashion as an industry. The process depends on highly exploitative by-products of consumerism and internationalisation. Third world countries like Bangladesh, Korea and China have become the sites of the mass production of fashion for the west because of low wages and minimal worker protection. Stringent efforts are made to 'prevent the clothes from being released on to the local market' (Khan 1992: 66; cf. Coleridge 1989: 283–90). Nonetheless, there is considerable leakage between competing systems offering a choice of dress techniques to consumers everywhere.

A similar process of modified and interdependent fashion systems has occurred among blacks in America and Europe. They have developed a distinctive but interrelated system of fashion alongside dominant western modes. One instance was the zoot suit, which was popularised among American blacks in the 1940s. It was not just a style, but 'an emblem of ethnicity and a way of negotiating an identity' (Cosgrove 1989: 4). It was both a symbol of racial tension and the focus of racial conflict. Attempts were made to ban the zoot suit and vigilante parties hunted down zoot suiters and stripped them of their distinctive frock coat and trousers. The suits were a means of expressing resistance to white culture and of rebellion:

In retrospect, the zoot suit's history can be seen as a point of intersection, between the related potential of ethnicity and politics on the one hand, and the pleasures of identity and difference on the other. It is the zoot suit's political and ethnic associations that have made it such a rich reference point for subsequent generations.

(Cosgrove 1989: 20)

Out of the zoot suit came the dandy of the 1950s, as young blacks continued to assert a separate identity and assume a distinct lifestyle based on black music and associated subcultures (Tulloch 1992: 85–6). With the growth of popular music as the focus of youth culture, came recognition by white youth of the richness of black culture. Stylistic elements began to percolate through white fashion and culture. During the 1960s, black style was acknowledged as a fashion system and encapsulated in the figure of the Rude Boy (Jamaica and UK) and Cool Cat (US). Style was explicitly a sign of rebellion and active resistance: 'priorities of subversion, materialism and a little violence for diversity' (Tulloch 1992: 87). Musically, black style was expressed in reggae, soul and later rap. The growth of Black Power, Rastafarianism, policies of non-discrimination, and a Black is Beautiful rhetoric combined to consolidate the transformation of subcultural fashions into mainstream systems. Throughout the 1980s, experimentation with black style merged with popularisation and embodiment in urban fashion more generally.

An index of greater confidence within black culture, greater acceptance of black fashion and tolerance towards black culture, has been reflected in a greater emphasis on casual, sportswear and leisure clothes in black fashion. Correspondingly, black musicians have 'consciously promoted themselves as a positive cross-cultural tangram bent on world domination' (Tulloch 1992: 93). Ironically, as the distinctiveness of black style has been acknowledged, so too has it influenced trends in white western fashion. Black designers, themselves, have recognised this. Tulloch cites the 1991 'One World' collection of Joe Casely-Halford:

> He proved that one need not be an overt black expressionist in order to filter segments of one's cultural heritage and views into designs whilst capably delivering the goods to a non-black clientele to incorporate into their own lifestyle: 'locksed up', barefooted white models in waif-like slip dresses shielded themselves with giant silk scarves . . . depicting a world map of three globes – Africa being the focal point – held in black hands and incorporating the slogan, 'No more first, second and third world, just one world'.
>
> (Tulloch 1992: 96)

One of the most interesting recent interventions in western fashion has been the success of Shammi Ahmed, an Asian Briton, who has created the highly popular label, 'The Legendary Joe Bloggs'. He has challenged western fashion on its own terms by producing his own line of leisure wear: 'the unmistakable Joe Bloggs T-shirts, the improbably baggy, wide-bottomed jeans'. Despite – or because of – the ironic appropriation of these quintessentially western garments, Ahmed has become a multimillionaire as a result of this foray into fashion (Khan 1992: 73).

Indeed, significant inroads have been made into the European domination of western fashion. Perhaps the most radical force has been the penetration of Japanese design. Numerous designers – in particular, Issey Miyake, Rei Kawakubo of Comme des Garçons, Yohji Yamamoto, Kenzo, Kansai and Matsuda – have infiltrated both Parisian couture and street fashion (Nicklin 1984:

58; Koren 1984; Steele 1991: 183–9; McDowell 1984: 178–9). Considered together, the Japanese designers seem to share the influence of three key elements of Japanese aesthetic philosophy – irregularity, imperfection and asymmetry (Steele 1991: 186). They have collectively challenged many of the tenets of design as well as rejecting 'formal' ideals of clothes in favour of wearable ones.

Miyake has been credited with smashing 'the image of *haute couture* as the standard bearer of fashion, as well as the idea that clothes transform those who wear them' (Isozaki 1978: 55). Instead, he has played with the space between the fabric and the body, reducing their relationship to the minimum:

> In western clothing the fabric is cut to the bodyline and sewn. The form of the attire is modelled after the body, with a shell similar to the shape of the body thus being created. In so doing, the space between the two is eliminated. In the case of Japanese attire, a technique which simplifies cutting to the minimum is predominate [*sic*]; the set width of the material itself, like an invariable constant, given importance.
>
> (Isozaki 1978: 55–6)

Miyake has emphasised the space between the body and cloth by asymmetrically draping the cloth over the body as if it were wrapped up in anarchic layers: a 'symbolic gesture made against the methodical structure of the parisienne *haute couture*' (Isozaki 1978: 56). His clothes have drawn on elements of Japanese design, nationalism and philosophy:

> His clothes are active, not passive, and they make demands. They are not clothes for fitting in . . . His clothes also often use certain historic Japanese shapes and exotic combinations of material that are, in some cases, almost ancient (like paper), but all for modern means.
>
> (Cocks 1988: n.p.)

Other Japanese designers have also played with a mix of traditions that challenge conventional tenets of fashion. Kawakubo, for example, presents an 'eclectic combination of global cultures . . . chopp[ing] away at the traditional trench coat and clipp[ing] up the tail of the dinner jacket, mixing Western tradition with Indian elegance and Japanese style' (T. Jones 1992: 72). Unlike Parisian couture, Matsuda claims that his 'clothes are not made to shock or to be framed and hung on the wall; they are made to be worn, to be comfortable, functional and look good' (quoted by Nicklin 1984: 62).

The Japanese influence has partially re-drawn the boundaries of fashion away from 'western' ideals of the body, body–space relations, and conventions of clothing. The principles of western fashion have incorporated non-European influences, traditions and forms into mainstream practice.

Distinctions between fashion systems obscure their interrelationships and interdependence. Not only have fashion systems become internationalised, so too have discourses surrounding fashion. Thus consumer fashion simultaneously draws on discourses of exoticism, the primitive, orientalism and authenticity.

Figure 2.5 Japanese revision of western fashion: swirling asymmetrical cape by
        Issey Miyake.

While these terms reiterate distinctions between western and other fashion systems, in fact their deployment crosses such boundaries although it is geared towards specific conditions of social interchange and environments. In this process, exotic impulses merely allude to sites of difference, insecurity and transgression in each cultural milieu.

Chapter 3

Fashioning women
Techniques of femininity

FROM FEMALE TO FEMININE

> All the things that adorn woman, all the things that go to enhance her beauty,
> are part of herself . . . making . . . the woman and her dress, an indivisible
> whole.
>
> (Baudelaire 1972: 423–4)

Western culture is obsessed with sex (e.g. Adams and Cowie 1990). The topic of
women has preoccupied countless philosophers and feminists. The sex–gender
distinction is one dimension of this interest. If sex is determined by biology, then
gender is learned and acquired as a set of social trainings about how female
bodies behave. Mauss (1973: 84) observed that 'Nothing is more technical than
sexual positions'. As well as techniques of sexual acts underpinned by an array
of sexual morals, there is an even more bewildering array of techniques of
gender.

It is also possible to distinguish techniques associated with the occupancy of
a female body (being female) from techniques that deploy gender as a social
strategy (being feminine). While techniques of being female include practices
associated with fertility, nurturing and caring, they also include techniques
associated with domesticity and the management of everyday life. Techniques of
femininity are related to these (and obviously there is a fine line between the two)
but are characterised by techniques of display and projection of the female body.
This chapter explores some of the relationships between these two sets of techniques, especially where the two are in tension or conflict.

Fashion systems – and techniques of dress and decoration more generally –
manifest techniques of gender specific to any cultural formation. Western fashion
became preoccupied with techniques of femininity as 'the woman question'
gained ascendancy from the eighteenth century onward:

> Devotion to fashion in dress was adduced as a natural weakness of women,
> something they could not help. This view was strengthened in the nineteenth
> century, when masculine and feminine clothing became so much more
> different in fabric, trim, and construction. Elegant men's clothing during this

time was actually no less complex, demanding, and uncomfortable, but it tended to be more subdued and abstract in the way it looked. Women's clothing was extremely expressive, almost literary, and very deliberately decorative and noticeable.

(Hollander 1980: 360)

The emphasis on techniques of display was double-edged. On the one hand, these techniques were geared to articulating appropriate forms of conduct and facilitating social intercourse. On the other, signs of display had to be intelligible to

Figure 3.1 Demure formality and Victorian femininity. (America 1905.)

the observer and a credible reflection of the social position and location of the wearer. Techniques of display were shorthand for moral qualities. Women, in particular, were at risk of being damned by their garb. Depictions of women's fashions were frequently tinged with moral condemnation as in the following description of the women in the new colony of Sydney in 1811:

> the European women in the settlement spare no expense in ornamenting their persons, and in dress, each seems to vie with the other in extravagance. The costliness of the exterior . . . is meant as a mark of superiority; but confers very little grace, and much less virtue, on its wearer, when speaking of the dashing belles who generally frequent the Rocks.
>
> (Quoted by Sanders 1992: 144)

The ways in which bodies are fashioned through clothes, make-up and demeanour constitute identity, sexuality and social position. In other words, clothed bodies are tools of self-management.

The peculiar inflection of western fashion stems from the philosophical oppositions between subject/object and male/female. Women are constrained by representational codes which position them as passive vehicles of display and the object of the look. In turn, the look is structured by the normative male gaze, as objects of desire and repositories of pleasure (e.g. Berger 1972; Pollock 1977). Fashion has been singled out as a domain of representation and practice in which exploitative relations are central. Because femininity is defined in terms of how the female body is perceived and represented, 'a woman's character and status are frequently judged by her appearance' (Betterton 1987: 7). The body 'is the site on which feminine cultural ideals can be literally manufactured' (ibid.: 8): 'Paintings, advertisements, pornography, and fashion are all practices which produce particular ways of seeing the feminine body' (ibid.: 9).

According to Sawchuk (1987), the link between fashion and femaleness has three sources: explanations of capitalism that equate men with production and women with consumption (Veblen 1970); art history that associates the development of western art with the portraiture of the female nude (Berger 1972; Pollock 1977); and psychoanalytic accounts of the gaze as gender-coded (Mulvey 1975). These preoccupations construct a reductionist framework of explaining fashion: 'as a reflection of the social onto the body, fashion as the repression of the natural body; fashion simply as a commodity to be resisted; fashion as substitute for the missing phallus' (Sawchuk 1987: 65). In other words, women 'are sold their image in the form of commodities' (Betterton 1987: 13).

From this standpoint, fashion constitutes an effective and pervasive means through which women become objects of the gaze and of male sexual desire. If women are confined to the role of display, and 'measured' by the standards of achieving desirable 'looks', they are caught up in a vicious circle:

> Women's love of clothes, cosmetics, jewellery, their obsession with style and fashion, reinforces the myth that we are narcissistic and materialistic. In turn,

this reinforces capitalism, which depends upon this obsession with our bodies for the marketing of new products.

(Sawchuk 1987: 64)

Sawchuk questions the essentialist basis of the equation between economics and gender. She argues that it is both 'repressive and homogeneous in its effects', as well as depending on a transparent relationship between representations and texts upon readers and viewers (ibid.). Instead, western fashion should be seen as culturally and historically specific. Western consumer fashion was shaped by the legacy of Christian morality and Victorian respectability. Changing circumstances have changed the parameters of western fashion. A significant number of commentators have revised the ways in which gender should be conceived in techniques of representation and cultural production (e.g. Betterton 1987).

Some of this work has specifically addressed the subject of women and fashion (e.g. Ash and Wilson 1992; Garber 1992; Hollander 1980; Kidwell and Steele 1989; Shields 1990; Steele 1991; Wilson 1985). Common to this work is the argument that gender identity is a multi-faceted process that implicates not only sexual desire but a range of learnings, orientations, identifications and sexual knowledges. These are gained from a variety of sources in processes of prestigious imitation. Sources of knowledge of gender techniques include overtly instructional 'manuals' (such as etiquette guides and women's magazines), role models (prestigious or influential women) and specific techniques of the body. This chapter explores some of these feminine trainings.

INSTRUCTING FEMININITY

Overt forms of instruction about techniques of being female and feminine have been shaped by changing ideas about gender. Since the eighteenth century, techniques of femininity have been organised around body techniques, interactive modalities and mental dispositions through which 'feminine' attributes are displayed. Weibel (1977: 176) relates this to the 'vast separation in male and female roles that came in with the Industrial Revolution'.

The development of the class system as an outcome of economic growth and restructuring, coincided with changing perceptions of gender. With it came 'the increasing identification of a particular class, the bourgeoisie, with the attributes of a particular gender, the feminine, newly defined wholly in terms of a domestic and private sphere' (Ballaster *et al.* 1991: 74). Women were the visible correlate of the economic and social standing of their menfolk. Becoming feminine was a 'task' of learning about the attributes of femininity, 'a task wholly identified with the world of leisure, and a task that can be a pleasure, not a labour' (ibid.).

The convergence of class with gender, and the association of femininity with 'leisures and ornament', were central to the production of advice for women on how to be feminine. Advice came in the form of admonitions on moral conduct, steps to realising feminine 'nature', information about clothing conduct and fashion, deportment and social etiquette, as well as guides to fertility, family and domestic management. The intertwining of personal and social identity were central to European notions of femininity.

The politics of the body were elided with domestic, social and public politics. During the eighteenth century, the publication of magazines specifically addressed to women took up these concerns. While magazines such as *The Tatler* appealed to the social snobbery of the upper echelons, new magazines appealed to wider audiences. They were akin to training manuals for the masses. Dominated by 'domestic' magazines, they concentrated on 'the struggle to achieve marital happiness and perceiv[ed] "women's issues" as determined solely with regard to this single "career"' (Ballaster *et al.* 1991: 59).

The format of these magazines set the tone for subsequent publications. Ballaster *et al.* (1991: 71) cited the *Lady's Magazine* as the forerunner of modern women's magazines:

> Every feature common to the twentieth-century form we know so well appears at one time or another in its pages; the agony aunt, occasional news reporting with a 'woman's' slant, features on famous women (past and present), cookery recipes, sewing patterns, medical advice, readers' letters, regular contributors. Like the modern women's magazine . . . the *Lady's Magazine* was not constructed to be read from beginning to end, but rather according to the reader's interests and priorities, article by article.

The popularity of women's magazines grew enormously. Early magazines stressed the qualities of virtue and morality that were associated with femininity. Later, the Victorian ideal shaped the format of magazines including sections offering tips on household management, dressmaking, essay competitions, fiction, literary criticism, gardening, hygiene and healthcare, and 'courtship' advice (C. White 1970: 45). Other magazines focused on beauty, dress, and taste.

The late nineteenth century witnessed an explosion of women's magazines which reflected major changes in economic circumstances, social mobility and mass production. Between 1870 and 1900, fifty new titles appeared in Britain and women became 'consumers of magazines on a scale unimaginable a century earlier' (Ballaster *et al.* 1991: 75). Advertising and consumerism had a growing importance in addressing women in their role as housewives (as opposed to house managers). Several titles, including Isabella Beeton's *Englishwoman's Domestic Magazine*, established in the 1850s, 'set the pattern for middle- and working-class women's magazines for the next fifty years' (ibid.: 83).

There was a tension between the promotion of beauty aids and new fashion trends and attention to domestic chores and problems, childrearing and personal concerns. While some women advocated emancipation, employment and independence, others wanted to be 'a quite unillustrious, more or less hampered and dependent wife and mother', as one correspondent put it (C. White 1970: 89). Ballaster *et al.* (1991: 84–5) suggest that domestic ideology 'was neither monolithic nor static; indeed, it was deeply contradictory'. Women's magazines were consumed by women readers with very different circumstances of existence. Gradually, magazines began to identify specific readerships by structuring their appeal and content:

> the relatively expensive (sixpenny) weekly ladies' paper aimed at the upper-class woman; the good-quality middle-class domestic magazine, which cost up to sixpence per month; and the penny weeklies aimed at the or working-class woman.
>
> (Ballaster *et al.* 1991: 92–3)

The differentiation of the readership of women's magazines reflected changes in definitions of femininity from the eighteenth to nineteenth centuries. Gone were the moral and religious emphases on women's 'nature' and duty, being replaced by an emphasis on women's labour and achievements. The new woman was defined primarily as a 'homemaker' undertaking practical (household management), economic (managing the household finances) and moral (reproduction, caring and nurturing) (Ballaster *et al.* 1991: 88). Magazines reflected this orientation toward domestic activities by reiterating the work of the household as the organising principle of women's lives. This was increasingly 'balanced' by the insertion of specials on fashion and beauty:

> On the one hand, woman's role was to be beautiful, dressed in clothes which expressed the social status of her husband or father and her own desirability. But the domestic role demanded that her sexuality could only be expressed through maternity.
>
> (Ballaster *et al.* 1991: 89–90)

Thus the magazines offered contradictory and competing roles for readers, sometimes resolved by the insertion of a paper pattern enabling the reader to labour to produce the desired fashionable mode. In this way, the magazine could be both a 'work manual' and 'purveyor of pleasure'. By the late nineteenth century, yet another model of femininity could be identified, that of consumer. With the growth of advertising, the manufacture of beauty products and the use of visuals in magazines, the definition of woman became bound up with appearance and dress, which 'depended in turn on her spending power and discrimination as a consumer' (Ballaster *at al.* 1991: 97). Whether women had the opportunity, or could afford, to indulge in conspicuous consumption, women's magazines – be they 'ladies', homemaker, or escapist penny papers for working women – all played on the contradictions and tensions between different roles and orientations for women.

Nonetheless, Ballaster *et al.* (1991: 107) stressed that 'womanliness was ever the site of competing definitions based on generation, class, status and wealth'. Although these concerns have persisted to set the agenda of women's magazines, subsequent shifts in the definition of femininity can be found. Thus, while the genre of the women's magazine has remained constant, its specific appeals and addresses have varied. SINCE FILM + MEDIA DEVELOPMENTS

Another strong indicator of the source of feminine trainings came in the huge demand for etiquette guides. Women's roles were specifically associated with etiquette as the 'preservers of morality and arbiters of taste' (Windshuttle 1980: 70). A distinction was made between public and private etiquette, with the lion's share being associated with the domestic sphere and the private home. Etiquette consisted of manners, rules of social intercourse, knowledge of what counted as 'taste', rules of dress, and an appreciation of social hierarchies. Victorian notions of femininity were interspliced with codes of etiquette.

As the changing conditions of women's lives accelerated through the 1920s, 1930s and 1940s, so the contradictions and conflicts multiplied. In the home, women increasingly 'did' for themselves. The highly visible role of (middle-class) women as the 'social' face of family life which developed in the nineteenth century declined. A woman was now seen 'as guardian of her family's health and happiness rather than of its social place' (Davidoff 1973: 99). This change was reflected in the changing foci of the contents of household management and etiquette guides. Advice was now offered on social etiquette, household help, beauty, self-improvement and fashion. Women's bodies (rather than moral qualities) became the currency through which success could be achieved in these diverse spheres. Clothes and body silhouettes were the visible markers of style.

Yet, despite the long history of women's magazines, their significance as technical guides has only recently been acknowledged. Despite their long-term success and enormous readerships, women's magazines were not defined as an industry until after World War II (Ballaster *et al.* 1991: 109–15). This belated recognition was initiated by advertisers who realised the potential benefits of appealing to this special consumer group. Academic interest in the content of the women's magazines has developed even more recently (e.g. C. White 1970; Millum 1975; Winship 1978, 1987, 1991; Ballaster *et al.* 1991). These studies have centred on how women's magazines create 'a world of woman: woman to woman', and on the images of women that they offer. Most studies have noted the lack of fit between the ideals of femininity and the practical conduct of women.

During the twentieth century, the established formats of women's magazines have persisted. On the one hand, they offer advice, information and instruction specifically for women (practical techniques of being female), while on the other hand, they offer images of femininity, fashion and beauty (techniques of desire and femininity). During the 1920s and 1930s, the number of women's magazines mushroomed and experimented with new formats. Generally, the newcomers addressed middle- and lower-middle-class women rather than the leisured wealthy class. For example, the British magazine *Woman* sought to 'entertain you with vivid, vital stories and touching every side of life and human interest' as well as giving 'you practical help and inspiration concerning your home' (C. White 1970: 97). By contrast, *Good Housekeeping*, launched in 1922, extolled 'home-making as a full-time job with its own kind of professionalism . . . in a double process of encouraging high standards of household management and providing work-manuals of basic skills' (Ballaster *et al.* 1991: 121).

The functions of magazines became more explicitly demarcated between service (especially concerned with housework as domestic science), fashion and beauty, lifestyle and consumerism, and self-improvement. This was the fore-runner of niche marketing. Different consumer groups were being distinguished by their attributes.

Meanwhile, 'a new and all-pervasive preoccupation with sex' emerged in the twenties (C. White 1970: 107). At first, magazines were circumspect, but gradually sex became the centrepiece of the rhetoric and visual presentation of women's magazines. The frivolity of the 1920s turned to an obsession with consumerism in the 1930s, concerns that were muted during wartime. Instead, women were mobilised first to support the war effort and later to actively contribute to it. Although women were still primarily managing home and family, they were also offered new options and occupations as a consequence of the war. The change was short-lived. Magazines of the 1950s returned to pre-war con-cerns of family and consumerism:

> The bride replaced the working woman. She was used to sell soap, stockings, soap powders, aspirin and tea. By the 1950s her 'dewy loveliness' was also selling crockery, lingerie and linen. As a newly-wed she supervised a modern home equipped with the latest devices of electric servants, which make her 'a home-manager instead of a home slave'.
>
> (Anon 1973: 13)

Advertising came to dominate the magazines in ways which disturbed the editors and moral guardians. Advertisers used 'the sexual sell', playing on emotions and fantasies

> calculated to focus attention on their domestic role, reinforce home values, and perpetuate the belief that success as a woman, wife and mother, could be purchased for the price of a jar of cold cream, a bottle of cough syrup or a packet of instant cake-mix.
>
> (C. White 1970: 158)

The tension between the advocacy of techniques of beauty and self-presentation versus techniques of homemaking were sharpened with the development of mass produced cosmetics and consumer fashion:

> 'Make-up' became not only respectable but essential for feminine beauty. Cosmetic advertisements and advice on their use in advertorials thus brought together consumption and the representation of women as object of the gaze, linking both to the work of femininity.
>
> (Ballaster et al. 1991: 122)

Despite the emphasis on 'the look' of femininity, magazines continued to advo-cate a 'maternal, nurturative role' for women as supportive and resourceful counterparts to men, while women who sought other roles were portrayed as 'selfish, or fractious' (Anon 1973: 13).

In the 1960s, two changes occurred. On the one hand, the influence of advertisers increased to the point where they determined the look, focus and success of magazines. On the other, in response to new ideas of consumer sovereignty and the opportunity for consumers to make choices between products, magazines became less dogmatic and more interactive. They were training women to be consumers by encouraging readers to contribute and participate in the pages of the magazine – for example, through letter pages, diverse advice columns, reader makeovers, and fashion features. Domesticity and new social problems dominated the content. Magazines offered discrete sections which corresponded to the different departments of women's lives, and offered advice to improve the management of these arenas. Homemaking was structured as a blend of work and leisure and a happy home as the product of hard work:

> the home is simultaneously *just* an arena of leisure for women, and one of leisure and *work*, where 'work' is justified as such (even when we might not think of it as work – the work of beauty) by resort to the masculine concepts of work – efficiency, planning, etc.
>
> (Winship 1978: 137)

The strategies of magazines became more precise as techniques of market research were borrowed from the advertisers and used to characterise the profile, lifecycle and consumer patterns of readers. Readerships were distinguished in terms of ideal types such as the housewife, the young married woman, the teenager, the fashion sophisticate, and the 'with it generation'. Although a range of new titles appeared, including *She*, *Nova*, *Cosmopolitan*, *Options* and *Elle*, 'none of these magazines took the world of paid work as the ground for an alternative definition of the feminine' (Ballaster *et al.* 1991: 123).

Nonetheless, magazines were changing as was their appeal. For example, in 1965, Helen Gurley Brown used her magazine, *Cosmopolitan*, to transform girls from 'timid mouseburgers', constrained by the 'gender gap' in romance and the 'glass ceiling' at the office to the glossy, confident Cosmo Girl (McCarthy 1990: 58). The Cosmo Girl was proactive – not only concerned with finding a man, but forging a career, living an independent life, and acquiring consumer goods. In keeping with the tradition of earlier magazines, the transformation was the outcome of self-improvement, of setting goals and fighting to attain them. Unusually, *Cosmopolitan* endorsed feminism and (hetero)sexual enjoyment at the same time, as well as taking a stand on a number of controversial issues. Betty Friedan commented that she:

> was very grateful for the support of Helen Gurley Brown in our early battles for equality. I enjoyed having that sexy Cosmopolitan Girl say that she loved her sports car and her new Chanel suit, but any man who wanted to attract her had to be for the ERA.
>
> (Friedan 1991: 66)

Attempts were made to engage with new agendas for women and to reflect the 'inexorable movement towards greater independence, responsibility and social mobility for women' (Harrison 1991: 228). While *Cosmopolitan* tackled 'the tangled relations of work and pleasure' through sexuality (Ballaster *et al.* 1991: 124), other new magazines, such as *Nova*, tried to develop a formula that addressed women as intelligent and responsible readers. *Nova* was a complex and provocative magazine with an editorial policy 'predicated on the shared disillusion of a generation turning its back on the shining brave new world' (Harrison 1991: 228). One of its most memorable features was its use of 'punchy, graphic and unabashedly sexy photographs' (Harrison 1991: 228). The magazine eventually failed though it remains one of the most radical experiments in women's magazines. While its less radical contemporary *Cosmopolitan* has surived, so too has the explicitly feminist magazine *Spare Rib*, perhaps surprisingly (Ballaster *et al.* 1991: 112). These deviations did not stop either the persistence of the home-and-family orientation of the majority of women's magazines, nor halt the declining circulation of women's magazines as a whole.

The 1970s and 1980s saw some shakeouts in the market as new titles appealing to the 'new woman' jostled with the evergreen service magazines. While distancing themselves from explicitly feminist publications, the most innovative titles have been aimed at 'women who are not readers of women's magazines', that is, to women who do actively dislike the 'service' and domestic emphasis of traditional women's magazines, but who want magazines that address the circumstances and interests of working women who also value their home lives (S. Williams 1990: 84). The idea of gender-specific appeals has also been questioned in relation to the perpetuation of the separate 'Women's Page' in newspapers (Braden 1991).

On the whole, however, most women's magazines still concentrate on offering advice about femininity and providing entertainment for women (C. White 1970: 276). Nonetheless, women's magazines construct a 'privileged space, or world, within which to construct and explore the female self' (Ballaster *et al.* 1991: 176). C. White (1970: 299) described women's magazines as constituting an arena of femininity:

> Turning the first page of a mass weekly is like entering a women's club – a woman knows she is on 'home ground' in more senses than one. This is her territory, her profession; she knows the rules and she shares the implicit goals and values. Here she finds warmth, friendship and identification, as well as a little harmless escapism. There is colour, humour and vitality to raise her spirits, and often a money-saving offer to give a fillip to her wardrobe. Over the years a special relationship can grow up between readers and their magazines, a strong bond compounded of trust, loyalty – and habit.
>
> (C. White 1970: 299)

Against these habitual readerships, magazines and their readers became the object of scrutiny in the 1970s and 1980s. Critics have argued that women's magazines portray a shallow range of role models for women as well as relying on the sexual sell as the basis of advertising and guides to personal presentation. Millum (1975: 160) concluded that women's magazines in the 1960s and 1970s offered women just four roles: hostess, mannequin, self-involved narcissist, or wife and mother. According to Millum, the limited range of roles offered by advertising acts as a social regulator that preserves the status quo by moulding women's points of view and legitimating the lack of choice for women:

> The roles offered, the life-patterns indicated, the stances offered, are all consistent in their occurrence and their form, and it must be remembered, cumulative. Not only this, but the magazines themselves in most cases support the advertising in the maintenance of these roles . . . The reification of the female, loss of individual independence, introversion, the retreat into the womb of the home, woman as the natural half of humanity, guardian of the past and the future, the emphasis on sexual attraction, competitiveness . . . all these occur again and again, the same roles are proffered again and again, consistently and cumulatively.
>
> (Millum 1975: 179)

Despite the persistence of these themes, the range of women's magazines and changing patterns of circulation and readership suggest that women consume and use magazines in complex ways. Magazines of the 1980s and 1990s are organised around diversity and choice as the basis of customised techniques of femininity. This approach accords with the general popularity of the 'psy' complex in contemporary western culture. Women's magazines offer readers a smorgasbord of identifications, practical skills, objects of desire, and competing sources of prestigious imitation. The revised techniques of femininity supplant the choice between domesticity versus self-presentation with a tension between work and family in a lifestyle characterised by activity and independence. By casting women in this proactive model, women's magazines construct women's culture around individuality and achievement rather than around conformity and duty. Even Betty Friedan, the well-known American feminist, has endorsed the 'new look' women's magazines:

> Actually the world depicted in women's magazines today is much more progressive than it was 25 years ago. There is a much greater diversity of women in those pages – black, Asian, and Hispanic. And the very advice they give out implies autonomy, independence, and a lack of complete credulity or passivity on the reader's part. There's a complex richness to women's culture today that is a beautiful mix of feminism and femininity.
>
> (Friedan 1991: 66)

Even so, the new femininity is still complex and contradictory, posing work against home, conservatism against progressiveness, and habit versus change. The different sections of women's magazines not only place these oppositions side by side, but invite selective reading strategies. Women 'dip into' bits and pieces of magazines explicitly engaging with the 'severely contradictory, if not incoherent, discourses of femininity simultaneously' (Ballaster *et al.* 1991: 162). Not only are readers selective and inconsistent in their reading patterns, they are also sceptical – even cynical – about what they eagerly consume.

Women read magazines as 'small treats' (Winship 1991: 148), as illicit pleasures, and as 'time out' from hectic schedules (Craik 1991). According to Winship, the revival of crafts and homemaking in the 1980s is not a nostalgic hankering for simpler pasts, but sublime 'surrogacy for practices that might construct another self; another place for women' (Winship 1991: 149). It is a way in which women can reconcile multiple demands by fantasising about leisure while at the same time vicariously asserting '"independence", which currently means doing it all: child and husband care, paid work' (ibid.: 148). The appeal of the image of home cooking, arts and crafts, and home sewing (even if readers are too busy to actually make something) is precisely the way in which work is constructed as leisure. It also reflects the widespread popularity of DIY (do-it-yourself) within the home because it seems to 'undo' mass consumption – and the dependence on supermarkets, department stores, seasonal sales and the like (cf. Tomlinson 1990: 68–9). Recipes, instructions, patterns and surveys also constitute practical competances and knowledges associated with femininity. The reason why many topics recur in women's magazines relates to the role of providing popular education about cultural mores. In that way, women's magazines are akin to oral cultures, where the circulation of 'potted' versions of certain topics is a way of reproducing skills and knowledges across generations and different cultural groups.

DESIGNING WOMEN

> A woman then, *to attract a man*, should:
>> Be easy on the eyes;
>> Be happy and self-confident;
>> Be feminine, tender, kind, and thoughtful;
>> Be poised;
>> Be dependent;
>> Be well-groomed.
>
>   (Tolman 1969: n.p.)

While we may have moved a long way from the etiquette of the *ancien régime*, in which dress 'was clearly invested with a precise socio-political role of self-confirmation for some and subordination for others, fixing each in his [*sic*] place by signalling the position of each' (Perrot 1981: 161), clothing still articulates the attributes of the person. In western culture, these have been organised by the priorities accorded to aesthetics, sex and class under capitalism:

> The practical function of clothing being inseparable from its aesthetic function, itself inseparable from its sexual function (modesty or enticement) or social function (prestige and distinction) this commercialism may

over-stress some of them for the better dissimulation of others that are not as admissible, opportune or persuasive.

(Perrot 1981: 161)

The emphasis on sexuality has been especially prominent in the consumer fashion system. Changes in style and line of cut systematically relate to changing mores of sexuality such as the prominence of specific sexual and sensual bodily features. According to Perrot, 'there is a periodicity of place and appearance of the erogenous zones or those that are sexually stimulating, in which clothing is necessarily and profoundly involved' (Perrot 1981: 165). Because western culture has been so preoccupied with the 'problem' of femininity, women's fashions have responded frequently to discourses about sex.

Through processes of prestigious imitation, young girls construct a social persona from techniques of femininity including body trainings, codes of dress and decoration and mental techniques (acquired through imitation of friends, siblings, relatives, popular role models, magazines and television). Social and sexual identity is lodged in the way the body is worn. Gender – especially femininity – is worn through clothes. But although clothes allude to persons as sexual beings, they do not automatically denote sexuality. This is most clear in the case of children's clothes. Although girls and boys are dressed differently according to sex, they are not expected to behave in a 'sex-typed' manner (Paoletti and Kregloh 1989: 40)).

The separation between sex, gender and sexuality runs through codes of dress and decoration in complex ways. Furthermore, understandings of these distinctions are not necessarily shared by women and men. For example, some evidence suggests that the model of the 'male gaze' as the basis of codes of looking and ways of seeing may be just one arrangement. In terms of dress behaviour, there may be multiple understandings of allusions to sexuality. Despite the rhetoric that women dress to please men, other evidence suggests that women primarily dress to please other women. Further, there is no clear pattern as to whose 'eyes' women view other women through.

Moreover, men and women have very different ideas as to what constitutes a fashionable look. For example, the Australian magazine *Cleo* invited men to rate various clothes, assuming that the 'sexy' looks would rate best (Anon 1987). In fact everyday looks (casual top and skirt or jeans) were preferred while the 'way out' high fashion looks scored poorly. These results suggested that the fashion behaviour and circulating techniques of interpreting dress and decoration are complex and variable.

One of the features of western consumer fashion has been the rise of fashion designers as authoritative sources of advice about clothes – and by extension – related techniques of femininity. Often, they have been likened to dictators making pronouncements on what's in and out and what's feminine and what's not. Their rise to influence began in the 1920s and has lasted, despite the declining popularity of couture fashion and the expansion of mass-produced fashion.

Figure 3.2 Silken smiles and the new femininity. (Shanghai 1917.)

The reason for their success stems from their role in defining body–habitus relations through the line and cut of clothes. Individual designers are typically celebrated for introducing a new cut or a new look as a sign of their creative genius and ability to impose their will. But, as well as promoting modish fashions, designers have also extolled an extreme version of a fashionable lifestyle characterised by leisure, pleasure, elitism and conspicuous consumption. The most successful designers – usually men – have become arbiters of taste and social etiquette. As American designer, Oscar de la Renta, reflected:

> In the old days fashion designers – seamstresses really – made and sold only dresses; *today we sell a lifestyle to the whole world.* We have moved into more and more areas of influence, and this has made a huge difference to how we are perceived. It has made the career more socially acceptable. And I think in the end all social structures come to depend on power and influence. And, of course, on the influence and power that money brings.
>
> (Quoted by Coleridge 1989: 5; my italics)

While the world of designer fashion (couture) is big business and extremely competitive, its influence on everyday consumer fashion is perhaps overstated. Although couture design is regarded as the apex of the fashion world, in practice it is geared towards a small, rich clientele. The large design houses in Paris have only about 3,000 customers of whom less than 700 are regulars. Of these, about 250 are American and 250 are European (made up of French, Germans, Italians, and 'half a dozen' British); of the remainder, ninety are from the Gulf countries, fifty from South America, and thirty from the Far East (Coleridge 1989: 170). Americans account for about two-thirds of world sales, suggesting that Parisian design has a greater impact on fashion in the New World than in Europe. While this group is cultivated and monitored as select guests at the seasonal shows of each designer, their fashion choices do not necessarily influence fashion trends. In fact, only about 'fifteen to eighteen women' are regarded as trendsetters. If they take up a new fashion idea, the design is often popularised and modified for mass production and everyday consumption. In general, however, Paris couture is an exclusive club associated with a small section of the fashion industry. It seems plausible to question the amount of influence ascribed to either the designers or regular clients. But in pandering to their preoccupations and prejudices, designers recycle historical themes, icons of femininity and fantasies. Coleridge observed that:

> The long pedigree of couture is taken seriously by couture customers and permanently bolstered by designers. Historicism has, of course, a certain currency in ready-to-wear too, but allusions tend to be general, to a puritan collar, or a pioneer petticoat. In couture a collection is inspired, they tell us, by Madame de Pompadour, the Duchess of Windsor, the Marchesa Casati, the Duchesse de Guermantes. The allusions are specific. In a quite calculated way, by evoking Madame de Pompadour in a $15,000 bias-cut silk satin evening

dress, the designer is selling not only an evening dress but, by association, a stake in the eighteenth century itself. Aligned in this way, its price . . . is hiked into a different league of expectation . . . The revival of the *haute couture* has been achieved by marketing hand-built clothes as a sure-fire cultural talisman.

(Coleridge 1989: 174)

Designer fashion markets dreams, lifestyles and fantasies for a tiny elite for short-term pleasures. While researching his book, *The Fashion Conspiracy*, Coleridge (1989: 305–10) visited a Kuwaiti dry-cleaner shop which specialised in handling high fashion clothes. The back of the shop was filled with almost 300 unclaimed designer gowns, worth about $400,000. Some of the clothes had been there four or five years but were unlikely to ever be collected because the customers 'no longer like to wear that outfit' or have bought the new season's fashions. This 'elephants' graveyard' of abandoned couture underscored the 'pointlessness' of fashion as the failed amulets were rejected in favour of new ones. The clothes acted as technical props for high fashion women but could never live up to the expectations held of them.

While this 'dilemma' confronts few women in such an extreme form, many women are influenced by general trends in fashion and follow – albeit at a distance – the activities of the fashion industry. The relationship between couture (elite designers and consumers) and everyday fashion (high street designers and consumers) is complex. In both cases, it is mediated by fashion magazines but everyday fashion is also influenced by the system of 'looks' generated by high street designers, endorsed by the editors of fashion magazines and the buyers for large department stores and fashion boutiques. When Coleridge asked Grace Mirabella, former editor of American *Vogue*, where the power in the fashion triangle (designers, buyers or magazines) lay, she isolated magazines:

Which is not to say that individual designers don't make important statements. Or that store buyers aren't the first on their block. But fi-nally, fi-nally the magazines dictate what's at the top. We don't design clothes, but we can be very selective in our reporting. The insistence by us on a certain ease and modernity has been decisive, and we try to resist moving away from that.

(Quoted by Coleridge 1989: 250)

The role of the fashion editor is to follow the new 'shapes' offered at seasonal collections, select the ones that will be influential, devise a thematic 'story' to unify a selection of clothes, photograph them on location, then present them as a coherent fashion feature (Coleridge 1989: 254). Magazines like *Vogue* must also give their readers the kind of images and looks with which they can identify.

Although national editions of *Vogue* and *Elle* cater for specific tastes, in general the fashion industry makes a distinction between European and American looks. In fashion photographs, the difference is that '"American" means the model jumping in the air on a sidewalk, grinning energetically from behind a shillelagh of blonde hair. "European" means more restrained, serious and artistic'

(Coleridge 1989: 250–1). The tension between American and European 'looks' goes back to the shifting power relations within the fashion industry in the 1920s and 1930s, when American customers began to patronise the Paris designers while alternative fashion systems were developing to meet the specific needs of the large American market. For a long time, the position of Paris was maintained through sheer snobbery. The European look was touted as more sophisticated and French women promoted as role models for Americans.

This divide was perpetuated ruthlessly. Yaeger Kaplan (1987) has commented on the taste wars between French and American culture in the wake of World War II. She cites a writer in *Life* magazine who promoted 'The French Look' in a feature accompanied by photographs of a 'typical' pair of legs (short and slim), (small) bust in a brassiere, and a hand (featuring large and expensive jewellery). The photographs were presented in 'a crude form of pseudoanthropological race cataloguing' (Yaeger Kaplan 1987: 162). The French women were defined as '"sexier" than their American counterparts', making the most of their 'natural attributes' and generously employing 'artificial aids' where necessary. Beauty was something to be worked at and achieved, the product of labour and technical interventions as much as natural body attributes. The article implied that American women should smarten up their looks for the returning GIs by adapting elements from their French sisters. In this context, the photographs were designed to be used in the way store catalogues could be, by coding the language of fashion in visual terms and breaking it down into consumer items. This visual packaging of women was, Yaeger Kaplan (1987: 164) suggests, a forerunner of 'industrialised surrealism or postwar "consumer cubism"'. Codes of dress and decoration were accompanied by aesthetic codes and labour rituals.

High street designers are thus in the business of meeting the requirements of the magazine editors, the store buyers, fashion photographers and advertisers, and the practical circumstances of high street consumers. Although they follow the couture trends, their own collections are shaped by more pragmatic concerns. Above all, fashions must be wearable and suit lifestyles that involve active doing (work) rather than being (leisure). Consequently, successful high street designers must be attuned to the patterns of everyday life and stylistic trends among ordinary consumers. According to Sahlins:

> we think of designers as plucking their ideas out of thin air. But the fashion expert does not make his collection out of whole cloth; like Lévi-Strauss's famous bricoleur, he uses bits and pieces with an embedded significance from a previous existence to create an object that works, which is to say that sells – which is also to say that objectively synthesizes a relation between cultural categories, for in that lies its saleability.

(Sahlins 1976: 217)

The challenge for designers is to gain the support of key fashion leaders, in particular fashion editors and department store buyers. Designers must compromise between showing something daring and new while at the same time ensuring that it is wearable (at least in a modified form) and recognisable (draws on previous fashion styles).

Thus, there is always a tension between the promise of fashion and the lived experience. While fashion and advertising are invested with transformative properties which promise to revolutionise body–space relations, the practice of fashion is limited by practical concerns. Everyday consumers constantly negotiate fashion fantasies within the conditions of everyday life. The adoption of new styles entails a compromise between designer innovations and wearability. Because of this, the majority of fashion consumers are extremely selective and reject fashions that are inappropriate to their lifestyles.

In this process, the tension between techniques of being female and techniques of femininity is a major imperative in the transformation of ideas of clothes into systems of everyday fashion. It is perhaps surprising, then, that the vast majority of famous designers have been men. Despite the involvement of women in fashion design since the early days, the impact of women designers has fluctuated and few have become household names – the exceptions include Chanel, Schiaparelli, Vionnet, Vivienne Westwood and Donna Karan. But as Steele (1991: 9–19) argues, the reasons for the male dominance of fashion relate to widely held prejudices and to power structures within the fashion industry. Men are often regarded as more creative than women, and as designing more 'flattering' clothes for women. Because 'women dress to please men', women prefer male designers who do not impose their 'personal design restrictions on their product'. Other reasons put forward to explain this male dominance included the belief that male designers are misogynists who come up with styles that ridicule women yet appeal to the masochistic streak in women. It is also demonstrably easier for male designers to get support and financial backing.

Although the number and success of women designers has been increasing in recent years, it could be argued that they have had a far-reaching impact on everyday fashion and gradual changes in styles and comfort of clothes. Women designers are often more concerned with how clothes can be worn rather than solely with the aesthetic dimensions of design. One woman designer commented that:

> A woman creates clothes that correspond to her . . . There is an *identification* – whereas men who create clothes *sublimate* the women that they dress. It is, perhaps, for that reason that the clothes made by women are less spectacular, because we know the needs of other women, the defects that one wants to conceal and the advantages that one wants to show. Today women designers are the equal of men designers, although they do not create clothes in the same way – sublimation for the men, identification for the women.
>
> (Quoted by Steele 1991: 140)

As western fashion has escalated in size and scope, its concerns have accommodated the demands of contemporary women consumers. The idea of clothes as the packaging of inner feminine qualities has been supplanted by a concern with clothes as the technical props for active living. One reflection of this has been the development of fashions for working women, a market niche that has been especially attractive to women designers. In other words, the technical demands made on clothes have changed in accordance with new circumstances in which clothes are necessary accoutrements.

In the process of extending the fashion system to everyday consumers, guides to fashion and style have been appended to other sources of feminine instruction: through etiquette manuals; fashion, teen and women's magazines; role models including pop stars, television characters and royalty; as well as friends and relatives. The process of prestigious imitation has been combined with technical advice. One example of this heady blend was offered in a book entitled *The Princess of Wales Fashion Handbook* (James 1984). This book was ostensibly about how the Princess of Wales acquired a sense of 'style' and built up a wardrobe, make-up and set of 'looks'. The book also took her 'look' and used it as a role model for ordinary women. In other words, the book used the fantasy of the Princess as the basis of a modern 'etiquette' manual. It is just one of many such books and an example of the sub-genre of manuals based on an iconic role model (such as an actress or model).

James's book primarily addressed young working women who had not yet cultivated a sense of style, developed a multi-purpose wardrobe or learned the behavioural rituals associated with special occasions. The theme of the book was that 'your clothes talk for you, and it is important that the first impression is good' (James 1984: 65). As an instructional manual, the book used examples from Diana to teach readers how to wear their bodies and to give their bodies a language appropriate to their circumstances.

Style was defined as a combination of simplicity (understatement), practicality, and suitability (appropriate to the occasion). As well as sections on grooming, health and make-up, the book adapted the Princess's clothes for ordinary readers. Although Diana's clothes were hardly suitable for everyday wear, James took specific examples and adapted the 'look' for a basic wardrobe. This included coats, winter casuals (leisure and sporting coordinates), everyday wear (skirts and tops), holiday wear, suits, 'classic' dresses, evening wear, wedding dresses, and maternity wear. These clothes identified the key departments of women's lives. Each example was illustrated by taking one of Diana's outfits and adapting her 'look' for other body shapes.

Diana's thin (model-like) body was endorsed as the ideal body shape. Clothes that suited this canonical body would not suit other bodies so the outfits were adapted for four 'flawed' body shapes: hourglass; pear-shaped; short-waisted; and top-heavy. The adaptations involved disguising the body flaw. For short-waisted people, clothes should be shaped in order to take the emphasis away from the waist (for example, using longer line jackets, tubular shapes or dropped waistlines). Top-heavy types should use wrap-over, asymmetrical tops and jackets in plain colours. In addition, 'off-centre buttoning is good for big-busted women because it takes the eye away from the centre of the bustline' (James

Figure 3.3 How to adapt the Princess of Wales' evening dress to suit four body types: pear-shape, short-waisted, top-heavy, and hourglass.

Source: S. James, *The Princess of Wales Fashion Handbook*, London: Orbis Publishing, 1984, pp. 98–9.

1984: 72). Hourglass figures invited emphasis on the waist 'but without making your bust or hips look bigger' (James 1984: 55):

> Ballgowns and traditional evening dresses are very flattering to this shape. Always make sure that you have a definite waistline; this, together with a fine elasticated neckline, will show you at your best. A deep sash or cummerbund is ideal, and can even be tied in a bow to give a touch of extra femininity.
>
> (James 1984: 97)

On the other hand, straight-cut dresses belted at the waist 'would look awful – a sack of potatoes tied around the middle' (James 1984: 99). Pear-shaped bodies are the most problematic. One should avoid clothes that emphasise the waist because it 'will only call attention to your problem' (ibid.: 55). Instead, emphasis should be given to the top with skirts and pants designed to minimise the bulk of the hips. Moreover:

> There is no way of making a style that is too body-hugging look good on someone with big hips. At the other extreme, a large 'sack' shape will only make you look frumpy and bigger. The best way to get over the problem is to go for a striking top half that will combine well with a softer skirt to give you an overall slimmer appearance.
>
> (James 1984: 98)

The theme of these adaptations was not only that everyday body shapes did not conform to the ideals of the fashionable body, but that misshapen bodies should be regarded as 'problems' to be rectified or disguised. The language of the makeovers was accordingly instructional, authoritative and critical. Readers (ordinary women with ordinary bodies) could not achieve the Princess's perfect look, just an approximation to it depending on the severity of their body faults.

James also stressed the importance of dressing for the occasion. In a break from earlier style guides, this book emphasised the need to create a working wardrobe. This was illustrated by advice for choosing clothes which were suitable for job interviews which James described as 'one of those occasions when your clothes talk for you':

> The clothes you wear will depend largely on the type of job you are applying for and the impression you wish to make. The right outfit for someone applying to work in a trendy boutique would be entirely wrong for the girl who is being interviewed for a job with a bank. However, some rules apply, whatever the situation. Always try to be yourself, and dress comfortably. If you are uncomfortable, you will lack confidence in your clothes and it will show . . . Looking smart doesn't mean looking dull . . . And try to dress to a standard that you can maintain should you get the job.
>
> (James 1984: 65)

The tone of this fashion handbook indicates the fluid and dynamic relations between body and habitus inflected through clothing, behaviour, personal demeanour, and occasion. The style conveyed by choice of clothes articulates the contours of our habitus. Whether calculated or habitual, wearers construct themselves through clothes. As Angela Carter observed:

> Clothes are the visible woman – the detachable skin which expresses inner aspirations, dreams and fantasies; they are the signs of our status to ourselves and to other people. Nevertheless, we are never fully in control of our appearances. There are movements in the wearing of clothes – movements not completely dictated by the fashion industry.
>
> (A. Carter 1978: 51)

The idea that clothes constitute a language and means of communication has been central to the proliferation of the fashion industry and its promotion through women's magazines and by sanctioned role models. The identity and social position that are established through dress codes include the ascription of femininity. Women are fashioned by the desire to re-form or mould the body itself. The reconstruction of body shape is part of the acquisition of a particular range of body techniques, concerning posture, and specialised body movements. Reshaping the body itself is merely another technique.

MANAGING THE FEMININE BODY

> The intelligible body includes our scientific, philosophical, and aesthetic representations of the body – our cultural *conceptions* of the body, norms of beauty, models of health, and so forth. But the same representations may also be seen as forming a set of *practical* rules and regulations through which the living body is 'trained, shaped, obeys, responds', becoming, in short, a socially adapted and 'useful body'.
>
> The intelligible body and the useful body are two arenas of the same discourse; they often mirror and support each other . . . But the two bodies may also contradict and mock each other.
>
> (Bordo 1989: 25–6)

The desire to manage the body is the key to producing the social body. It is, of course, culturally specific. Bartky (1988) has considered fashion and beauty practices as modes of *body disciplines* concerned with: body size and shape; gesture, posture and movement; and producing the body as an ornamented surface (cf. Corrigan and Meredyth 1992). She argues that these practices produce self-regulating female subjects through the demonstration of control over the physical body. Although body disciplines are not unique to western culture, the obsession with the physical body as a visible index of moral qualities is specific. Prior to the nineteenth century, dieting and fasting had been associated with the development of the self. Moreover, these qualities had been identified with the select few who were deemed capable of attaining self-mastery and moderation:

> In the late nineteenth century, by contrast, the practices of body management begin to be middle-class preoccupations, and concern with diet becomes

attached to the pursuit of an idealized physical weight or shape; it becomes a project in service of 'body' rather than 'soul'. Fat, not appetite or desire, is the declared enemy, and people begin to measure their dietary achievements by the numbers on the scale rather than the level of their mastery of impulse and excess. The bourgeois 'tyrany of slenderness' . . . had begun its ascendancy (particularly over women), and with it the development of numerous tech-nologies – diet, exercise, and, later on, chemicals and surgery – aimed at a purely physical transformation.

(Bordo 1990: 83,85)

Body management became a means of 'normalising' the body in the process of reproducing gender relations and power relations more generally (Bordo 1990: 85–6). Through processes of self-monitoring and self-regulation of the body, multiple demands and conflicts placed upon it could be accommodated. Bordo hypothesises that the 'preoccupation with the "internal" management of the body (i.e., management of its desires) is produced by instabilities in the "macro-regulation" of desire within the system of the social body' (ibid.: 96). Bodies have become the 'site of struggle' over politics generated elsewhere but conducted through body techniques (Bordo 1989: 28).

Concern with body management is also gender coded within western culture. Bordo (1989: 20–2) argues that dieting and eating disorders are ways in which women can simultaneously express protest and retreat against prevailing defini-tions of gender and techniques of femininity. By controlling the intake and physical form of the body, women exhibit mastery over the body and their habitus. Moreover, they demonstrate 'male' qualities of 'detachment, self-containment, self-mastery, control' that are perceived to offer 'freedom (from a domestic destiny) and empowerment in the public arena' (Bordo 1990: 105). Such displays undo associations of femininity with excess, over-indulgence and lack of control. The threat of femininity (and its manifestation in a 'womanly' body) is neutralised.

According to Bordo, women with eating disorders are merely the extreme version of the widespread desire for 'a slender body' prompted by the opposition in consumer culture between discipline and excess. Indeed, she suggests that eating disorders characterise the modern western 'self':

bulimia emerges as a characteristic modern personality construction, precisely and explicitly expressing the extreme development of the hunger for unre-strained consumption (exhibited in the bulimic's uncontrollable food-binges) existing in unstable tension alongside the requirement that we sober up, 'clean up our act', get back in firm control . . . (the necessity for purge – exhibited in the bulimic's vomiting, compulsive exercising, and laxative purges).

(Bordo 1990: 97)

As the conditions of women's lives alter with higher formal education, incorpor-ation in the workforce, assumption of careers, greater mobility, and voracious consumption of images of ideal bodies, the incidence of eating disorders has increased. They are a correlate of body techniques associated with the changing roles and definitions of self.

The incidence of bulimia nervosa (one to two per 100 women) and anorexia nervosa (one per 1,000 women) of western women suggests a social pathology. A recent survey of readers of the popular Australian magazine, *Cleo*, suggested that almost 15 per cent of 20- to 24-year-old respondents were anorexic or bulimic; 11 per cent and 19 per cent of 25- to 30-year-olds were anorexic or bulimic respectively; as were 18 per cent and 14 per cent of 31- to 40-year-olds (Goodyer 1992: 76). These results correlated with respondents' extreme concern about their body image, self esteem and ability to cope with stress (cf. Myers and Biocca 1992). Respondents over-estimated their own body size and identified over-thin models as their ideal body shape. Almost all women said they disliked something about their bodies, most commonly citing their thighs (71 per cent), bottom (58 per cent), stomach (56 per cent), hips (40 per cent), legs (32 per cent), breasts (22 per cent), and upper arms (17 per cent) (Goodyer 1992: 77). These results endorsed the view that dieting is 'the peculiar consequence of a culture fascinated by individual competition, dietary management, the narcissistic body and the presentational self' (B. Turner 1990: 166). In an article concerning 'the elastic body image', Myers and Biocca (1992: 115) suggest that objective body shape is significantly greater than the internalised ideal body which, in turn, exceeds the socially represented ideal body:

> As one's internalized ideal gets further away from one's objective body shape, the individual may experience a kind of self-loathing that exaggerates the perceived 'deformity' of one's objective body shape. This is supported by the observation that anorexics and bulimics, individuals who pathologically pursue an extreme internalized ideal, experience the greatest body image distortion. But body image distortion appears in normal populations as well, especially young females.
>
> (Myers and Biocca 1992: 117)

Lynch argues that the mismatch between the slender ideal of role models and the fleshy attributes of ordinary women contribute to a 'lived tension of disembodiment' in the inability to fulfil the ideal. Increasingly, analysis of anorexia has been linked to feelings of powerlessness. But what begins as a refusal to be part of the power structure becomes a form of power and control in the behaviour itself: *not* eating becomes the locus of power and focus of attention in the anorexic's life:

> The anorexic avoids the shameful world of eating, while simultaneously achieving personal power and a sense of moral superiority through the emaciated body. Their attempts at disembodiment through negation become the symbol of their moral empowerment.
>
> (B. Turner 1990: 163)

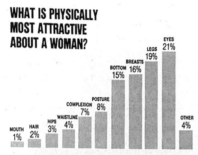

WHAT IS PHYSICALLY MOST ATTRACTIVE ABOUT A WOMAN?

EYES 21%
LEGS 19%
BREASTS 16%
BOTTOM 15%
POSTURE 8%
COMPLEXION 7%
WAISTLINE 4%
HIPS 3%
HAIR 2%
MOUTH 1%
OTHER 4%

What's a woman's single most appealing feature, we asked, listing breasts, complexion, hair, bottom, hips, waistline, eyes, mouth and posture? Like us, you probably guessed breasts. Wrong. Eyes got the biggest score of 21 percent, followed by legs which 19 percent of men liked best. What this shows, of course, is the difference between what women think men like and what men really *do* like. To give you some comparison, we checked *Cleo's* 1985 survey on women's attitudes. The features women thought were most attractive — skin and hair — were given a low rating by men. Only five percent of women thought that their legs were an important asset.

What do men find a turn-off?

Wondering what they found unattractive about women, we asked men to rate — as very unpleasant, somewhat unpleasant and not at all unpleasant — a list of features which other men have told us they dislike in women. We were amazed to find that the kind of problems women agonise over, like stretch marks and dimpled thighs and buttocks, aren't a big deal. Less than one in five described them as being very unpleasant and about a quarter of men didn't mind them at all. Being flat-chested wasn't an issue either. Almost half the men (mainly the young singles) rated it not at all unpleasant. Bad breath, however, was found to be unacceptable to 98 percent of men, and underarm hair is another turn-off with 77 percent rating it very to somewhat unpleasant. Bikini line hair seems to be more acceptable, with 38 percent of men finding it not at all unpleasant!

We also provided our men with some space to add any dislikes of their own. A few added smokers, facial hair and unwashed hair, while one-off complaints were a fascinating mixture, including: "women who fart"; "body odour"; "dirty, bitten fingernails"; "over made-up, 'plastic' faces"; "girls who look manly, with short hair, etc"; and "tattoos".

What fashion "look" do men like best?

You might have tipped the sexy black skirt (A) as the likely winner, reasoning that spiky heels and tight leather were a universal turn-on for men. How wrong can you be? It was the little blue mini that scored the highest points, with 65 percent approval, with the jeans and shirt (F) following close behind at 64 percent. Both sexy, yes, but in a sweeter way than the more aggressively seductive look of black leather.

Third came the well-groomed look of a big-shouldered suit which 54 percent of the men liked, sexy again, but with more restraint and class. Less than half the men (43 percent) liked the black leather skirt and only 27 percent fancied the tailored pants and jacket (too masculine perhaps?). The very different look of E barely rated. Eighty-four percent of our men (bless their conservative souls) didn't like it a bit.

Figure 3.4 Fashioning gender: men's perceptions of female attributes and fashions.

Source: *Cleo*, October 1987, p. 125. (Courtesy of Australian Consolidated Press.)

This argument fits into Elias's claims for the existence of a shame frontier and moral codes as the basis of European cultural behaviour. The physical components of the condition are subordinate to its moral dimensions. The anorexic is prompted by the inability to cope as an adult woman (not the ideal shape, unable to communicate, compete and achieve) and appears to become powerful through the condition:

> The classic anorexic is the master (the gender-specificity of 'to master' is another complexity) of disguise and deception, only acting as if she had no appetite, while being fascinated by food.
>
> (B. Turner 1990: 167)

While 'looking good' (attractive to the opposite sex and able to compete with other women) may be one of the factors leading to anorexic behaviour, Turner notes that, in fact, the condition leads to sexual and social unavailability, and ultimately to exclusion. Anorexia functions as a moral, ascetic defiance of contemporary culture. The complexity of the issue suggests that it would be misleading to over-emphasize the influence of specific role models in its incidence. But it does confirm Caputi's (1983: 191) suggestion that a woman's body becomes her 'enemy and obsession for life'.

In a similar vein, Bordo compares the habits of dieters with those of body-builders engaged in 'the quest for firm bodily margins' (Bordo 1990: 90). Although body-building appears to 'have the very opposite structure from anorexia . . . building the body up, not whittling it down', many body-builders 'talk about their bodies in ways that are disquietingly resonant with typical anorexic themes' (ibid.: 98). As a technique, body-building entails self-denial, purity, pain, a sense of the body as alien, and of mastery:

> Most strikingly, there is the same emphasis on *control*, on feeling one's life to be fundamentally out of control, and on the feeling of accomplishment derived from total mastery of the body . . . The technology of dictating to nature one's own chosen design for the body is at the centre of the bodybuilder's mania, as it is for the anorexic.
>
> (Bordo 1988: 99)

The recent popularity of aerobics and fitness – as adjuncts to the diet industry – are generalised manifestations of these approaches to body management. Firm bodies, muscles and 'working out' have been redefined as 'a symbol of correct *attitude*; it means that one "cares" about oneself and how one appears to others, suggesting willpower, energy, control over infantile impulses, the ability to "make something" of oneself' (Bordo 1990: 94–5; cf. Lynch 1987: 136; Wolf 1991: 198). In short, the feminine body is the site of severe conflict and prodigious labour. Body management constitutes a bewildering array of techniques aimed at realising the *intelligible* and *useful* body that can cope with the practical circumstances of one's habitus. For women, in particular, this involves reconciling techniques of being female with techniques of femininity appropriate to a particular cultural milieu.

Chapter 4

Fashion models
Female bodies and icons of femininity

GENDER AND CONSUMER CULTURE

The previous chapter considered the ways in which femininity was acquired as a purposeful practice. Much less academic attention has been given to other pervasive sources of knowledge about being female and feminine. For example, while there are studies on women's magazines, shopping and role models, there is little on the influence of fashion models in the formation of gender identity in western culture. In this chapter, the development of modelling is sketched and related to changing ideas about gender. The model constitutes the technical body of western consumer culture.

The history of 'femininity' in western culture was entwined with consumerism and iconisation of key cultural symbols. Through the nineteenth and twentieth centuries, there were competing and successive definitions of femininity that were articulated in diverse techniques. The role of 'prestigious imitation' (Mauss 1973: 73) was increasingly accorded to figures in popular culture – first publicity-conscious aristocrats, then film stars and heiresses, followed by models, pop stars and television stars. This chapter explores the development of the profession of fashion modelling in the context of changing techniques of femininity and new forms of consumer fashion. Modelling came to epitomise dominant characteristics of western femininity: the importance of appearance; fetishisation of the body; manipulation and moulding of the body; the discipline and labour associated with 'beauty' and body maintenance; the equation of youth with femininity; and feminine lifestyles.

The precursor of modelling was the feminisation of consumerism. Although 'the consumer' is a non-gendered term, 'it was women – specifically housewives – to whom it was applied' (E. Carter 1984: 194). The association of women with domesticity through household management was replaced by associations with modernity (through consumer goods and household appliances), leisure and pleasure. The image of 'The Girl' became synonymous with the exchange of value attached to consumer goods, 'the coin in the exchange of desire':

> Because The Girl is the Paris yard of desire, she is the measure of need. She
> makes desire intelligible by giving it form and she does this by establishing

and controlling what is acceptable as pleasure . . . or as exchange for sexuality
. . . She is the standard in the social construct of the economy of freedom as
control.

(A. Clark 1987: 200)

Consumer behaviour was central to the acquisition of a sense of self and women's
sense of self became modelled on the image of The Girl (ibid.: 201–2). This
nexus was reflected in the development of advertising which accompanied the
growth of shopping facilities (e.g. Benson 1986; R. Williams 1982; Kidwell and
Christman 1974). Reekie's (1987) study of the development of department stores
in Sydney showed how ideas about gender were crucial to shaping modern forms
of shopping. By the 1890s, shops began to exploit the fact that the majority of
customers were women. They constituted between 70 and 95 per cent of all
shoppers and spent three times as much as men (Reekie 1987: 175). As one trade
journal proclaimed: 'Man is essentially the earner, woman the shopper' (ibid.:
177). This declaration has remained the catchcry of consumerism.

Shops responded by instituting gendered departments to display 'gendered'
goods. Departments for 'ladies' wear were physically separated from 'men's'
departments – and the sex of the staff matched the sex of the commodity (Reekie
1993: 65). Particular sensitivities surrounded underwear departments which
necessitated 'close bodily proximity between seller and customer' (ibid.: 63).
Men sold men's underpants (although most of the customers were women) while
women sold women's underclothes. Even so, men supervised the stock in
women's underclothing departments because employers 'believed women lacked
sufficient business acumen' (Reekie 1987: 82). Other goods were also classified
along gender lines:

> Children's clothes (boys as well as girls) were categorised as women's goods
> because women were responsible for child care and for buying the clothes of
> their sons and daughters. Haberdashery, furnishings, manchester and most
> fancy goods were also women's commodities because of their affinity with the
> domestic sphere. Ironmongery, hardware (except for household items such as
> crockery and cooking utensils), workmen's tools and materials such as paint,
> smoking requisites, leather goods and sporting goods were male. Furniture
> occupied a peculiarly ambiguous position in the gendered world of commodi-
> ties, male by virtue of its bulk but female in its household association.

(Reekie 1987: 81)

Considerable effort went into creating gendered deparments that reflected desirable attributes of gender. Women's departments received the most attention: to
make them 'more seductively comfortable than men's, windows were deliberately more alluring, and female models were more extensively and carefully
deployed than male figures' (Reekie 1987: 297). The gendering of commodities
was reflected in advertising techniques. Masculinity and femininity were translated into specific appeals for particular goods: 'beauty was associated with

femininity, utility and practicality with masculinity' (ibid.: 285). Appeals to men emphasised practicality, action and male occupations by constructing a confident, solid, chunky masculinity (ibid.: 303–8). While advertising appeals to men remained little changed between the 1890s and the 1930s, those for women were transformed.

Shopping itself was designated 'a female pursuit' (Reekie 1987: 176) and as a result, by the 1920s, advertisers were directing their appeals to women. Advertisements for women reflected changing notions of the female body shape away from the severe body cant to angular boyish shapes. Increasingly women were portrayed as young with 'baby doll' faces and in poses that were decorative or implied leisure (ibid.: 301–8).

The contrast with images of masculinity also reinforced the message that 'women belonged to the world of leisure and men to the world of work'. The retailers':

> presentation of bourgeois images of womanhood helped to sell the high status value of a leisured lifestyle to female customers of all classes. It was also to retailers' advantage to promote women as consumers rather than producers if they were to cultivate a section of the unpaid labour force exclusively devoted to the social work of shopping.
>
> (Reekie 1987: 311)

Through the public site of shopping, women took advantage of the opportunity to operate outside the home, command an expertise, mingle with friends and other women, and derive pleasure from the activity. The organisation of shopping into types of goods correlated with the organisation of women's lives into different departments of existence. Even for young women, shopping provided an important point of identification between the worlds of home and work. While young women mostly shop for the present (buying fashion, cosmetics and leisure goods), they also begin to prepare for their future home (buying soft furnishings, homeware and furniture) (E. Carter 1984: 200). By contrast, young men primarily shop for leisure and entertainment goods and possibly a few clothes. Their trainings for adulthood are not bound up with the experience of shopping.

As well as offering pleasures of anticipation and consumption, shopping also constitutes a habit and a discipline. Since shopping plays a major role in the lives of many women, it contributes to the formation of self and gender identity. The dimensions of femininity derived from shopping combine practical trainings about selection, quality, value and utility with trainings about leisure and pleasure. Shopping also contributes to the process of self-formation by offering ideal images of femininity as goals to be worked towards. The female body is constructed as a surface to be worked on and a volume to be sculpted and moulded, through 'beauty' regimes, clothing and lifestyle. Shopping, advertising and women's magazines employ consumer behaviour as a set of techniques – instructions, principles and instruments – out of which a practical femininity can be constructed (E. Carter 1984: 207). The culture of consumerism is less important for its materialist basis than for the practical models for everyday living offered through it (cf. Nava 1991).

Even so, the assumption of femininity 'is at best shaky and partial' (Walkerdine 1984: 163). The ideals and fantasies offered to women are points of orientation for the realisation of a gendered self. While the creation of role models provides 'a set of pleasurable moments' for women, their significance is the dissemination of lessons about 'hard work, its costs and rewards'(McRobbie 1984: 160). Femininity is the product of hard labour. The message is made palatable by using fantasies and dreams to secure identification with ideals and commitment to goals and practical actions. To this end, the media have provided the means for promoting desirable images and icons of femininity, because they can be endlessly reproduced and widely consumed. Thus role models have been drawn from aristocrats, beautiful women, fashion devotees, film and television stars, models, and popular musicians. A. Clark's (1987) article on 'The Girl' distilled one role model into a particular recipe for femininity. But it was not the first example of feminine imagery.

THE LEGACY OF THE GIBSON GIRL

The forerunner of modern images of femininity was the Gibson Girl, a phenomenon of the 1890s. She was drawn by American illustrator Charles Dana Gibson as the embodiment of the wealthy Langhorne sisters. They were outspoken, privileged women who defied contemporary conventions about female passivity and domesticity. The best-known sister, Nancy, became Lady Astor, who was the first woman to sit in the British House of Commons in 1919 (Ewing 1974: 22). The signature of the Gibson Girl was her distinctive clothes and demeanour. In her tailored shirt and skirt – a comparatively pared down form of female apparel – she epitomised the changes which were propelling women to break out of Victorian restrictions:

> This 'Big American Girl' was determinedly self-assured, part college girl, part fashionable beauty, her hat perched jauntily on her pompadoured head, followed everywhere by male admirers. This new American girl was not just exceptionally pretty, she could look you straight in the eye, had a firm handshake, and strode from the nineteenth century into the twentieth century emancipated, confident and chic.
>
> (A. Bailey 1988: 92)

Although the Gibson Girl was encumbered by her tight-waisted bodice and huge billowing skirt which trailed on the ground, she became popular because she embodied new definitions of gender and lifestyle. Her distinctive S-shaped body dominated the iconography of women into the 1900s. Not only did she establish a new model of the female body, she spawned an industry of Gibson Girl 'media tie-ins' – Gibson Girl shirtwaists, skirts, shoes, corsets, wallpaper, posters and the like. Her image was copied by every fashion and popular illustrator: 'In 1910 and

1911 *Vogue*'s pages are haunted by the Gibson Girl's ubiquitous influence, dulled by the continued requirement of absolutely meticulous presentation of every dressmaking detail'(Seebohm 1982: 168). The popularity of the Gibson Girl spread first to Europe, then further afield, making her the first truly international role model. Local variations of the look were popularised through department store catalogues (Joel 1984: 42–3). Her success was due to the conjunction of her image (a relatively unrestricted mode of dressing, active lifestyle and outspoken confidence), with major cultural, political and economic changes in western societies.

The Gibson Girl also heralded a new approach to clothing and fashion. Her clothes could be reproduced simply and cheaply. They suited the practical circumstances of women. The proliferation of clothes in the Gibson Girl style aimed at working women as well as leisured ones, and, made available in department stores and through mail order catalogues, typified changes occurring in the fashion industry. Clothes could be produced in large numbers and sold to mass markets. Developments in reprographic techniques and expansion of the press enabled fashion ideas to be disseminated to a popular audience and large market. Fashion was being democratised and made available to large numbers of people (Kidwell and Christman 1974).

At the same time, an elite fashion industry was emerging, especially in Paris. Fashion designers replaced the traditional dominance of women in the dressmaking trade and established a different kind of relationship with their customers. The designers fawned over favourite clients yet also dictated what they should wear; the clients loved it. Thus, the new approach to fashion was schizophrenic. On the one hand, fashion was democratised as more people had access to the images and clothing preferred by the trend setters. On the other hand, fashion producers were setting the styles. Other changes were also occurring in the fashion industry. The aristocracy was supplanted as the elite fashion community and role models. Socialites, artists and movie stars offered alternative sources of inspiration. These role models offered desirable images and behaviour that were no longer based on emulating one's social superiors. Individualism and modernity prevailed.

Nowhere was this clearer than in the emergence of the fashion industry in America. Not only was America the home of the Gibson Girl, it was also the catalyst in democratising fashion. Part of this process depended on the establishment of networks of stores nationally which, with the development of department stores, saw the emergence of efficient national outlets. Retailers also saw the potential of home dressmaking with the marketing of efficient sewing machines. The paper-pattern industry proved a bonanza since it offered ordinary women the opportunity to create new styles for themselves (Walsh 1979). Women could experiment with fashion at home. Thus, while Paris remained the apex of couture fashion, new techniques and ideas about fashion from America were constantly feeding into the Paris industry. The interdependence between Parisian and American fashion was enhanced by the growth of Hollywood. The cinema popularised new fashions and produced new female icons. Paris designers were hired to dress the stars whose images were adapted by the movie fans. As an industry, Paris took off as the fashion heart because of Hollywood.

Ewen (1980: S59) has identified three feminine types that developed in Hollywood movies – the vamp, the gamine and the virgin. Each exuded an ambiguous sexuality which highlighted changes and tensions being experienced more widely in America. Whereas the vamp and gamine 'projected images of sexual freedom and social independence', the virgin was 'the last holdout of the patriarchal tradition' (ibid.: S60). Ewen argued that the movies held special appeal for immigrant women, caught between the traditional cultures of their parents and the new conditions of America. For these women, 'these new movies were manuals of desires, wishes and dreams'(ibid.: S63). Movies combined fantasy with 'practical guidelines for change'; 'a visual textbook to American culture, a blend of romantic ideology and practical tips for the presentation of self in the new marriage market of urban life' (ibid.: S63). American culture was actively promoted through films that endorsed shopping as a leisure activity, ready-made clothing, mass-manufactured goods, cosmetics and advertising. While women took up these activities and opportunities with enthusiasm, Ewen concluded that these changes represented a new set of rules and techniques that were just as restricting as the old:

> As women moved from the constricted family-dominated culture to the more individualized values of modern urban society, the form and content of domination changed, but new authorities replaced the old. In the name of freedom from tradition, they trapped women in fresh forms of sexual objectification and bound them to the consumerized and sexualized household.
>
> (Ewen 1980: S65)

The model of femininity offered by the cinema was composed of ideas about 'dress, manners, freedom, and sexual imagery' (Ewen 1980: S65). Femininity was constructed as a process of selecting an ideal image and adapting available clothing and cosmetics to realise an approximation to that ideal. The attributes of femininity were also shaped by the practicalities of everyday life, particularly that of striking a balance between work and leisure.

In accordance with the increased mobility of women, the Flapper became the image of womanhood in the 1920s (Pumphrey 1987). She epitomised modernity, a commitment to new ways of living that explicitly rejected the old. Pumphrey calls her 'an ironic realization of modernist principles' committed to an active life. She needed special clothes for 'travelling, shopping, lunching, weddings, outdoor amusements, tea, dining, theatre, dancing' (ibid.: 186). This highly *public* life of the new woman was a catalyst for the rapid expansion of consumerism. While the values of romance, home and family suffused this rhetoric, women were not banished to the home. Rather, they revelled in public visibility, though perhaps not to the degree that the image of the Flapper would suggest. Ewen cites the recollection of one immigrant woman who distinguished herself from the images offered in the movies:

We dressed plainly. We wore long dresses that were different than the styles in the movies. I knew about flappers from the movies, but I never dressed that way. None of my friends dressed that way. There was a flapper in my building. I guess . . . it was her nature. She was Italian and went to speakeasies. Her mother was upset at her daughter's behaviour, but she didn't bother anybody.

(Quoted by Ewen 1980: S64)

This memory not only suggests that fashionable female types were adopted by a minority of women but that such followers of fashion were marginalised within their social milieu. In other words, actual practices of femininity cannot be elided with the representations, role models and fashions of a period. The latter function as markers of extremities and tensions within a cultural milieu, alluding to aspects of self-formation in which body and habitus are in conflict.

FROM DEMOISELLES DE MAGASIN TO MODELS: SELLING CLOTHES AND IMAGES

Who is that girl prancing on the hood of a Rolls, strutting along a beach on ice skates, fording a stream on a water buffalo, serving tea in a space suit, climbing a tree in a cocktail dress?

Who else but that rag-bone-and-hank-of-hair known as a High-Fashion Model. She is supposed to be showing off the new clothes for the readers of *Vogue*, *Harper's Bazaar*, and fashion pages of general magazines. Is she succeeding? No, scream a growing gaggle of fashion designers, who claim their clothes are being downgraded to mere props for far-out photography.

(Anon 1965a: 42)

Throughout the twentieth century, one feature of femininity has dominated a succession of female icons – the look. In contrast to the self-actualising potential of the Gibson Girl and the Flapper, subsequent icons have been fetishised for appearances. Feminine identity in western culture hinges on the display of female attributes. The female body – unclothed and clothed – has been invested with sensual, erotic and desired impulses. While fashion models epitomise the objectification of the body – being 'used as a piece of flesh', as one top model put it (Hartman 1980: 77) – the cult of the body has structured the appeal of other role models as well, especially that of movie stars and pop stars.

The idea of using models for displaying clothes – modelling the mode – developed out of couture design. Marie Worth, wife of English-born designer Charles Worth, is credited with being the first professional model although de Marly (1980: 101) disagrees. Gagelin, Worth's employer, had used models, known as *demoiselles de magasin*, since the 1860s. They were retained by the salons to display the latest styles for regular customers. However, Worth extended the practice by using the models outside the store as well. Marie Worth became 'a walking advertisement' wherever she went (ibid.: 102). Her reputed elegance redefined modelling as an artform: 'she gave the role of model a dignity it had not possessed before, and which it has lost since' (ibid.).

The marketing of fashions and the designation of certain physical features as desirable 'feminine' attributes were the impetus to the wider use of models. Live models, instead of wax mannequins, were being used in store displays as early as 1916, when one retail trade magazine criticised the use of '"shop and factory girls" who were ungainly, wore too much face colour and had pimply backs' (Reekie 1987: 292). Models not only displayed the latest fashionable clothes but the atmosphere associated with them through the creation of feminine tableaux – such as the bedroom, the office, a wedding, or an outdoor setting (cf. Barthes 1984: 300–2). Shop windows, catalogues and in-store fashion parades became 'popular free forms of entertainment' and the source of fashion information (Reekie 1987: 295).

While modelling was gradually recognised as a profession in countries like England and America, it was not professionalised in Paris until the 1950s (de Marly 1980: 102). At first, modelling 'was considered very fast and loose and no model girl was received in polite society' (Keenan 1977: 111). According to a former model of the respected house of Molyneux, Madame Vera, even in the 1930s, 'models had little social standing' (quoted by Shrimpton 1965: 150). On the other hand, models were very popular with rich young men who often supported them. Models became fetishised by admirers. The 'mystic mannequin', Sumurun, recalled one appearance which attracted attention:

Molyneux designed a slap-up Oriental thing for me. Underneath the tunic there were electric lights and a jewel in my turban lit up, and my earrings, too. Two little black children threw rose petals at my feet. Men in the audience ran and picked them up and kissed them – the petals I had walked on – imagine! Some of my young boyfriends were waiting at the end of the catwalk. One of them came up and – with my hand on my heart this is true – he gave me two boxes with diamonds and emerald jewellery in them. That kind of thing happened in those days.

(Quoted by Keenan 1977: 113)

Modelling began its climb to respectability in England with the establishment of Lucy Clayton's model agency in 1928 (Keenan 1977: 114). The curriculum covered a broad range of social skills and gender trainings: including classes on applying make-up, dress sense, making entrances and exits, social graces, deportment, haircare and styling, shoe selection, professional manicure, medical problems, personal hygiene and depilatories, photography and television advertisements (Shrimpton 1965: 30–1). About the same time, Poiret began to take his models on tours, first to Longchamps, and later, to other European capitals (de Marly 1980: 103). He photographed the models and these photographs began to replace those of aristocrats and actresses that had previously appeared in fashion magazines. Magazines soon formalised this shift and engaged professional photo-graphic models specifically for their purposes.

The greatest fillip to modelling came from Jean Patou who recognised the potential of the American market. First, he had to persuade the buyers of the fashion stores to handle his clothes. He decided to recruit American models for this purpose, and advertised for girls who were 'smart, slender, with well-shaped feet and ankles and refined of manner' (Keenan 1977: 113). Amid considerable publicity, Patou travelled to New York and chose six models from five hundred applicants, an indication of the attractions of this new career for women. He chaperoned his troupe carefully and 'introduced a little touch of showmanship' into the parades. According to Keenan (1977: 114), 'Patou succeeded in his aim of drawing the American buyers, but he also gave the model a new status and importance'. Modelling was set to become the new glamour industry.

The reality was rather different. Working as a model was an insecure and volatile business with long periods of inactivity and boredom punctuated by 'frenzied activity' (de Marly 1980: 104). Normally, the models stayed in the salon, 'perfectly groomed at all times, ready to show dresses the moment a customer called and then waiting around until the next customer appeared' (ibid.). At other times, they 'had to stand and pose for hours' while a designer fitted cloth and clothes on their body. The periods of the seasonal collections, on the other hand, were busy times for models: 'It was hard work and badly paid, but . . . she could have her moments of excitement, wearing the most beautiful clothes in the world' (ibid.: 105).

Photographic models fared no better. Photographers were often disparaging about their subjects. For example, although Cecil Beaton was charming to models at photographic sessions, behind their backs he called them 'silly cows'. In 1938, he announced that he had had enough 'of taking fashions on young models who survived just as long as their faces showed no sign of character' (Harrison 1985: 24). Despite the reservations of Beaton and others, the popularity of modelling grew. Gradually, the job was professionalised and routinised. Models were trained to hold formal, frozen poses for a sequence of still shots. These conventions began to change in the late 1930s as concepts of realism and the moving image influenced the more experimental fashion photographers (see Chapter 5).

The expansion of modelling was put on hold during World War II though the war experience had an impact. It revolutionised women's priorities, boosted the mass market and marketing techniques, internationalised cultural influences, and developed realist techniques of reportage. American ex-model, Lee Miller, became a war photographer but also continued her interest in fashion through some stark yet spectacular fashion spreads for the English *Vogue*. She even succeeded in getting the English and American editions of *Vogue* to publish her photographs and stories on the liberation of Europe (V. Lloyd 1986: 8; Hall 1985: 45–63).

The post-war period created the perfect conditions for the transformation of modelling into a major industry. Modelling was an attractive option for young women who wanted a job and indulgence. The glamorous profession was coveted by debutantes and well-bred young girls looking for an amusing job before they settled down. Because of the ready supply of potential models, working conditions were highly exploitative. Models were at the beck and call of their agencies and employers. Designers, for example, had their favourite models whose careers depended on remaining in favour. Successful models made it because of the way they wore the clothes, not because of their looks. Their bodies were traded as commodities, separated from their sense of self.

Dior's 1947 'New Look' collection epitomised this feeling. The new clothes emphasised the waist and shapely (feminine) contours. They were promoted as light-hearted and frivolous, and relevant to post-war euphoria. During the 1950s, the main role models were still movie stars, while models popularised the new fashions anonymously. Despite the glamour, modelling was still not held in high regard within the fashion industry. Chanel, for example, was ambivalent about her housemodels, saying:

> They are beautiful, that's why they can get these jobs. If they were intelligent they'd give them up. All they think of is money. They don't care a single damn about you. They come here looking like housemaids on a day off and they leave looking like scrubwomen.
>
> (Quoted by Keenan 1977: 124)

Modelling developed two main branches – catwalk (later called runway) modelling for collections and fashion parades, and photographic modelling for magazines and catalogues. Within this division, there were various types of modelling work. While some models secured a permanent modelling job in a high fashion house, most worked on a freelance basis in wholesale or retail fashion, as well as modelling couture fashion, or doing photographic (and later television) work. One of the most lucrative types of modelling work is done by models who specialise in particular body parts, such as hands, feet, legs or breasts.

Runway models had to be supple, move well, and have a sense of rhythm in order to bring the clothes they were modelling to 'life'. The model's job was to act out 'what any piece of clothing can and cannot do' by 'projecting the appropriate expression and capturing the mood' conveyed by the fashion (Hartman 1980: 57). Their bodies had to be well proportioned so that the clothes would hang well. Because the emphasis was on the clothes, runway models potentially had longer careers than photographic models among whom lines and wrinkles were feared. As the model, Wilhemina, remarked:

> If you're good as a coat hanger, there's no reason why a few wrinkles will keep you out of the business. An audience gets a quick image of a model and doesn't see every inch of her, as does the critical eye of the camera.
>
> (Quoted by Hartman 1980: 74)

In general, runway models could be taller and bigger than photographic ones, since the technology of the camera distorts size and therefore suits the proportions of smaller models. Photographic modelling also required photogenic (not necessarily beautiful) facial features. According to Jean Shrimpton:

Photogenic girls are rare. Not pretty ones. There are plenty of those. But girls whose bone structure is enhanced by the camera, and who look good from every angle. The best compliment a model girl can be paid is that one can't take a bad picture of her.

(Shrimpton 1965: 36)

Although the division between runway and photographic modelling persists, many models have been doing both kinds of work since the 1980s. The most important requirement for modelling is to meet precise bodily specifications. These have changed over time, generally imposing smaller limits. In the 1970s, for example, models were required to be tall, flat chested, small hipped and broad shouldered. They also needed wide-set eyes, slender legs, healthy hair and skin in a 'lean and lithe' body and the ability to project charisma (Hartman 1980: 67). Agencies impose strict weight limitations, usually below a model's 'natural' weight, by imposing penalties on models who exceed their target weight. Although models in the 1980s were more generously proportioned, new criteria stressed fitness, muscles and cosmetically enhanced bodies.

One of the most controversial features of the modelling industry has been the manipulation of the body to conform to requirements. Cosmetic surgery has become endemic (Perrottet 1993). Even in the 1950s, one of Dior's favourite models, Lucky, had several facial cosmetic operations before she was considered suitable to be a model (Keenan 1977: 121). Removing the back teeth is common among print models to achieve a hollow-cheeked look. Some have the lower rib removed to reduce the size of the waist. Verushka had one joint removed in each foot to make her feet smaller (Hartman 1980: 70). Shrimpton was under pressure to have cosmetic surgery to remove the bags under her eyes which were disguised by careful upward lighting:

Those bags were an enormous nuisance all the time I was modelling. Fashion editors and photographers were constantly saying to me: 'You must get to bed earlier.' But it was nothing to do with lack of sleep or anything else. God had given me bags under my eyes, in the same way as he had forgotten to give me a bosom and shoulders. No one who worked with me would accept this simple fact. I was under great pressure to have them removed by cosmetic surgery, but this is something I have never believed in. Bailey did not really mind. Except when they were causing him photography problems, he quite liked my bags – he did not want me to be perfect.

(Shrimpton 1990: 63–4)

The acceptance of cosmetic surgery as a norm prompted an editor of *New York* magazine to characterise modelling as a collection of 'plastic-surgery-enhanced behinds' on people 'who have no existence other than their surface' (*Mode*, September 1991: 74). Face lifts, lipo-suction, breast and lip enhancement have become commonplace. Fashion collections have been likened to 'going to the circus, but instead of elephants you find skinny women with surgery enhanced behinds, and designers who are obsessed with their own self-importance' (ibid.).

The 1960s were the turning point for the profession. In 1964, Courrèges launched his 'space age' clothes, and Mary Quant her pop clothes. Both collections offered a new look for teenagers and young people. Courrèges and Quant also challenged the staid forms of presentation and many pretensions of the fashion industry (Quant 1967: 48, 103; Steele 1992: 134). Quant wanted to design clothes for young people that broke the rules of conventional dress. When she could not buy what she wanted, she experimented with designing and producing clothes and accessories herself. Part of her approach included display. For example, she wanted to get away from conventional window dressing with fixed poses and grand expressions:

I wanted figures with the contemporary high cheek-boned, angular faces and the most up-to-date hair cuts. I wanted them with long, lean legs, rather like Shrimpton's, and made to stand like real-life photographic models in gawky poses with legs wide apart, one knee bent almost at right angles and one toe pointing upwards from a heel stuck arrogantly into the ground. It was just at this time that photographic models were beginning to use the leaping about style.

(Quant 1966: 51–2)

Her clothes were 'fun' clothes that recreated childhood and teenage fantasies: tunics, knee-high boots, leggings, short skirts, knickerbockers, shifts, PVC and animal-patterned jackets. Quant won the *Sunday Times* Fashion Award and was voted Woman of the Year in 1965 (Quant 1966: 139, 142). Accepting an OBE (Order of the British Empire) the following year, Quant wore a mini and cut-away gloves to Buckingham Palace. Despite this controversial entrance, the award showed that youth fashion and street design had gained respect:

The old order was coming to accept the rebel youth culture. But unavoidably this culture was being absorbed by the Establishment and capitalised upon by large manufacturers throughout the country.

(Bernard 1978: 64)

Models benefited from these changes. The new designers had very different ideas about how their clothes should be worn. Quant, for example, showed her clothes to a background of pounding music, a riot of colour with the models running and dancing down the catwalk to create a sense of speed and movement. She chose photographic models for the job because she:

wanted to show the clothes moving, not parading, and these girls move beautifully and naturally. They walk swingingly and when they are still for a moment, they stand arrogantly.

(Quant 1966: 99)

Quant's approach was controversial and influential. She opened a Paris showing with an 11-year-old girl wearing a shiny mock-crocodile batwing top over black tights, her long fair hair hanging over her shoulders:

She looked wild as she ran down the catwalk with the other girls, like greyhounds, pounding along behind. There were [*sic*] none of the mincing up and down, stop and start, stylised movements of the usual fashion model. These girls were all primarily photographic models so that when they stopped in their tracks, they automatically took up the sort of arrogant positions you see in the fashion pages of the glossies.

(Quant 1966: 132)

The new clothes were relevant to the lifestyles of the models. High fashion was no longer elite and stuffy but was found in the high streets. Models became both living advertisements for clothes and well-known individuals. The conventions of fashion photography were also challenged by experimental young photographers who thrived on the spectacular. The new look also dictated a new body shape. Conventional tenets of modelling were repudiated by the models, photographers and designers.

Even so, many models still came from wealthy families who could afford to pay the cost of taking modelling classes, and regarded modelling as a glamorous interim job. Jean Shrimpton, Verushka and Lisa Taylor were typical of this generation of models. Taylor, for example, accounted for her six-year reign at American *Vogue* during the 1970s as being due to her 'listless indolence and fresh-scrubbed Oyster Bay breeding' which appealed to the class-conscious fashion people (Sherrill 1992: 86,88). While a good background helped models enter the industry, the world they encountered was very different, full of wild parties, drugs, egocentrics, and people from very different backgrounds. Coming to terms with these new opportunities was not always easy. Taylor dropped out in 1977 and although she missed the nightlife and friends, she did not miss the modelling:

I didn't like having men come on to me . . . I didn't like feeling taken advantage of or being treated so poorly, like I was just a stupid girl. Models are basically treated like objects – by everybody. Fashion editors and photographers and even hairdressers.

I never felt in control as a model. I never knew what was going to happen to me next. And the girls who really lasted, or who got great deals – like Cheryl Tiegs – never were the best models; they were just the ones who had these great business advisers telling them what to do.

(Quoted by Sherrill 1992: 88,114)

The dependent relationship between models and their mentors has been a source of tension. Shrimpton recounted how her world was turned upside down by one of the radical new photographers, David Bailey, who was renowned for his ruthless and sexist attitude to models. His memory of meeting Shrimpton underlined this:

I walked into the *Vogue* studio and saw Jean Shrimpton doing a Kellogg's advertising shot with Brian Duffy. 'God, Duffy,' I said, 'I wouldn't mind a slice of that one.' 'Forget it', he said, 'she's too posh for you. You'd never get your leg across that one.' We bet ten bob, a lot of money when you're breaking the ice to have a shit. Three months later, I was living with her.

(Quoted by Di Grappa 1980: 7)

Shrimpton's memory of this encounter was telling for her naivety:

Bailey popped his head around the curtain. He had come to check if my eyes were as blue as they were supposed to be. I was far too nervous to take much notice, and too busy reciting 'Humpty Dumpty' [to relax her], but I did notice that the owner of this little head with long, black hair (pre-Beatles), black, suspicious eyes and a wary expression was very attractive. He never said a word, just stared at me and grimaced. It was such a stern little face that I thought: 'Ooh, he doesn't think much of me.' And then the face vanished.

(Shrimpton 1990: 43)

The disparity between these recollections highlights the nature of the relationship between the model and photographer or model and designer. Models are important for their ability to project moods and create an image as well as in their ability to be transformed by make-up, clothes and the camera. One fashion director recalled:

I noticed a child with a plump face, curly red hair, and no make-up. Within a short time she transformed herself into a raving beauty and began to use her body and facial expressions in an amazing way.

(Quoted by Hartman 1980: 58)

The interplay between the model, the props, and the desired image is orchestrated by the photographer. This 'creative' tension is organised around the body of the model as an abstract entity. Photographer Horst commented:

Magazines pick the models, the makeup people and hairdressers today. But I always tell the makeup people the girl must look natural and not made up. The hair should look like the girl did it herself. If the accent is on the hairdo, one forgets about the girl. It's like being overdressed. Chanel used to say, 'If a woman walks into a room and people say, "Oh, what a marvellous dress," then she is badly dressed. If they say, "What a beautiful woman," then she is well-dressed.' The girl must look like a person. The dress and makeup and hair are only to help.

(Di Grappa 1980: 73)

The desired image is the result of extensive manipulation of the model's attributes. This is the key to the success of models. Justin de Villeneuve, who managed 1960s model Twiggy commented on her makeover:

She looked really extraordinary when she emerged at the end of that day. I'd always thought her head was the most beautiful shape, but now her hair was cut so cleverly to show the shape – she was an amazing sight . . . There was this little Cockney girl in a little white gown, with her long neck and her huge huge eyes – she looked like a fawn. She looked like Bambi. I knew then that she really was going to make it.

(Quoted in Twiggy 1975: 36)

Twiggy herself dwelt on the technical details of the transformation:

I was in Leonard for eight hours . . . he cut it, coloured it, re-cut it, did the highlights. They kept drying it to see if it felt right. Those short haircuts have to be absolutely precise. The back was just an inch long, with a little tail, and the front very smooth. I thought it was marvellous.

(Twiggy 1975: 36)

Twiggy's transformation created a look that she projected. It also captured popular tendencies in images of femininity. So she came to symbolise the new model of femininity:

Twiggy was the perfect model for the time. She weighed six and a half stone and took size six in dresses. She was flat chested and stick legged, she was guaranteed to look good in a mini. She had a small, thin face capped with boyish haircut and large dark eyes underlined with pencilled lashes . . . Her line 'It's not what you'd call a figure, is it?' became a standard joke, and suddenly everyone was slimming.

(Bernard 1978: 64)

Media reports emphasised her childlike qualities:

Twiggy radiates the precious innocence and image of youth. Her figure, a frail torso of a teenage choirboy, with a mini-bosom, trapped in perpetual puberty, and four straight limbs in search of a woman's body, is a figure belonging to the youngest of Venus's handmaidens.

(Quoted by Twiggy 1975: 63)

The attraction of Twiggy was her immature body and androgynous hairstyle. The new femininity rejected the curvaceous signs of femininity in an attempt to break out of the conventions of women's lives. Thinness was a sign of weakness, asexuality and hunger (Wolf 1991: 184). The ambivalence of the slender female body continues to underpin definitions of femininity.

It has also spawned a huge diet industry. Whereas Twiggy's thinness was natural, many other models struggled to achieve and maintain the new look. Dieting and eating disorders have become the norm for models; along with dancers and actresses, models are called 'vocational anorexics' whose condition is directly related to the requirements of their jobs (Caputi 1983: 195). American models now weigh 23 per cent less than the average American woman, rising from 8 per cent a generation ago (Wolf 1991: 184; cf. Myers and Biocca 1992). While the 'average model, dancer or actress is thinner than 95 per cent of the female population', these women constitute contemporary role models (ibid.:

185; Caputi 1983: 196). The pressure to manipulate and actively control body shape stems from the emphasis on appearance as the hallmark of contemporary western femininity. Accordingly, the desire to approximate perceived ideal body shapes is a prominent attribute of western women. The quest is predicated on a mixture of narcissism and self-loathing. The unmodelled body gives way to the elastic body (see Chapter 3). Models have reinforced (and propelled) changing body ideals.

SUPERMODELS AND SUPER BODIES

Whereas models had been an adjunct to the fashion industry, by the 1960s they were synonymous with it. The status of modelling reached a zenith. Individual models became household names and international personalities. Twiggy, for example, was named 'Woman of the Year' in 1966, an unthinkable occurrence previously. By the 1970s, models had become superstars, a trend that continued into the 1980s and 1990s. Supermodels were well-paid, high-profile, inter-national jet-setters.

Their changing status was reflected in their earning power. American models earned about $25 a day in the 1940s. This had increased to $5,000 a day for a top model in the 1970s, and between $15,000 and $25,000 a day by 1990. Highly successful models earned $250,000 a year, while about 30 earned $500,000, and a handful $2.5 million annually (Rudolph 1991: 72). Despite the potential earning power, most models have difficulty sustaining a regular income. Not only must potential models conform to criteria about their bodies, they must develop a distinctive trademark in their work. Crucial to the model is an updated portfolio of studio shots, 'tear sheets' (from jobs they have done) plus a 'head sheet' that includes vital statistics and rates. Modelling jobs are usually contracted through agencies who send out details of suitable models. Although models emphasise their individual attractions, they are usually chosen for jobs depending on whether they are 'the right type' for the client and the clothes. Even top models endure 'go-sees' and rejections (Hartman 1980: 64). The body becomes an all-consuming obsession for models and their co-workers. Models are judged on the 'perfection' of their body, yet are considered unintelligent because of it. Lauren Hutton commented:

> I've met people who apparently felt that by virtue of being attractive, I was dumb. It's still a prevalent cliché. Unfortunately by being attractive, women can get what they want; they don't develop their personalities or sense of humour. But it's a stifling way to live. Who wants to just sit around and be vacuous?
>
> (Quoted by Hartman 1980: 64)

Naomi Campbell has also described the frustration of being taken at 'face value' – as being no more than her image as a model:

Figure 4.1 Supermodels: Naomi Campbell epitomises the high status of fashion models.

Source: Time, 16 September 1991. (1991 Time Inc. Reprinted by permission.)

Part of the problem is that people only take models at face value. In a way, what we do is like acting, except that we don't speak. Because we don't speak, we don't have anything to say. What we try to do is project all our emotion and personality through our faces, but that can be misconstrued. These pictures are poses, that is not what we are like in real life at all. We are women too, we have feelings. When you have a very visual job, your appearance is taken to be the most important thing about you. There is no defence.

(Quoted by L.-A. Jones 1992: 10)

Moreover, the ideal body changes and models can be displaced overnight should their 'look' go out of fashion. Shrimpton discovered on a shoot in Portugal that she was becoming a has-been when the other model, the Dutch-born Willie, was given the best clothes and more shots because she was younger and fresher. Shrimpton's reaction was one of powerlessness: 'Even today I am not totally free of the sense of being a has-been' (Shrimpton 1990: 161). Modelling is a risky and transient business.

Each decade becomes associated with a particular image of femininity and of particular models who capture that look. Sometimes the look is associated with national images. Katie Ford of the Ford Agency identified German models with the 1960s, Italians with the 1970s, and English and Australians with the 1980s (Sheehan 1986: 64). These caricatures do not reflect the employment patterns in the industry as much as the encapsulation of successive idealised 'looks'. Even so, most of the successful models have conformed to western stereotypes of beauty because 'in every country, blond hair and blue eyes sell' (Rudolph 1991: 72). Although the majority of models are still white, the supermodels include some diverse looks and ethnicities. Even so, non-white models still experience ambivalence towards them within the industry. English-born black model Naomi Campbell suspected that many resented the fact that she has succeeded as a 'black tulip' rather than a 'typical English rose':

I should think that the people who really care about those things despise having me, a black tulip! Things are changing, of course, but will always be slow. Not a lot of ethnic girls – Hispanics, blacks, Japanese – do the endorse-ments, get awarded the big cosmetic contracts. We're good enough to model clothes, do the pictures, but that's it.

(Quoted by L.-A. Jones 1992: 10)

As the status of models has changed, so too has the profession. The dissolution of the distinction between runway and photographic models requires models who are flexible, have diverse skills and are more competitive. Successful models maintain a disciplined regime of body rituals to maximise their attributes, including constant dieting, exercise, massages, saunas, manicures and pedicures. At the Miss Venezuela Academy, which has produced four Miss Worlds, three Miss Universes and countless runners-up in the past decade, selected applicants are offered free aerobics training, diet advice, dental work, make-up applications, hair-styling, and 'the latest range of cosmetic surgery' – a popular option (Perrottet 1993). 'Getting the look' is one thing; keeping it is another. Elle MacPherson attributes her success to discipline – diet, exercise and punctuality – starting each day with 500 sit-ups and three litres of water (Lyons 1992: 12).

Despite, or perhaps because of, the enormous investment in their bodies, few models admit to being beautiful. Rather, they seem to be chronically dissatisfied with their looks. Even supermodel Cindy Crawford said: 'It's hard doing a runway show. You're surrounded by 40 of the most beautiful women in the world. You see all your own imperfections and none of theirs' (quoted by Rudolph 1991: 74). Models separate their 'professional' bodies from their 'lived-in' ones, regarding them as alien. One 14-year-old model commented on her first photographs for *Elle*:

> There was a lot of mucking around. You never really know how it's going to turn out. I was pleased with the pictures. But it's hard to relate them to being me. There's me at school and there's me in the magazine – they're completely different.
>
> (Safe 1990: 24)

Even top models are not immune from this sense of alienation and dissatisfaction. Although dubbed by *Time* magazine as 'The Body of Our Time', Elle Mac-Pherson has said:

> I don't particularly like the way I look, to tell you the truth . . . I often think I'm smarter than I look . . . When you're trying to sell how beautiful you are and you don't think you're that beautiful, it's a bit scary. I have an image, that's approachable to the public and it sells. That's great but it's different from being the most beautiful woman in the world. I know damn well what I see.
>
> (Quoted by Wyndham 1990: 23–4)

The obsession with their looks breeds extreme insecurity. Shrimpton recalled:

> I was bored, and we must have been exceedingly boring to others. I found life trivial then, and looking back I do not understand why I stuck with it. We were so vain that we continued to dress ourselves up and go out to be looked at . . . I was so insecure that I was always fiddling in the bathroom or running to the ladies to check my appearance. It was pathetic! Here I was, at the height of my fame, behaving like this. I was just an accessory.
>
> (Shrimpton 1990: 102)

Yet modelling continues to attract many young girls as a potentially glamorous and lucrative career. Many models are starting in their early teens. Photographers like them because they are still thin with perfect skin and clear eyes (Safe 1990: 26). Moreover, they are 'fresh' and untrained in the conventional poses and gestures of experienced models. Their attraction is their youth and naivety. As Vivien Smith of Vivien's Model Management, observed:

They want a brand-new face so people will ask, 'Who is this wonderful girl?' Another reason is that young girls don't have lines on their faces. They're like a fresh canvas and the make-up artists and photographers can create on them.

(Quoted by Safe 1990: 26)

The youth of up-and-coming models contrasts with the desire of the older top models to stay in the business. Ten years used to be considered the career span of a model. After that, they would get married or try to enter a related field, such as establishing their own agency, doing fashion design, photography or consultation, joining a public relations firm, or acting (Hartman 1980: 63). Increasingly, models are extending their modelling careers in other ways, through product endorsements, personalised calendars, and modelling for niche markets. The demand for older models (in their thirties and forties) has also grown. At the age of forty, Lisa Taylor was re-employed by Calvin Klein, after she chided him for employing young models to promote clothes aimed at older women. The ploy was highly successful, re-establishing Taylor's career, selling Klein's clothes, and prompting public pressure to see more 'role models of women when they're women, not children' (Sherrill 1992: 88). In other words, models are becoming career professionals.

Whereas models were at the beck and call of agents who discovered them, clients and designers who gave them work, stylists who decided on their look, and photographers who constructed their image, successful models have become tough negotiators. This shift in the power relations in the industry has created tensions between the old guard and the new 'Cool Club' of supermodels. They have become hard-nosed businesswomen, demanding higher fees, and negotiating the conditions of their contracts. As advertising has become more competitive and international, the supermodels have become 'one of the few reliable sales tools. Their beauty is a global ideal, as desirable in Tokyo as in Prague, Manila or Buenos Aires' (Rudolph 1991: 71). Equally, models are often better known than the designers of the clothes they wear, and attracting top models to show the seasonal collections has become an industry priority. According to Eileen Ford of the top New York agency, models are actively resisting being treated as 'this cute play thing or this air head' (*Mode*, September 1991: 72).

One of the most lucrative deals for models is an exclusive contract with a cosmetics or fashion designer or manufacturer since it guarantees an income and exclusive work. It brought fame for Cindy Crawford (through Revlon), Pauline Porizkova (through Estée Lauder), Isabella Rossellini (Lancôme), and Claudia Schiffer (through Guess?). The contracts for these deals are comprehensive, detailing the responsibilities of the model to the employer. A contract between American designer Calvin Klein and model Jose Borain to promote the perfume Obsession for a million dollars over three years, specified the following services:

all broadcast advertising, promotion and exploitation (e.g. network, local, cable and closed circuit television, AM & FM radio and cinema), print advertising, promotion and exploitation (e.g. printed hang-tags, labels, containers, packaging, display materials, sales brochures, covers, pictorial, editorial, corporate reports and all other types of promotional print material contained in the media including magazines, newspapers, periodicals and other publications of all kinds), including but not by way of limitation, fashion shows, run-way modeling, retail store trunk shows, individual modeling and other areas of product promotion and exploitation which are or may be considered to be embraced within the concept of fashion modeling.

(Quoted by Faurschou 1987: 90)

For her part, Borain was required to maintain her 'weight, hair style and colour and all other features of . . . physiognomy and physical appearance as they are now or in such other form as CK may, from time to time, reasonably request' (quoted by Faurschou 1987: 90). The contract also specified that her personal lifestyle should:

be appropriate and most suitable to project an image and persona that reflect the high standards and dignity of the trademark 'Calvin Klein' and that do not diminish, impair or in any manner detract from the prestige and reputation of such trademark.

(Quoted by Faurschou 1987: 91)

The contract could not be terminated by Borain, but Calvin Klein could do so should Borain be disfigured, disabled, suffer illness or mental impairment; should she 'come into disrepute or her public reputation [be] degraded or discredited'. It could also be terminated on the death of Borain or bankruptcy of Klein (Faurschou 1987: 91). Thus, the contract specified precise bodily features as well as the personal attributes of the model deemed to reflect the qualities associated with the product. Product endorsement has also become an important sideline for Elle MacPherson. Launching her 'Down-Underwear' line of lingerie for Bendon, she described herself as 'a saleswoman': 'As a model I sell products. I'm a very good saleswoman. It's very nice to have been a consumer, to be a salesperson and now to be a creator and a . . . realisateur' (Elle MacPherson, quoted by Wyndham 1990: 23).

Changes within the modelling profession have mirrored changes in the fashion industry as well as reflecting new ideas of femininity and ideals of the female body. Above all, modelling has placed a premium on particular constructions of beauty and female body shapes. Models currently epitomise the ideal female persona in western culture, making top models highly desirable companions:

if you're an ego-maniacal celebrity who doesn't consider the person on your arm to be a person rather than an accessory, what do you go for? You go for the accessory that is most sought after in that world. If what you are looking for is a good-looking woman, you naturally go looking in the modelling catalogue.

(*Mode* September 1991: 74)

Modelling epitomes techniques of wearing the body by constructing the ideal technical body. Through those techniques, the body is produced according to criteria of beauty, gender, fashion and movements. These change as codes of prestigious imitation alter. The emphasis in modelling is on self-formation through the body to the exclusion of other attributes. As the model Moncur said: 'It's an addiction, because you exist through others' eyes. When they stop looking at you, there's nothing left' (quoted by Rudolph 1991: 75). Models are trapped in their images. The increase in the use of male models suggests that the equation of femininity with appearance and bodily attributes has been an historical moment; constructions of masculinity are now undergoing a similar process of redefinition, a theme pursued in Chapter 8. Techniques of masculinity are highlighting the body as the site of discipline, labour and reconstitution in the production of a social body that articulates the self and fits its cultural milieu, and where 'the look' says it all.

Chapter 5

Soft focus
Techniques of fashion photography

AESTHETIC TENSIONS AND TECHNICAL CONVENTIONS

'It all depends on the picture,' says the designer Bruce Oldfield. 'A clear picture sells clothes, an out-of-focus one doesn't. We had a picture in *Harpers & Queen* – a navy-blue jersey dress, very simple, high neck – and my God that dress sold, hundreds of them. Mrs Average could look at the picture and think, "That's a nice dress, it's got sleeves and I can wear it at Ascot, and it's got a long jacket which will cover my bum, and it's in *Harpers*." If the fashion editor plays around with the dress too much, and puts gold twigs in the girl's hair, then it doesn't stand a chance.'

(Coleridge 1989: 254)

Fashion photography has had a controversial history. On the one hand, it has fought for recognition as a legitimate form of photography with its own aesthetic conventions. On the other hand, it has been based on projecting images of femininity in terms of desire. By creating fantasies, fashion photographs stand for 'desire itself' (Evans and Thornton 1989: 107):

Both fashion and photography have been accomplices in the renewal of their objects, the one by 'modish' variations of photographic techniques and the other by the restructuring of the image of woman by which an age seeks to discover its own identity.

(Del Renzio 1976: 36)

These two themes have run through histories of fashion photography. The aesthetic theme has constructed a history of the creative genius of photographers and of a shift towards conventions of 'naturalism' and explicitness in technique. Decisive moments and turning points in fashion photography have been identified as successive styles reflecting new moods. Fashion photographs have been celebrated as capturing the spirit of an era. The relationship between successive techniques of fashion photography and techniques of femininity has been integral to the ways in which the fashionable body has been shaped through the twentieth century. Fashion photography has constituted both techniques of representation and techniques of self-formation. It has served as an index of changing ideas about fashion and gender, and about body–habitus relations. As well as constituting a record of fashion moments, fashion photography has become the main source of knowledge about clothes and bodies in a practical way and in processes of historical accounting.

Photography revolutionised the representation of fashion, not just in terms of the technical ability to depict clothes 'realistically', but by inventing ways to display the relationships between clothes, wearers and contexts. Fashion photography plays off the moment of the composition against abstract ideals of style. As Susan Sontag (1978) noted:

> The greatest fashion photography is more than the photography of fashion. The abiding complexity of fashion photography – as of fashion itself – derives from the transaction between 'the perfect' (which is, or claims to be, timeless) and 'the dated' (which inexorably discloses the pathos and absurdity of time.

The representation of clothing produces a contemporary image of 'what looks natural': 'In order that the look of the body might always be beautiful, significant, and comprehensible to the eye, ways developed of reshaping and presenting it anew by means of clothing' (Hollander 1980: 452). Fashion photography introduced new codes of 'naturalism' and new ways of thinking about fashion. Previously, conventions of portraiture structured the depiction of fashion. Among the wealthy classes during the Renaissance, 'as soon as one had a new costume, one had a new portrait done' (Barthes 1984: 300, fn. 16). Mirrors were often used as props to show the face of the sitter while the rest of the painting showed the details of the clothing and toilette. The mirror reinforced the identity of the sitter by 'seeing the self as a picture' (Hollander 1980: 398), underlining the fact that this was a portrait and not an abstract depiction of the clothes themselves.

The importance of photography was its apparent ability to transcend symbolic codes (of taste, emotions and narratives) and portray fashion stripped of meanings and associations 'into an undreamt-of condition of truthfulness' (Hollander 1980: 327). The photographic technique was welcomed because of its 'realism', though, in practice, it constructed other forms of representation that prompted new ways of seeing.

Throughout the nineteenth century, photography competed with illustrative methods. Illustration was associated with art schools and decorative styles while photography was classified as an 'objective' technique for recording objects and events. Because fashion designers and editors wanted their clothes to appear glamorous and exotic, the fashion journals favoured illustrations. Editors like Condé Nast realised the importance of the cover illustration to sell magazines and experimented extensively with different kinds of illustrations that combined art, mood and the quality of a poster (Seebohm 1982: 164). The most coveted fashion illustrations were Paul Iribe's hand-coloured, ink drawings that used a minimum of detail and emphasised colour and shape. He was also 'the first artist who dared to show models with their backs turned to the reader' (Seebohm 1982: 169).

Figures 5.1, 5.2, 5.3 Changing techniques of fashion illustration.

Source: From the collection, Cintra Galleries, Brisbane. (Reproduced by kind permission.)

2. Journal des Dames et des Modes
   Original hand-coloured engraving   1826

3. Journal des Jeune Personnes
   Original hand-coloured engraving   1856

4. Paul Iribe
   Three Gowns by Paul Poiret
   from "Les Robes de Paul Poiret"
   Engraving with pochoir   1908

5. Charles Dana Gibson
   "Gibson Girl"
   Pen and ink   circa 1900

Figure 5.2

6. "Lassitude" by Georges Lepape
   Dinner gown by Paul Poiret
   Gazette du Bon Ton
   Pochoir   1912

7. "Bata-a-Clan"
   Original design by Govpy. Paris
   Ink and gouache   circa 1930

8. Raoul Dufy
   One of a series of eight coloured
   lithographs commisioned by
   Bianchini-Ferrier to promote
   their fabrics designed by Dufy
   Supplement to Gazette du Bon Ton   1920

9. "Colombe"
   Original design by C. Ollret
   for Dior. Paris   circa 1950

Figure 5.3

The flights of fancy of the illustrators were in marked contrast to early fashion photography which adopted the conventions of pictorialism as the basis of the shot. Photographs consisted of formal poses that emphasised grace, elegance and status. This was underlined by the use of aristocrats and debutantes to model the fashions. This convention was established early on. The first recorded use of photography to depict fashion was an album of 288 photographs produced in 1856 of the Countess de Castiglione in her gowns. The Metropolitan Museum of Art commented that she 'was among the first women to have been seduced by the camera; no earlier collection is known of one sitter that reveals such a compulsive desire to be photographed' (quoted by Hall-Duncan 1979: 14). The scopophilic link between the camera and the sitter was already evident.

Most of the fashion photography between 1850 and 1880 consisted of 'social' portraits rather than commercial reproductions. The black and white photographs were often hand coloured. The development of the halftone printing process in 1881 allowed the reproduction of photographs on the printed page (Hall-Duncan 1979: 22, 26). This was to become the staple technique for fashion photography until the development of colour printing (using colour transparencies and engraving techniques) and finally Kodachrome in 1935 (Hall-Duncan 1979: 121).

The popularity of photography increased during World War I with the recognition of its value as a recording device. Technical developments improved the clarity of the images helped by the new light-sensitive film. As cameras became smaller, easier to use and cheaper, so their use spread. Fashion designers recognised the value of photography to depict seams, shapes and details of garments 'accurately', without the distortion of artistic style (Seebohm 1982: 178). There was a backlash against the imaginative efforts of the illustrators. American *Vogue*'s editor-in-chief, Edna Chase, was particularly scathing of fashion artists:

> who shrink from clearly depicting the clothes they are sent to draw. If the great masters of old didn't think it beneath them faithfully to render the silks and velvets, the ruffs and buttons and plumes of their sitters, I don't see why it should be so irksome to modern-day fashion artists to let a subscriber see what the dress she may be interested in buying is really like.
>
> (Seebohm 1982: 179)

Although photography as an art-form was in its infancy, it was a flexible and cheap alternative to fashion illustration. Throughout the 1920s, illustration and photography appeared side by side in fashion journals, catalogues and stores. There were an estimated 6,000 working illustrators in New York and 4,000 in Paris (Seebohm 1982: 175). Meanwhile, fashion editors were building up a stable of photographers. Nast decided to jettison the 'wilful, wild, willowy, wonderful' drawings for 'practical fashion' photographs. He recalled that:

> My critics at the time failed to realize that my decisions were not against a young movement of the day, but were decisions in support of *Vogue*'s mission in life – to serve those one hundred and more thousands of women who were

so literally interested in fashion that they wanted to see the mode thoroughly and faithfully reported – rather than rendered as a form of decorative art.

(Seebohm 1982: 178–9)

The closure of the *Gazette du Bon Ton* in 1925 signalled the demise of fashion illustration. The fashion mood had changed in accordance with new cultural politics – the elitism of *haute couture* was being challenged by ready-to-wear, and Hollywood was the new source of images and role models (see Chapter 3). Fashion photography reflected the new feeling:

By the end of the 1930s, the history of the fashion print was almost played out. Their role had been taken over by the fashion photographer. Occasionally fashion impressions appear in glossy magazines as a faint memory of the influential past they once had. They live on only in the working drawings of the great fashion houses. Strangely enough what remains in fashion photography today is to a large extent the legacy of the situational fashion print of the *Gazette de Bon Ton* and the impression of a fashion ideal – the concept of chic a far more tantalising and marketable idea than a precisely detailed photograph.

(Maynard 1986)

The importance of the cover image was also recognised. Nast made detailed analyses of the sales and return figures for each issue of *Vogue* to rate the effectiveness of each cover. He found that photographic covers sold better than illustrated ones, and that 'informative' photographs were more popular than 'arty' ones. Covers with 'no poster value' and 'experimental' images sold worst of all. The best sellers were the colour photographs of Steichen, Hoyningen-Huené, Horst and Beaton who dominated fashion photography in the 1930s and 1940s (Seebohm 1982: 184–7; Squiers 1980).

The practice of using aristocrats, socialites and personalities to model the clothes persisted in elite fashion magazines and outlets. Professional models were associated with prostitution. It would have been 'shocking' to use potentially dubious women to promote respectable clothes (Hall-Duncan 1979: 9). Consequently, designers, photographers and fashion magazines preferred women who epitomised the acceptable social values of the elite to endorse the new styles. This attitude changed as photographers became confident in exploring new techniques borrowed from new artistic movements and moral codes were relaxed. Modernism, realism and surrealism shaped the fashion photography of the 1920s and 1930s (Hall-Duncan 1979). In time, photographic techniques began to influence artistic developments, especially the use of light, the manipulation of focus and the distortion of images (Tausk 1973). Modernism encouraged geometric lines, angular arrangements, decorative motifs, photomontage and experimentation; realism inspired apparently 'honest' snapshot-like poses and the incorporation of images into (or juxtapositioned with) everyday scenes or settings; while surrealism celebrated experimental and manipulative distortions and 'solarisations' of the photographic image to produce dreamlike super-realism.

These technical conventions were reflected in emerging images of femininity, beauty and gesture. For example, Man Ray's use of mannequin dummies for a *Vogue* cover in 1925 'were not only striking at the time but established the dummy in the canon of fashion photography's iconography' (Harrison 1985: 20). Cecil Beaton was convinced that 'his precocious ideal of feminine beauty had been created by a photographic image' (ibid.: 23). Two other changes were also significant. Photographers began to photograph models in action, a trend that accompanied the popularity of sportswear for women. One of the first action photographs was Jean Morel's shot of Lillian Farley 'on the move and on the street', taken in 1932 (Harrison 1991: 11). This was upstaged by Munkacsi's famous photograph of model Lucile Brokaw running towards the camera which was shot in 1944. Carmel Snow, editor of *Harper's Bazaar* recalled that:

> such a 'pose' had never been attempted before for fashion (even sailing features were posed in a studio on a fake boat) but Lucile was certainly game, and so was I. The resulting picture of a typical American girl in action, with her cape billowing out behind, made photographic history.
>
> (Quoted by Harrison 1985: 33)

Peter Rose Pulham was another to experiment with action. He explained:

> Miss Tilly Losch has not so much posed for these photographs as allowed the camera to pose for *her*. Tired for once of the single photograph of a static dress suspended from action like an unconscious person, we have taken a sequence of ten photographs which show, not the shape of the dress, but the way it moves . . . the camera has recorded ten movements the dress made, each during a tenth of a second.
>
> (*Harper's Bazaar* January 1935: 6–7)

Action photography became more sophisticated with its applications to sport and influenced the photography of sportswear. The 'realist' imagery of sports' fashion photography 'offered the modern woman a vision which she could apply to her own life' (Hall-Duncan 1979: 77). In 1926 *Vogue* pronounced that 'sport has more to do than anything else with the evolution of the modern mode' (Harrison 1985: 34). Photographer Norman Parkinson was typical of those who rejected the rarefied, elitist image of women in fashion, asserting that 'my women behaved quite differently. They drove cars, went shopping, had children and kicked the dog. I wanted to capture that side of women' (quoted by R. Clark 1982: 45). Women led active lives as workers and consumers, images reflected in the burgeoning advertising industry and acknowledged in fashion photo-graphy. Parkinson's 'running, jumping' pictures of women had an enduring impact on fashion photography. Static poses largely disappeared, replaced by moments of a narrative, fleeting impressions, and blurred actions. The trend was reinforced by the popularity of casual and informal clothing styles.

Increasingly, fashion photography was characterised by experimentation. Photographs were designed to shock (Barthes 1984: 302; M. Carter 1987: 6).

Photographers resisted the restrictions placed on them by fashion editors. Cecil Beaton rebelled against the 'artificial' and elitist ways of representing women:

> One afternoon in 1936 I was about to photograph a number of girls in sports suits when I suddenly felt I could no longer portray them languishing in the usual attitudes of so-called elegance. I made them put on dark glasses and stand in angular poses with their elbows crooked and their feet planted well apart. Instead of looking like mannequins unconvincingly pretending to be ladies of the *haut-monde*, they suggested ballet dancers at rehearsal. Today it seems odd that these pictures should have created such an uproar in the editorial department of *Vogue*. I was called in for a special conference. What did I mean by making my models look so unladylike? Was I trying to have a bit of fun at the magazine's expense? I retorted that, for me at any rate, the days of simpering were over.
>
> (Quoted by Hall-Duncan 1979: 114)

The relationship between the photographers and the fashion editors was characterised by conflict. Norman Parkinson related this to the attitudes held by photographers towards women, and to their sexual preferences:

> I was a different sex. I wanted my women to live and live with me and be my friends. I didn't want to immortalise them in some porcelain area. I wanted them to be out there in the fields jumping over the haycocks.
>
> (Quoted by R. Clark 1982: 37)

Parkinson strove to capture 'girls to look as though they breathe and live and smell' (quoted by Shrimpton 1965: 89) in the hope that: 'When they come to write my obituary I would like them to say that I took photography out of the embalming trade' (quoted by R. Clark 1982: 45).

Fashion photography was both shaped and constrained by the fashion industry. In aesthetic terms, photographers sought an unusual angle or setting that distinguished a particular photograph and challenged the conventions of the moment. But photographers were constrained by the fashion editors of the publications for whom they worked. These arbiters of taste functioned as gatekeepers between changing codes of photography, changing images of women, new fashions and styles, and the limits of public standards. Editors were ruthless in their selection of images even though they cultivated an elite coterie of photographers. David Bailey recounted a battle with Diana Vreeland, editor-in-chief of American *Vogue*, over covers:

> Vreeland and I always argued about the white background on the *Vogue* covers. A coloured background was never used, but I got the first blue background in years, and only because the model wore a white hat. Covers were a tricky business. On the same day, six photographers shot a cover. At that time, it was always Bert Stern, Avedon, Penn, myself, and the trendy young photographers living with models that *Vogue* wanted. Six photographs would be put up on the wall and one chosen. The light was always on the

model's right, and her eyes were looking toward it, to draw the viewer to the type.

(Quoted by Di Grappa 1980: 9)

Conventions of fashion photography have undergone a series of changes due to a myriad of technical, cultural and economic forces. The 1930s was a period of significant change. Technically, the process of colour reproduction improved the possibilities for popularising fashion photography, although it was still a complex, expensive and prestigious process. Due to its associations with modernity, colour photography became the lingua franca of fashion photography. The first colour photograph appeared on *Vogue* in 1932, and it was not until 1950 that a black and white photograph was used again (Hall-Duncan 1979: 121).

GENDERED IMAGES

One of the distinctive features of fashion photography has been the centrality of gendered images of clothes: clothes for different genders, and different genders through clothes. Fashion illustration and photography increasingly emphasised women between 1900 and 1920. While conventions for depicting men were unchanged through to the 1930s, images of femininity went through several modes and gradually became homogeneous (Reekie 1987: 309). Moreover, the emphasis on aesthetics was competing with the pressure to represent fashion as a commodity. Abstract appeals to ideals of beauty were replaced by the transformative potential of commodities. Realism, modernism, photomontage and photo-journalism were the techniques used to enhance the 'realistic' impression of the photograph. The framework of that realism was consumerism:

Influenced by the New Photography of the 1920s, an approach which attempted to emphasise the 'essential nature' of objects by drawing attention to their forms and meanings, fashion photography increasingly represented women as commodities.

(Reekie 1987: 290)

Identification with a fashion photograph depended on identification with the properties of the advertised product. Photographs became synonymous with 'the modern look' which encapsulated Hollywood glamour, new urban lifestyles and new freedoms for women (Australian National Gallery 1986: 2). Fashion photographs were 'quite conspicuous constructions' portraying an 'unreal', glamorous world designed 'to seduce and to captivate the viewer': 'Images such as these promise an easy life, for those with the looks and the money – a life whose passing is marked only by the never-ending parade of fabulous new products' (ibid.: 4).

There was a close connection between the development of the film industry and the development of fashion photography. Films threw up the new role models, images of a consumer society, visually-based fantasies and narratives,

Figure 5.4 Redefining female sensuality with touches of androgyny: a rare back profile on a *Vogue* cover.

Source: *Vogue* (Australia), January 1982. Photographer Patrick Russell. (Reproduced by kind permission: *Vogue* Australia © Condé Nast Publications Pty Ltd.)

and new codes of representation. Cosmetics were developed *for* the cinema to enhance the appearances of the film stars and to accentuate character (Keenan 1977: 79–80). Naturally, the use of cosmetics was extended to fashion photography. A 1937 British manual entitled 'Photography in the Modern Advertisement' gave the following advice for representing sexual difference: 'the studied expression of skin texture gives desired character to male subjects. Men's faces should not be retouched. The shadow side of the face should be full of detail'; while for women: 'modelling can be slightly over-emphasised to give pattern in repro- duction. Careful skin retouching helps to preserve delicacy of complexion' (quoted by Stephen 1983: 43). The use of cosmetics and the calculation of their 'effects' was geared towards constructions of femininity:

> Portraits of models and film stars . . . suggest physical perfection: surfaces are black, white, matt and smooth; lighting effects accentuate contrasts, light and shadow; blemishes or irregularities are inconceivable. The self-conscious arrangements of the bodies and the construction of their completeness make even the glamorous men in the portraits appear feminine, as if the art itself was by definition feminine.
>
> (Reekie 1987: 290–1)

The representation of gender was based on body shape and gesture. As defini- tions of gender changed, the ideal female form altered from an S-shape at the turn of the century to 'more upright and less corseted posture' by the 1910s:

> The figures appeared less fragile and static, more confident and solid. Faces, for example, began to look plumper and healthier than their 1890s counter- parts. This solidity was emphasised by the trend towards a more stylistic portrait that de-emphasised facial heterogeneity. Similarly, the age range began to narrow. Mature faces became less common, and many assumed a youthful, almost tomboyish appearance. The post-War women looked out of the page in a more playful and challenging manner than their predecessors would have dared ten years earlier.
>
> (Reekie 1987: 303–4)

The modernist influences of the 1920s and 1930s contributed to representational techniques that emphasised form over content. The representation of gender became increasingly stylised. By the 1930s, faces were doll-like and blemish-free, bodies were angular and geometric, and the models were 'uniformly youthful' (Reekie 1987: 304). In illustration and photography, the aesthetic codes elided notions of art with ideals of femininity: 'advertising set up a form of vision grounded in notions of seduction, possession, dominance and control' (Carrick 1987: 117). Advertising and fashion photography offered images of femininity through identification with the tableaux depicted in the image:

> 'Woman' and 'art', as established fetishistic signs, were transformed within the poster into the visual and conceptual equivalents of the commodity itself.

When linked to advertised products, these symbols exerted an extraordinary power of appeal.

(Carrick 1987: 118)

As Maynard (1986) has noted: 'The impression and style was everything. As an ideal, the impossibly willowy fashion model was born' and photography was the preferred medium to portray that ideal.

Photography could be used to emphasise fetishised parts of the body and to downplay other parts. In 1926, a columnist in *Shop Assistant's Magazine* complained 'that various parts of women's bodies (knees and ankles) were too often used as sexual advertising bait in posters, newspapers and magazines' (Reekie 1987: 315). Advertising and marketing increasingly drew on psychology as the rationale for consumer appeal. The psychological wisdom of the time claimed that women were the main shoppers because of a 'psychological buying instinct'. Since the basis of that instinct was deemed to be emotional, advertising was designed to appeal to women's 'obsessions' with fantasy and romance, family welfare and human interest (Reekie 1987: 323). Thus modernist imagery was allied to psychological formulations to construct 'modern' notions of gender and sexual identity. Femininity became co-extensive with the fashion photograph.

THE MODELMAKERS

World War II was a transition period for fashion photography. Fashion photography became more political and critical, reflecting wartime preoccupations. Displays of excess, frivolity and indolence were discouraged by fashion magazines. Fashion photography experimented with relating the impact of war on the lives of ordinary women and men. Lee Miller was one of the wartime photographers who excelled at producing social documents through her fashion photographs. Nast wrote her a complimentary letter on a series of photographs taken in 1942:

> The photographs are much more alive now, the backgrounds more interesting, the lighting and posing more dramatic and real. You managed to handle some of the deadliest studio situations in the manner of a spontaneous outdoor snapshot.

(Quoted by Seebohm 1982: 244)

The impact was lasting. Post-war photography had a new maturity that combined technical experimentation with new perceptions of women and a climate of 'charm and ease' (Hall-Duncan 1979: 122). It also had another element – sexuality – which became the central motif of fashion photography (Harrison 1991: 14). After the austerity of wartime fashions and restrictions on the use of fabric, post-war fashion celebrated the female form with attention to shapely contours and signs of femininity. Dior's New Look epitomised the new fashion, though when it was first shown, it created controversy: 'models wearing the new style actually had the gowns ripped from their bodies' (Hall-Duncan 1979: 135). This probably guaranteed the success of the look which became the leitmotif of fashion photography of the 1950s. Technically, fashion photography combined techniques of the documentary with social commentary: photo-journalism, contrived spontaneity, action and passion. The work of Irving Penn and Richard Avedon became synonymous with these techniques. While Penn emphasised anthropological and sociological elements in his photographs, Avedon created dramas which explored 'the looks, mannerisms, and gestures of human beings' (Hall-Duncan 1979: 140, 147, 154). With the new maturity towards photographing fashion, the profession gained respect and popularity. Photographers were sought after and, in turn, they sought out individual models whom they photographed exclusively.

Fashion photography was in the ascendency. Fashion was everywhere; fashion photography attracted a new generation of photographers and models; and models achieved status and prestige as role models for young women. Inevitably, the success of fashion photography led to standardisation and conservatism. Photographers, such as Penn, lamented the pressure to produce 'an artificially manufactured image created as much by make-up artists, stylists and hairdressers' as it was by the photographer (Harrison 1985: 37). Even the seemingly conservative Cecil Beaton rejected the conventions of the fashion editors:

> I want to make photographs of very elegant women taking grit out of their eyes, or blowing their noses, or taking the lipstick off their teeth. Behaving like human beings in other words . . . It would be gorgeous instead of illustrating a woman in a sports suit in a studio, to take the same woman in the same suit in a motor accident, with gore all over everything and bits of the car here and there. But naturally that would be forbidden.
>
> (Quoted by Hall-Duncan 1979: 202)

Tensions began to crack the façade of the 'image makers'. By the 1960s, dissatisfaction turned to open revolution and fashion photography became a sign of the turmoil of the 1960s generation. The dominance of couture was shattered by the success of street designers, fashion boutiques and new ways of representing clothes and models. The new fashion appealed to younger women who identified with the models promoting it. Model Jean Shrimpton attributed her success to the fact that she epitomised ordinariness:

> I looked like every other young girl of my age: my hair was shoulder-length and flipped-up at the ends; I hadn't yet quite mastered the eye make-up which was to become a sort of trademark; and I was stiff and uneasy before the camera. Word had got around that I had the most amazingly blue eyes, but other than that all I did with any degree of success was to embody ordinariness – which is, of course, a hugely marketable quality.
>
> (Shrimpton 1990: 43)

Fashion photographers capitalised on the 1960s spirit. Avedon typified the photographers who were intent on creating social statements that rejected the strictures of fashion photography and reflected contemporary women in these 'disturbing times' (Harrison 1985: 38). He incorporated 'a range of poses and gestures' from the American Ballet Theatre into his photography which created new conventions of gesture and display (ibid.: 39). Avedon rejected realism in favour of creating the perfect picture by regularly doctoring the photographs:

> All the models who worked for him knew perfectly well he would give them a different body if their own was not up to his exacting standards. I have seen my head on someone else's body – he had doctored a photograph of me he took for Revlon, the cosmetic house. He had photographed me with a teddy bear, but when I saw the advertisement the hands holding the teddy were not mine. They were much better hands, with longer nails. It did not worry me. It was still a privilege working for him.
>
> (Shrimpton 1990: 100)

The result was that photographers came to determine the nature of 'the look' and construct the 'fashionable self' (Derfner 1976: 42). Their power within the fashion industry increased accordingly. Fashion photographers became heroes whose lifestyles epitomised the young generation: 'young fashionable male[s], rolling in money, success and women' (Imrie 1984: 29). The so-called Terrible Three – David Bailey, Terence Donovan and Brian Duffy – working-class Londoners with an irreverent attitude to the pretensions of fashion and a low opinion of its protagonists (including the models), typified the photographer-hero (Hall-Duncan 1979: 159–61). Brian Duffy described the trio as 'violently hetero-sexual butch boys. We didn't just treat models as clothes horses. We emphasised the fact that there were women inside the clothes. They started to look real' (Duffy quoted in Shrimpton 1965: 86). A *Sunday Times Colour Magazine* feature on the three 'modelmakers', published in 1964, credited them with setting the 1960s style and creating 'a certain way of looking' (quoted by Imrie 1984: 29–30). It concluded that:

> They have little in common with the pre-1960 conception of fashion photography; it is their straightforwardly sexual interest in women, combined with an unbroken attachment to their East End origins, which has enabled them to interpret the mixture of toughness and *chic* peculiar to their time. 'We try and make the model look like a bird we'd go out with.' Very often, the model and the bird are the same one.
>
> (Quoted by Imrie 1984: 28)

The glamorous world of fashion became the object of scrutiny in films such as *Qui êtes-vous Polly Magoo?*, a 1966 satire on the ephemeral world of *Vogue*, and Antonioni's *Blow Up*. In the latter, David Hemmings depicted the life of the photographer-hero as wild, chaotic and sexy and modelled on the image of the Terrible Three. Bailey and Duffy acknowledged that taking fashion photography was 'a most definitely sexual thing. The only thing between you and the girl is the camera. A three-legged phallus' (Hall-Duncan 1979: 161). Women were badly treated by many of these photographers, used as mere accessories and as decoration: 'women had to know their place' (Shrimpton 1990: 48–9).

The explicitly sexual nature of the relationship between the photographer and the model was a feature of 1960s photography. According to Donovan, a good picture depended 'on a chemical thing between you and the girl' (Imrie 1984: 28), while Duffy strove to achieve 'complicity' between the photographer and the model (Shrimpton 1965: 87). Photographs of this period toyed with direct confrontation between camera and subject, spontaneity, blatant sexual overtones and overtly sexualised bodies. Shrimpton reflected back on 'a strong sexual atmosphere' during photographic sessions (Shrimpton 1990: 44): 'Photographers do have a lure for models, and a photographic session can be a very seductive time. Locked together in a studio, a sexual buzz gets going which normally ends when the session ends' (ibid.: 77).

While public attention was focused on the Terrible Three, Shrimpton credited photographer John French as the unacknowledged influence on their approach to photography. French recognised the importance of capturing the 'personal projection' of a model. He likened great models to alchemists: 'their personality suddenly bubbles and bubbles and you realise that they react and make that fantastic rapport between the photographer and the model which makes for a lively and exciting picture' (French quoted by Shrimpton 1965: 95). The models appreciated his:

> gift of making women look fantastic, but in a more modern way [than Avedon], and he knew exactly how to get a model to give her best. He made us all feel he was totally in love with us right up until the moment when the last superb picture was taken.
>
> (Shrimpton 1990: 99)

Bound up in the intimate relationship with the photographer/camera, models displayed a sensuality bordering on sexuality. It became second nature and could easily be misconstrued. When Shrimpton was photographed with actor Steve McQueen for a *Vogue* series, he was puzzled by her display. She recalled the encounter as follows:

> Avedon is very theatrical when he shoots. Disco music was pounding, and his instructions to me were to gaze very lovingly at this man. I knew what he wanted: he wanted me to come on strong.
>
> Steve McQueen was not entirely comfortable, probably because acting and modelling have nothing in common: they are two entirely different skills. Avedon began to shoot, and while he clicked off his first twelve exposures I sat even closer to McQueen and held his ear gently between my thumb and forefinger. I did what was required – I came on strong looking lovingly into his bright blue eyes just a breath away.

Avedon was urging: 'Fine, beautiful, hold it. That's it! Still now. G-r-e-a-t . . .'
Models learn to count the clicks of the camera without knowing they are
doing it. As soon as I was aware that the twelve exposures had been taken I let
all my muscles go loose and relaxed into lethargy until Avedon was ready to
shoot again. I think McQueen suspected I really was coming on strong with
him. I wasn't: that's how models work. I was not turning on my sexuality for
any reason to do with him; I was simply doing my job. It was an automatic
reflex: turn on, stop, sit back, wait, and then turn on again until the
photographer was happy . . .

These sudden switches of mood surprised McQueen. He said with a sort of
academic interest: 'You just turn it on and off.'

I shrugged. 'It's my job.'

(Shrimpton 1990: 95)

The explicit sexuality of 1960s fashion photography paralleled the features of
new-wave film. Increasingly, filmic techniques were incorporated into fashion
photography (Harrison 1985: 49), rejecting 'the rules of haute couture refine-
ment, of pose and attitude, of sexual discretion, and polite society' (Hall-Duncan
1979: 183). In the process, the clothes became 'more and more incidental . . .
mere props for far-out fashion photography' (ibid.: 180). As fashion photography
became more outrageous, tensions between the photographers and the designers
and fashion editors came to a head. Designers complained that the photographers
had lost sight of the fashion 'because the photographer gets involved in the model
or the scene he is shooting – everything but the dress' (*Time*, 3 December 1965:
42). One designer commented:

Actually, it's the reader who suffers, but then maybe she really wants to see
clothes in awkward poses in bizarre settings. On the other hand, it's my selfish
purpose to see clothes looking beautiful; it's the photographer's selfish purpose to be famous; it's the art director's selfish purpose to have a striking,
stylish page; it's the magazine's selfish purpose to sell ads and issues. With all
these selfishnesses, you just come up with one big crumbler.

(*Time*, 3 December 1965: 42)

The fashion industry resented the power and disrespect of the photographers and
they applied pressure on them to conform. For their part, the photographers
upped the ante by shooting more and more outrageous photographs. Eventually,
public opinion began to turn against the photographer-heroes and the cult of the
fashion photographer waned. Nonetheless, the revolts of the 1960s forged new
conventions and aesthetics for fashion photography. These converged with
changes to fashion magazines under the impact of cinema, television and video.
The emphasis on the visual content became paramount and the roles of photographer, art director and editor became 'blurred or interchangeable' (Harrison
1985: 50). In response, photographers found new ways to rebel. Helmut Newton
and Guy Bourdin epitomised the trend towards conventions of brutal realism and

eroticism. They pushed the limits of fashion photography to produce images that shocked by questioning the foundations of fashion and making intertextual references to other cultural debates. Central to the photography of the 1970s was an obsession with sexual motifs – 'homosexuality, transvestitism, and miscegenation, as well as voyeurism, murder, and rape' (Hall-Duncan 1979: 196). Newton was:

> the prime mover in wresting fashion photography from its years of naivety and innocence. His startling images, for all their nostalgic references, are completely of our time. Their ambiguity confounds his critics, who are unable to decide whether his women are remote or seductive, dominant or submissive. As Beaton once said, Newton 'plays tricks on his audience'. He enjoys provoking the viewer but his integrity is intact.
>
> (Harrison 1985: 52)

Their allusions to female sexuality and gender relations created a storm of femininist criticism. Newton and Bourdin were attacked for being sexist, exploitative, regressive and misogynist. Defenders suggested that the new images were not so much the 'intrusion of the "real world" into fashion photography', but the acknowledgement of the centrality of brutality in popular culture, especially cinema and television (Brookes 1980: 2).

Retrospective accounts have argued that this photography was only forcing the audience to confront fantasies, myths and stereotypes about sexuality. Bourdin pushed the conventions of erotica even further to question the superficiality and transience of glamour. His photographs were so explicit that it was 'difficult to imagine the reader-spectator, whether male or female, identifying with anyone in the photograph' (Harrison 1985: 52).

The male dominance of fashion photography was challenged in the 1980s when a number of female photographers, such as Deborah Turbeville (a former fashion editor) and Sarah Moon (a former model), became well known. They questioned the conventions of photography and the artifice of modelling through caricatures of poses and gestures. Turbeville's photographs:

> featured models who combine passive, laconic poses with expressions of unease and disenchantment . . . Her women appear independent, self-contained, but also vulnerable. Her photographs suggest a narrative but the story is not explained. They recall instead brief snatches of poetry.
>
> (Harrison 1985: 53)

Turbeville's photographs confronted the contradictory identities of women: 'the models' bodies refuse even while they mimic the standard pose – their faces convey dejection, boredom, sometimes fear; the bodies convey the pose in its failure' (Griggers 1990: 87). Her pictures neither glamorised the clothes nor the models. Rather, they conveyed a sense of alienation, despair and suffering: 'the camera seems always to intrude into a private world of quiet despair, the masquerade is only ever half made, and the woman in the pose suffers in spite of and because of its failing' (ibid.: 90). Finally, the ambivalence of the models towards their work was exposed directly by the 'off-centre composition, the dissociated sense of isolation, and the evocation rather than the statement of fashion' (Hall-Duncan 1979: 217). Considered together, the photographs of Turbeville, Newton and Bourdin emphasised 'not just kinky sex' and 'bizarre story lines' but 'underlying tensions' of people tottering 'on the brink of some unfathomable abyss: their poses are intimately linked with psychosis and despair' characteristic of our self-destructive society (De Neve 1976: 26). The clothes in the photographs were of little importance. Instead, fashion photography embraced cynicism and parody. The promotional function of fashion photography had been re-defined and undermined:

> to catch and engage the reader's attention, to hold a subgroup of readers in the audience who enjoy reading fashion parodically, and to capitalise on the average middle-class reader's ambiguous relation both to the commodity sign and to her own subjective positions within the socio-discursive field.
>
> (Griggers 1990: 95)

The new conventions reflected new ideas about gender and sexuality as well as reflecting widespread questioning of consumerism. Female photographers, in particular, articulated the conflicting points of identification and circuits of desire that confronted women (Griggers 1990: 100). The female spectator can reject identification with the totalising image and engage with the 'impossible network of gazes' inscribed in the image:

> For the female reader, the experience of the discourse is the experience of ambivalence – ambivalence towards power, toward motherhood, toward marriage, toward a homoeroticism dressed in leather and pearls, toward fashion, toward social investment, and toward representation itself.
>
> (Griggers 1990: 101)

According to Griggers, women can adopt a range of viewing positions based less on voyeurism than on the structure of spectacle and the inscription of 'a vestimentary "package"': 'Clothing and other kinds of ornamentation make the human body culturally visible . . . clothing draws the body so that it can be culturally seen, and articulates it as a meaningful form' (Silverman 1986: 145).

The network of relations between bodies and clothes, and between clothed bodies and their social context, have inflected changing conventions of fashion photography: from the classic formal poses of early photography; to the use of gestures and location shooting; to 'leap[ing] and sprawl[ing] a la sixties' (M. Carter 1987: 7); and indiscernible clothing in 'a pleasing blur or swirl' (ibid.: 7). In the 1980s, fashion photography dispensed with tableaux (formalised settings and possibly implied narratives) (Barthes 1984: 300–2) and replaced them with the imperatives of video through the use of moving images: the 'attire and its wearer have been held in the grip of a long, slow dissolve' (M. Carter 1987: 7). Fashion photography faces another cross-roads. On the one hand, fashion photography has become a respectable art-form, represented in galleries and museums and celebrated in retrospective exhibitions which:

> invite us to look in a different, more thoughtful, more abstracting way. Time has changed them, too. Seen in this retrospective form (compiled in a book, on the walls of a museum), images that started out as fashion photographs become a commentary on the idea of the fashionable.
>
> (Sontag, quoted by Harrison 1985: 14)

But on the other hand, fashion photography has repudiated its rationale as an effective technique for representing fashion. It has become introspective, concerned more with technique than with the subject of the images. A former owner and editor of *Harpers & Queen* magazine commented:

> Today magazines have actually regressed into the past. There isn't the same kind of arrogance that we developed and that led us in all kinds of directions. I could almost do the next issue of *Harpers & Queen* now. Advertisers actually used to ring up *Queen* in the '60s and ask for the photographer because that was one of our strengths – I can imagine now some of the editors ringing up the advertisers. This is a bad state of affairs.
>
> (Perkins and Woram 1991/2: 37)

As powers relations between the photographers and employers shift again, fashion photography also faces criticism about its images, especially of femininity and sexuality.

EROTIC CODES

> Anybody who sits down to be photographed feels it's contrary to their natural instinct. They feel narcissistic, immodest. They're doing everything that is contrary to their pure, classical nature. You have to take hold of that area [between the lens and the sitter] and make people enjoy it. You're like a snake watching a mongoose. You give your whole attention to them. You never turn your back. You persuade, you talk, you have asides to your assistant, but you never take your eyes off your subject.
>
> (Norman Parkinson, quoted by R. Clark 1982: 40–1)

Parkinson's view of the role of the photographer highlighted the peculiar relationship between the camera and the object, a relationship that is simultaneously intimate and disinterested. The photographer must coax the sitter to perform shamelessly for the camera lens while, at the same time, manipulating the situation (the pose) to achieve a certain effect. The photographer manipulates the space between the camera and the sitter to create an illusion of sensuality. This characteristic has been accentuated by the experimental priorities of fashion photography.

The relationship between sensuality and sexuality, and between scopophilia and male desire, have become the focus of feminist work on representation. Laura

Mulvey's analysis (1975) of the relationship between the cinematic look and visual pleasure has underpinned this appraoch. She examined the contradictions between scopophilia (the pleasure of the look) and narcissism (identification with the image). Whereas the scopophilic look invokes an active viewing position, narcissism entails a passive relationship with the image. Moreover, according to Mulvey, this relationship is necessarily gendered – as if from a male point of view. She concluded that the viewing positions of female spectators were inherently circumscribed and over-determined by the structure of the two kinds of looks. Voyeurism and fetishistic scopophilia are established by the look as normative pathologies of viewing:

> The object is normatively female . . . ; the subject is normatively male. This doesn't of course mean that women are excluded from positioning themselves as the subjects of visual discourse: different degrees of inclusion/exclusion are operative along the spectrum from pornography to romance. But in all cases, including that of most texts specifically designated for women, their inscription . . . occurs in subordination to the forms of the male gaze, through a negation of the difference of femaleness.
>
> (Frow 1984: 35)

Women see themselves as objects, as visions to be surveyed. Equally, women learn to conduct themselves as surveyed objects through specific codes of dress, gestures and interpersonal communication. While the patriarchal implications of Mulvey's arguments have been resisted by recent critics, no comprehensive alternative account has been offered, apart from the idea of subversive readings 'against the grain'. At best, women construct feminine pleasures and points of view that are not based on voyeurism. The 'soft porn' tendencies of much recent fashion photography challenge the prospects for progressive points of view because the visual registers of advertisements and fashion photography:

> depend upon a process of narcissistic identification – perhaps the female equivalent of phallic competition – which provokes no resistance but which carries the same codes of control, objectification and to-be-looked-at-ness as are at work in pornography proper. Soft pornography mediates between hard pornography (transforming the spectacle of castration or its fetishistic substitutes into the unthreatening spectacle of submission) and romance (transferring its mechanisms of sublimation onto the commodity).
>
> (Frow 1984: 37)

The soft porn image plays in the space between these two registers even when the object of the look is male. In fashion, men too adopt 'postures of submission – the receptive smiles, the body cantings – which constitute the political ceremony of femininity' (Frow 1984: 37). These images do not simply transfer notions of femininity but construct the body – or bodily parts – as commodities and as signs of fetishised sexuality. The 'multiplication of areas of the body accessible to marketability' and their associated sexualisation (Coward 1987: 54) are bound up with the presentation of the sexualised body *and* of the social self.

Figure 5.5 'Easy does it': modish men composed by new techniques of representation and leisure suits.

Source: *Mode*, September 1992, p. 111. (Reproduced by courtesy of Australian Consolidated Press.)

Fashion photography provides a commentary on changing definitions and critiques of sexuality through authorised erotic images which are acceptable because they are produced for fashion rather than gratuitously. Fashion erotica is characterised by a distanced quality that estranges the image from the spectator and disrupts and subverts conventional stereotypes about sexuality and roles (Myers 1987: 62). Over time, distanciation itself is incorporated into registers of sensuality and privileged codes of viewing that are related to, but distinct from, pornographic codes: 'Extraordinary liberties are taken precisely because it is "only" fashion' (Evans and Thornton 1989: 82). Fashion images are consumed both compliantly and deviantly by readers who lust for the pleasures of the image as much as the clothes they depict. Brookes (1980: 1) confronted what she saw as the 'intimacy of the double-page spread' which projected a feeling of *jouissance* between the model and each viewer/reader. Sexual desire is heavy in these images yet meaning is denied by the transience of the image: 'Just looking, just speculating, one can "become" this woman who walks away and attract oneself or attract another's gaze' (Evans and Thornton 1989: 106–7).

Fashion photography has entered a new phase of controversy with the sexual preoccupations of the 1990s: post-feminism, the new masculinity, ambivalence towards homosexuality, and sexual well-being. As a result, men have become the object of desire and the subject of fashion photography. According to Harrison (1991: 276; Triggs 1992: 29), photography has drawn on the classical Greek tradition of depicting the male nude to look at men as objects and as repositories of sexual desire. Male sexuality is depicted through physicality, sensuality and camaraderie. The new mood has been captured in high-street fashion through the advertisements, such as those for Calvin Klein, which emphasise 'youthful eroticism' (Harrison 1991: 276; Triggs 1992: 27; Grant 1992: 20). The radical character of depicting male sexuality is already being absorbed into the conventions of the genre as transgression, repudiation and parody.

Fashion photography provokes viewers and consumers into confirming their own identity through structures of desire. It is in this way that fashion photography exceeds the seams of the clothes it portrays by playing with current definitions of sexuality and identity. Its conventions are neither fixed nor purposeful, instead constituting a nexus between fashion and selfhood – and above all, embracing the instabilities, conflicts and contradictions in sexuality. As a representational technique, fashion photography has far-reaching practical consequences.

Chapter 6

States of undress
Lingerie to swimwear

TECHNICAL BODIES AND GENDERED CIVILITY

A sweet disorder in the dress
Kindles in clothes a wantonness.

(From a poem by Herrick, quoted by Crawley 1965: 49)

These lines evoke the ambiguous registers associated with the relationship between clothing and bodies. States of undress, or the partially clad body, invite
particularly ambivalent responses. Nudity itself has also been the subject of
intense controversy because the naked body is titivated or covered in accordance
with social and cultural edicts. The term 'lasciviousness' (meaning lust or
wantonness) is often applied to discussions of the nude as if the sight and site of
the body incite sexuality. The figure of the body is ambiguous: on the one hand,
the body is the site of sexual conduct; on the other hand, it is a focus of the sexual
desires of others. In the first scenario, the body must be disciplined to control
sexual impulses; in the second, the body requires protection. The invocation of
these scenarios depends on contextual factors, or what Goffman has called 'the
orientational implications of exposure' (Goffman 1965: 50).

Guidelines on clothing conduct and 'situational *déshabille*' are highly variable
yet, in specific contexts, they are decisive because they equip the body to perform
in specific social occasions. As Freadman (1988: 147) has proposed, 'dress is the
fabric-ation of a body and its wearing'. She cites the example of clothing codes
in post-revolutionary France. Whereas men's clothing was homogenised and
standardised, women displayed the power and position of their families
(husbands and fathers) through their clothes (ibid.: 126). Clothes and the gestures
of women reflected 'the whole training of the feminine body' in the 'rules of
coquetry' (ibid.: 129). Women learned to manage the internal and external
components of the body in ways which were ascribed as 'feminine'. Being
decked out as a woman had its consequences: it restricted movement and, in
winter, it was cold. Fashionable shoes wore out because they were not designed
for walking. A woman's clothes had the effect of excluding her from
participating in many public activities. While these were the basis of gender
etiquette, it appears that many women ignored the restrictions on their clothes

and activities. As a result of 'transgressions' of clothing conventions, legislation was passed forbidding the wearing of male clothes by women (ibid.: 127; Steele 1988: 162–4).

The poet George Sand was one of the most notorious cross-dressers. She deliberately chose to adopt male clothing in order to participate freely in Parisian literary circles and to live, as she saw it, the appropriate life of a writer. By dressing as a man, she could abandon the coquetry of the feminine body and the need to behave 'as a woman'. Conversely, by dressing as a man, she could behave like one. Of course, her decision was controversial, as indicated by the enormous variation in portraits of Sand, some depicting her as a younger brother, others emphasising her feminine shape (waist, breasts and hips). Freadman comments: 'The caricaturists are intent on showing that the female form admits of no disguise, despite Sand's assertion that the disguise she had adopted had the helpful property of hiding the waistline' (Freadman 1988: 133). The response to Sand was both an attempt to restore her to her 'natural' place as a woman while acknowledging the 'sexual appeal of women in male attire' (Steele 1988: 164). Indeed, cross-dressing – especially in theatre and prostitution – has a long history of sexual incitement (cf. Garber 1992).

As this example illustrates, clothing is a key component of patterns of sexually coded rules of conduct. For these reasons, 'such apparently petty matters of "mere" etiquette' are of particular significance (Goffman 1965: 52). Yet the partially covered body has often received even more ire. Steele has asked:

> Why is the partly clothed figure often perceived as being sexier than the nude? Underwear provides an important clue. In the apparel industry, underclothes are known as 'intimate body fashions', a highly revealing expression. All clothes are body fashions, but the more intimate the connection between body and clothes, the sexier the clothes will be . . . the sexual power and charm of the body 'rub off' onto the clothes. But the clothes are then perceived as providing an additional erotic stimulus of their own.
>
> (Steele 1989b: 55–6)

The frisson between bodies and clothes is the theme of this chapter. It is difficult to separate the discussion of bodies from issues such as bodily movement, gender, sexuality and civility. In the past decade, these issues have come together in many studies of the bio-politics of the body. The theme of recent work is the way in which techniques of the body graphically construct an index of social behaviour. One review of recent studies of the body cites the influence of modernity (contemporary obsessions with newness and futurism), feminism (gendered patterns of social relations) and Foucault (the role of institutional ethics in bio-politics) as the sources of bodily motifs (Frank 1990: 133; B. Turner 1984). These have inspired Bryan Turner's discussion of bodily functions in terms of reproduction (patriarchy), regulation (external), restraint (internal) and representation (commodification) (Frank 1990: 133). The fashionable or fashioned body echoes each of these themes. The successful deployment of the body entails discipline and pleasure through the packaging and presentation of the body (cf. Featherstone 1982: 18).

Body work (exercise, sport, gesture, manners) is defined by a conjunction of notions of gender and codes of sexuality. Codes of civility were established through the conjunction of body techniques associated with social conduct, etiquette, power relations, and political behaviour (Elias 1978). In other words, the body does not behave 'naturally' but acquires an expertise in techniques, actions and orientations specific to a group or society (Mauss 1973: 73). The body is a contested and problematic player in social intercourse. Historical and cross-cultural examples of body work reveal a myriad of attitudes and behaviours. More often than not, however, prescriptions have differed for men and women though not always in the same way. For example, the naked male in ancient Greece symbolised heroism, divinity, athleticism and beauty while for women, nudity was shameful and immoral (Bonfante 1990; cf. Hollander 1980: 6–11). Respectable Greek women were covered from head to toe. Complex attitudes to women and femininity continue to reflect that problematic positioning of the female body in sexual and moral terms. More generally, the body has been an integral force in the articulation of codes of conduct.

Elias (1978) has argued that the development of civil society in Europe was predicated on codes of etiquette as the basis of social intercourse. One component of the new etiquette was the emergence of the 'shame frontier'. Until the sixteenth century, 'the sight of total nakedness was the everyday rule' for bathing and for sleeping (ibid.: 164). Both activities were communal – people ran naked though the streets to the bathhouse while visitors shared the family bed. Moral conduct and codes of etiquette were not attached to the sight of the naked body. Indeed, the wearing of clothes in bed 'aroused suspicion that one might have some bodily defect – for what other reason should the body be hidden?' (ibid.: 163).

Gradually, however, new notions of civility made strategic covering of the body central to acceptable social conduct. A shame frontier became attached to the naked body. In situations of intimate contact and bodily display, special clothes were devised to make the body respectable. This was the origin of bathing costumes, underclothes and nightdresses. While such garments covered sexually implied body parts, elaborate injunctions surrounded how such clothes should be worn. Rules about wearing clothes emphasised modesty for its own sake. Individuals internalised these injunctions as the dangers associated with shameful conduct. Although it was acceptable to display 'under' clothes to family members and intimates, the design of the garments was elaborated to make them look as 'respectable' (or publicly presentable) as possible. Pyjamas, for example, were a 'more "socially presentable" sleeping costume' than nightshirts so that 'the wearer need not be "ashamed" when seen in such situations by others' (Elias 1978: 165–6).

By the nineteenth century, children, too, were 'socialised' into conduct that preserved their modesty by the strategic covering of the body. These moral codes became 'second nature'. As Elias observes:

> Only if we see how natural it seemed in the Middle Ages for strangers and for children and adults to share a bed can we appreciate what a fundamental change in interpersonal relationships and behaviour is expressed in our manner of living. And we recognize how far from self-evident it is that bed and body should form such psychological danger zones as they do.
>
> (Elias 1978: 168)

For us, the display of body parts alerts us to the dangers signalled by the body as coded in a set of moral injunctions. Only under certain circumstances is body display acceptable. Moreover, because the sight of the body is invested with implications of unrestrained sexuality, its display is dependent on the existence and maintenance of restraining codes of conduct to prevent transgression rather than to positively achieve appropriate behaviour. Above all, European civilisation developed a high degree of individual internalisation of codes of restraint in civilised etiquette:

> One example is bathing manners. It would have meant social ostracism in the nineteenth century for a woman to wear in public one of the bathing costumes commonplace today. But this change, and with it the whole spread of sports for men and women, presupposes a very high standard of drive control. Only in a society in which a high degree of restraint is taken for granted, and in which women are, like men, absolutely sure that each individual is curbed by self-control and a strict code of etiquette, can bathing and sporting customs having this relative degree of freedom develop. It is a relaxation which remains within the framework of a particular 'civilized' standard of behaviour involving a very high degree of automatic constraint and affect-transformation, conditioned to become a habit.
>
> (Elias 1978: 187)

Despite a rhetoric of freedom and individuality which has accompanied explanations of fashion, Elias suggests that the more libertarian the behaviour or mode of dress, the greater the codes of constraint that govern that behaviour. Bodies are invested with far-reaching powers and political ramifications. They mediate contemporary etiquette and social conduct. From the nineteenth century, new styles in underwear coincided with new notions about desirable feminine shapes. Over time, these last eschewed the fleshy excess fetishised in the past in favour of increasingly slim contours and the highlighting of certain 'feminine' parts (bust, hips, waist). The body became a site upon which the wearer must work, through exercise and bodily disciplines (for example, diet, physical manipulation or constraint). The final product and desirable shape were enhanced by the shaping effects of underwear as the foundation for 'outer' garments and the achievement of desirable 'feminine' shapes.

EROTIC SECRETS OF UNDERCLOTHES

> Underclothes are secret garments, hidden under the outer clothing just as the body itself is hidden, to be revealed only in the privacy of the bedroom in the presence of intimate friends. A person wearing underwear is simultaneously dressed and undressed.
>
> (Steele 1989b: 56)

In western culture, underwear is a highly charged form of clothing. Despite being the object of popular speculation, there have been few studies of underwear as a generic clothing form. More interest has been generated in the most extreme form of undergarment, the corset. Histories of underwear (e.g. Cunnington and Cunnington 1981; Ewing 1978; Yarwood 1982) share the argument that underwear (as distinct from corsets and bodices) did not become an elaborated form of clothing until the nineteenth century. It had been common to wear a chemise and (for men) some kind of pants under outer clothing to protect the skin from chafing, and to prevent outer garments from being soiled. Linen was especially popular because of its softness. By the seventeenth and eighteenth centuries, most people:

> possessed several changes of underlinen so shirts and chemises could be washed frequently. Although baths were less usual until the nineteenth century, people were, in fact, much cleaner than is generally thought and the idea of wearing upper garments (such as dresses, trousers and sweaters) next to the skin as we do today would have shocked earlier generations.
>
> (Bath Museum of Costume 1980: 27)

Gradually, underclothing was differentiated and elaborated into separate garments. These included pantaloons, drawers, petticoats, and brassieres (bras). In accordance with the shame frontier, underwear was rarely referred to at all. Euphemisms such as underpinnings, unmentionables, indescribables and unwhisperables were used to allude to the unnameable (Yarwood 1982: 423). As the shame frontier reached new heights, so the emphasis on underwear intensified. Not only did the range of garments multiply, so too did the attention to detail. Women's underwear, in particular, was decorated with broderie anglaise, ribbons, lace and embroidery. The possibilities for creating new styles and following the contours of the body increased with the development of knitted fabrics. Silk was also a favourite. The health benefits of underwear were incorporated in the discourse of underwear along with ideas about personal hygiene.

Underclothing was an acceptable part of male dress much earlier. Shirts (or chemises) and drawers (or knickerbockers) were simpler garments apparently devoid of 'sexual' connotations. Yet opposition to women wearing underwear was in part based on the fear that these 'masculine' garments would sexualise women. Women's underwear gained acceptance slowly. According to Steele (1988: 164), throughout the nineteenth century women's underpants were regarded as 'demi-masculine' and were primarily worn by 'girls, sportswomen,

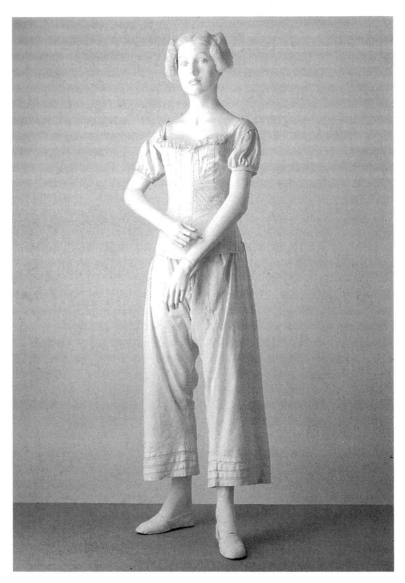

Figure 6.1 Early women's underwear: simplicity and concealment. English linen shift circa 1935 and cotton drawers circa 1834.

Source: Reproduced by courtesy of the Board of Trustees of the Victoria & Albert Museum.

and demi-mondaines'. One of the reasons why George Sand's male attire was so shocking was her preference for male drawers and chemise which were more comfortable and suitable for her outer garments.

As the nineteenth century witnessed the imposition of Victorian morality, an image of restrained and respectable womanhood contrasted with the elaborate and highly decorative underclothes worn by women. Sexual overtones were deliberately attached to the contradiction between the outer and the inner messages of femininity. In order to distinguish female and male underwear, the female garments were made as 'feminine' as possible by excessive attention to special cuts, 'soft' fabrics, and decoration.

There was a play between the public face of respectability and private pleasures of the Victorian woman. In a study of Victorian underwear, Finch (1991) used the example of a 1904 corset advertisement which depicted a fully dressed woman conversing with her corseted companion (in a shop dressing room). She contrasted these counterimages as the dual 'face' of the Victorian woman: 'Dramatically concretizing the "naturally" divided nature of "woman", this image imaginatively splits her clothed, publicly presentable side and her private, corseted being' (ibid.: 351).

Rather than disguising the body and hidden desires, the corset highlighted bodily parts and established an intimate relationship with the outer clothes. By moulding shapes and establishing vectors as to how outer clothes would fall, the corset imposed an invocation of sexuality on the respectable façade of the Victorian woman. As Finch puts it: 'the body in clothes and the body in underwear are ranged in a volatile relation' (Finch 1991: 351). Moreover, 'the new underwear not only constituted a site of charged sexuality but occasioned a collapse between the public and the private spheres' (ibid.: 355). According to Finch, such images were so provocative that new ways of presenting underwear were introduced. Underwear began to float in space in advertisements which showed the garments as if worn (filled out by an imaginery torso): 'the space occupied or, rather, not occupied by the female body is at once strangely empty and fraught (though ambiguously) with meaning' (ibid.: 347). Arguably, by not showing the body, the image further fetishised the body and its sexuality.

The sexual connotations of underwear were often appreciated by women. They chose garments which were not just decorative, and guaranteed to deliver the desired shape, but which were implicitly, and sometimes explicitly, seductive. It was no coincidence that the period from '1890 to 1910 was the great epoch of underwear and dishabille' (Steele 1989b: 51). It was also the period of 'the most rigid and agonizing corsets' of all (Yarwood 1982: 112).

The significance of corsetry has been the subject both of fascination and feminist concern (e.g. Wilson 1985: 91–116; Steele 1985a; Roberts 1977; Kunzle 1977, 1982; Davies 1982; Finch 1991). In Europe, the custom emanated in the twelfth century with outer corselets (front-lacing bodices which still persist in 'folk' costumes) (Yarwood 1982: 109–12; cf. Shorter 1982: 29). By the sixteenth century, the corset had become a rigid, elongated garment designed to enhance

Figure 6.2 Structural underwear: re-forming the female body. English cotton combinations circa 1895 and bustle circa 1884.

Source: Reproduced by courtesy of the Board of Trustees of the Victoria & Albert Museum.

the waist which was extended in length and constrained in girth. The central feature of this corset was the 'bask', a strip of wood, horn, metal, or whalebone inserted down the front of the garment from the bust to the hips. The bask made the corset 'an agonizing straight-jacket' (Yarwood 1982: 110).

Although the seventeenth and eighteenth centuries witnessed a relaxation of the corset, the nineteenth century produced the most extreme forms. Using new materials and technologies, the new corsets were moulded into sections (strips) which fitted the body and were fastened by back lacing. A metal spoon busk gave the corset a shape which was 'narrow at the top and widened below the curving waist into a pear shape' (Yarwood 1982: 110). It was this corset which attracted widespread denunciation and debate.

Subsequent corsetry was less extreme, epitomised in styles such as the Gibson Girl S-shape and subsequent flatteners and girdles. The popularity of corsets remained until the 1960s and has never disappeared. Indeed, corsetry made something of a comeback in the late 1980s as the uniform of popular female singers such as Madonna (courtesy of Parisian couturier Jean-Paul Gaultier).

As a garment, the corset packages the contours of the body to create certain possibilities and restrictions on movement. Yet this alone does not explain either why corsets became an enduring fashion or why they provoked such hostile reactions. Corsetry has become something of a *cause célèbre* among fashion theorists and feminists who decry its 'unnatural' implications (e.g. Roberts 1977; Davies 1982). For Roberts, the corset 'helped mould female behaviour to the role of the "exquisite slave"' (Roberts 1977: 557). Contemporary fashions for women reflected the exalted 'feminine characteristics' of frivolity, delicacy, inactivity and submissiveness (ibid.: 555). Through their clothes, women were subjugated into ornamental accompaniments to the social status of men. Leisure and inactivity (inevitable in corsets, tight sleeves, full skirts, multiple petticoats, crinolines (cages of hooped steel), and tiny slippers) were a perfect recipe for containing the model Victorian woman. The symptomatic and extreme mode of feminine containment was tight lacing.

The fashion for corsets reached its peak in late nineteenth-century England (Finch 1991: 343–4) becoming 'an imperative signifier of fashionableness in middle- and upper-middle-class women'. But it also became popular among working-class women and prostitutes. This cross-class appeal meant that corsets were associated with the contradictory rhetorics of respectability and honour as well as scandal and cheapness. One consequence of this was that women were 'reconfigured as an erotic field only problematically connected to a bodily physics of reproduction' (Finch 1991: 346): now 'the naked body and the body in clothes (or underclothes) revealed their truths simultaneously' (ibid.: 347).

This ambiguity was reflected in representational techniques that emphasised the play between the clothes and the body and 'mapped the body as the place where secrets hide' (Finch 1991: 347). Corsetry highlighted virtuous and erotic impulses simultaneously. Women endured the discomfort, physical manipulation, deformation, side effects, and permanent disabilities as a consequence of

Figure 6.3 Remoulding on a grand scale: corsetry and sexual titillation.
Source: Edwardian advertisement for C.B. Corsets (reproduced by courtesy of York Castle Museum).

the pleasures associated with tight lacing. Those who denounced the custom painted lurid and horrific pictures of the under-side of the custom. They argued that the practice caused significant anatomical and health problems – such as reduced fertility, complications in pregnancy and birthing – as well as making sexual activity uncomfortable and painful for women (e.g. Davies 1982). Wilson emphasised the sheer discomfort and physical distress caused by corsets with the following anecdote:

> Betty Ryan, a Wimbledon tennis star before the First World War, recalled that women's dressing rooms in English tennis clubs up to and during the First World War provided a rail near the fireplace on which the steel-boned corsets in which the women played could be dried: 'It was never a pretty sight, for most of them were bloodstained.'
>
> (Wilson 1985: 99)

Wilson concluded that it was too simplistic to assume that all women who wore corsets were victims, because fetishistic and auto-erotic elements were an integral part of the desire to wear corsets. Moreover, corsets had also been common for men, although the extreme forms of the garments and the denunciations of corsetry were aimed exclusively at women. Undoubtedly, the wearing of corsets related specifically to emerging notions of femininity in western Europe.

Yet some historians have questioned these accounts. Shorter (1982: 28), for example, argued that corsets were only worn by a small number of women (less than 5 per cent of the population) who were mostly aristocrats and the urban upper middle class; and that there is little evidence to prove that corsets harmed health. Rather, a moral panic about corsetry provoked outrageous claims. Shorter suggested that where 'symptoms' of the ill-effects of corsetry were identified, these were either coincidence or 'the work of overactive medical imaginations' (ibid.: 30).

Kunzle also questioned the way in which corsetry has been 'the scapegoat of costume history' and whose demise has been hailed 'as a victory for liberty, women, and social progress' (Kunzle 1977: 570). He has suggested that, rather than endorsing the emancipation of women, the vocal opponents of corsetry were generally conservatives who believed in the concept of the 'natural woman', namely passive (non-sexually aware) women devoted to childrearing and domesticity.

In contrast to Shorter, Kunzle believed that the practice of tight lacing was generally confined to lower-middle-class women and employed women. Thus, it was not: 'the uncorseted woman who was "in danger of being accused of loose morals" so much as the tight-laced one, whose practice was, on occasion, darkly linked with prostitution' (Kunzle 1977: 572).

On this reading, corsetry was adopted by those who were challenging the strictures of Victorian morality, which was the reason for the moral panic concerning the custom. In support of his argument, Kunzle claimed that defenders of tight lacing extolled 'the scarcely veiled sexual basis for this submission' in terms of the sexual and sensual pleasures and activities associated with the practice, whereas the desire to tight lace was also predicated on narcissism, a trait condemned in respectable womanhood (Kunzle 1977: 577).

The furore over tight lacing must also be located within the context of Victorian sexuality more generally. Although sex was rigorously confined to the bedroom, women were exhorted to remain ignorant about sex and be submissive in sexual encounters. Yet taboos about sex were predicated on an awareness of the behaviour which was counted as taboo. By the late nineteenth century, sexuality had become a lively topic of debate as conventions about sexuality were challenged. This was most evident in the development of sexology, or the study of sex, which espoused new ideas about sexuality including sexual morality, sexual trainings and 'marital harmony'. Sex was the noisy secret – repressed in 'polite' society yet ever lurking in moral codes, sex manuals, confessional modes and religious practices. Sex could not be spoken about, but, in order to enforce that censorship, sex was everywhere.

The silence about sex became a mechanism of 'increasing incitement' and created a 'veritable discursive explosion' of attention to sex (Foucault 1984: 12–13). Sex could not be named but had to be pursued. Every sexual longing, impulse and desire had to be located, named and exorcised. As an adjunct to this debate, the corset lurked under the respectable façade of respectability, as a constant reminder of impure thoughts and unconscionable acts. Kunzle concluded that:

It is not a historical accident that waist confinement was first manifested as a fashion, with its concomitant *décolletage*, in the mid-fourteenth century and that it survived, with decreasing validation, down to World War I. For waist confinement and *décolletage* are the primary sexualizing devices of Western costume, which arose when people first became sexually conscious, and conscious of sexual guilt in a public and social way. They did so both as cause and result of the particularly Christian sexual repression which reached a point of maximum intensity in the Victorian age.

(Kunzle 1977: 579)

The practices of binding, exposure and sexualisation of the body produced by corsetry enabled women to meet the ascetic, self-denying principles of Christian morality while simultaneously denying those intentions. Moreover, tight lacing withstood the campaigns of the reformers and only declined 'because other means were found for the sexual and self-expression of women, and men' (Kunzle 1977: 579), notably through the sexual libertarian movement that sanctioned sexual pleasure.

Not surprisingly, tight lacing has remained a controversial topic. Support for Kunzle's thesis comes in the prevalence of bondage and sado-masochism in prostitution and pornography with the celebration and exploration of the 'dark' (repressed) side of sexuality (see Garber 1992). Even in the general community, the use of corsets has remained popular. Kunzle (1982: 269) showed that various means of constraining the female body, including corsets, stiletto heels, boots and petticoats, have accompanied successive versions of the 'new femininity' of the twentieth century:

Of all of these, however, only the corset carried a historical dimension and was thus able to play a dual role, embody some of the purpose associated with the stays of old – sexualization – and at the same time offer freedom from their erstwhile rigour.

(Kunzle 1982: 270)

The new versions of 'structural underwear' had names which reflected the discourse of sexual freedom – 'foundation' garments, 'girdles' and 'sheaths'. Advertisers seized on the comparative freedom of movement offered by the new garments in advertisements that promised escape 'through associations with an age of elegance, leisure, and sexual privilege' (Kunzle 1982: 270). After the 'tubular' look of the 1920s, the wasp-waist returned in the 1930s under euphemisms like 'scissors-silhouette', 'spindle', 'wafer', 'champagne-glass' and 'hourglass' (ibid.: 271). Pragmatic considerations during World War II relaxed corseting, but Dior's New Look in 1947 re-established the 'cinched-waist' as the look of 'freedom'. This corset was even lighter and lacier, as reflected in its new name, the 'guêpiere' (ibid.: 273). In the 1950s, the Hollywood-inspired 'Merry Widow' silhouette required a front-hooked or zip-up girdle. Even in the mid-1950s, over six million Merry Widows were sold annually (ibid.: 274). Not until the 1960s did foundation garments cease 'sculptural modification' and allow smooth lines and clinging fit (ibid.: 274). Throughout the century, a spirited debate about the wisdom of wearing such garments and their impact on health continued in terms almost unchanged from Victorian times:

> As late as 1964, when the waspie was virtually dead anyway, we find a Dr. John Parr in an English daily vituperating in grand 19th century style about the stagnation of the lung base, restriction of vital capacity and even prolapsed wombs.
>
> (Kunzle 1982: 273)

Kunzle stressed that sexual connotations have surrounded changing styles and conventions of the female silhouette. 'Underwear, being an envelope of the body, easily and obviously lends itself to the role of lover – and love-substitute' (Kunzle 1982: 274). Marketers of underwear capitalised on such associations:

> Advertising and editorial copy abounds in the archetypal sexual and dream imagery of movement and suspension in air and water which was in no way impeded by the presence of light boning: flotation, ethereality, and sensuous oblivion in the breezes of bouffant skirts and cascades of ruffled tulle.
>
> (Kunzle 1982: 274)

Above all, women's underwear must be seen to be feminine, and definitely not masculine. Femininity is ascribed through the use of special fabrics, through decoration, line of cut, and associated symbolism. This attention to detail stems from the problematisation of female sexuality in western culture and its reflection in codes of clothing. Whereas the male body and male sexuality are aligned in a direct relation, men's and 'mannish' underwear for women delivers ambiguous and highly charged messages. Underwear conceals the body, but the design of women's underwear is calculated to display the fashionable contours of the female form. By highlighting female genitalia, underwear creates a package of 'the bridled sweeties' (A. Carter 1982c: 95).

Due to the erotic associations attached to underwear, variants of these garments formed the basis of the wardrobes of prostitutes and showgirls. As a consequence, models were reluctant to 'do lingerie jobs' because it was considered not 'respectable'. This attitude persisted long after underwear was transformed into luxury lingerie. By the 1920s, department stores began to model 'foundation' garments and to consciously design ladies' underwear departments as 'intimate' and 'refined' spaces to which women were, purportedly, 'particularly susceptible' (Reekie 1987: 281–2, 294). Ideally these departments featured 'soft colours, pretty furnishings, restful backgrounds and dainty accessories' (ibid.: 282). The choice of decor underlined the association of underwear with romance and femininity, instead of seduction and eroticism. Even so, lingerie retained some erotic connotations.

There have been three main changes to underwear in the twentieth century: the bra, new artificial fabrics, and stockings. Bras were not new – various garments

Figure 6.4 Underwear as active wear: differentiation of underwear for gender and lifestyle.

Source: Advertisement for Lincoln Underwear, *Women's Day and Home*, 1 June 1953.

had been devised to support and contain breasts – but the term 'brassière' was coined as recently as 1912 in America (Yarwood 1982: 49). Designs of bras have varied according to changing conventions about bodily shapes: to flatten the breasts (1920s); to enhance the contours (1930s and 1950s); to minimise and naturalise (1960s); to contain the breasts (1970s and 1980s); and to highlight attributes (1990s). The technical design of bras is reminiscent of surgical garments, possibly reflecting medicalised approaches to sexuality and femininity in western culture.

More recently, designs have followed the shape of breasts in accordance with the rhetoric of 'naturalism'. This trend was enhanced by the development of artificial fibres, such as nylon, rayon, elastic, lastex, lycra and spandex, that could be knitted into figure-hugging shapes. Used alongside the more traditional fabrics of cotton, voile, chiffon and silk, they have had a major impact on design and fit.

In the 1960s, corsetry declined in fashion as lightweight underwear in softer fabrics and lines gained in popularity, especially the 'natural' look created by lycra. Moulded cups replaced seams and underwire. Knickers followed a similar trend, becoming transformed from the basic white brief into colourful bikini briefs with high-cut legs, and cotton-elastane 'control' knickers.

By the 1980s, utility and practicality were in the fore, with more than a touch of androgyny: 'His Pants for Her' epitomised the adaptation of male pants – with minimum seaming, wide elastic bands and cheek-hugging fit. Both approaches evoked sexual imagery and fantasies. 'Feminine' themes with silk-like fabrics, lace and trimmings re-emerged in the late 1980s.

In the 1990s, corsetry has also made a return, improved by new fabrics and techniques. Bras have become less like 'under' clothes (plain and to be hidden) and increasingly like 'outer' clothes (coloured, decorated and patterned) and sometimes worn as, or combined with, outer wear (for example, bustiers, camisoles, French knickers). With the new fabrics, lingerie no longer conveys a message 'about cheap availability' but of luxury and sensuous pleasures (Hume 1992: 144).

Stockings have also been the beneficiaries of developments in artificial fibres. Fully fashioned (seamed) stockings in wool, cotton or silk had been the norm for decades. The potential for knitting stockings in fine fibres that moulded their shape to the body revolutionised the stockings industry. Yet, as Midgley (1973) has shown, it was a long time before circular-knit seamless stockings were accepted. Although seamless stockings had been available since the 1920s, and sold in roughly the same numbers as fully fashioned ones, it was not until 1953 (in the US) and 1957 (in the UK), that seamless stockings really took off. It was not until the fashion for the 'nude look' in legs, and shorter skirt lengths were popular that consumers changed their stocking preferences. Then, consumer behaviour changed radically and prompted significant improvements in fibres and technical production. Within a decade, seamed stockings had all but vanished. Midgley's study suggests that fashion behaviour may be shaped by intangible factors that influence the popularisation of a particular fashion item or fashion 'look'.

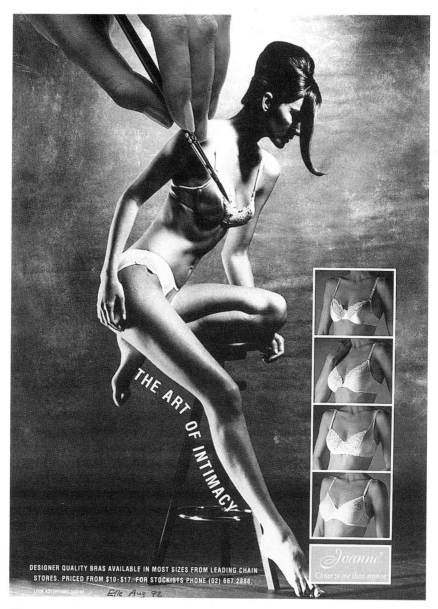

Figure 6.5 'The art of intimacy': depicting the sexual attributes of female contours.

Source: Advertisement for Joanne bras, *Elle* (Australia), August 1992. (Reproduced by courtesy of Wong Industries.)

Underwear has changed in accordance with a variety of forces and new looks. A sexual dimension has always lurked beneath the fashionable façade. Underwear of the 1990s explicitly acknowledges erotic connotations and impulses in the fetishisation of underwear:

> The erotic point is inescapable. The models are dressed up in undress, in a kind of clothing that is more naked than nudity. Their flesh is partly concealed by exiguous garments in fabrics that mimic the texture of flesh itself – silk, satin-finish man-made fibres, fine lawn – plus a sublimated hint of the texture, though (heaven forbid!) never the actuality, of pubic hair.
>
> (A. Carter 1982c: 97)

Underwear has become the acceptable face of erotic display, and modelling underwear is now regarded as a high-status modelling assignment. One model, Elle MacPherson, has even designed and promoted her own range of lingerie for Bendon. Aimed at a general market, MacPherson's line was designed to offer 'good quality, sporty, classy, reasonably priced and well-advertised, a combination of good Bonds knickers and a bit of class' (quoted by Wyndham 1990: 23). She wanted her underwear to reconcile women's lived bodies with ideals of the female body. Since 'three-quarters of women have small shoulders and big hips', her lingerie was designed to accentuate 'broad shoulders, small waist, small hips, the ideal body' (ibid.: 23).

The manufacture of signature lingerie associated with a female icon signals the acceptance of underwear as high fashion. Designers such as Jean-Paul Gaultier, Dolce and Gabbana, John Galliano, and Vivienne Westwood, have used corsets as the theme of numerous collections. The popularisation of underwear as outerwear, epitomised by the stage outfits of Cher, Madonna, Kylie Minogue and Annie Lennox, has explicitly exploited connotations of eroticism and post-Victorian sensibilities. Yet this will undoubtedly give way to other body shapes and erotic codes.

Women's underwear has produced a variety of female bodies; articulated conflicts in moral and gender codes associated with sexuality; and played off notions of the 'natural', untrained body against codes of civility and acceptable social conduct. In western culture, female sexuality has been problematised as a set of moral injunctions and body disciplines which have been reflected in changing fashions for underwear.

THE SEXUALISATION OF MEN'S UNDERCLOTHES

In contrast to the stormy history of women's underwear, men's underwear has diversified almost unseen. It was as if keeping men's underclothes plain and functional could secure male bodies as a bulwark against unrestrained sexuality. Shirts, singlets, long-johns and drawers constituted the range of men's underwear until 1939 when Y-front underpants were first produced (Rutt 1990: 76). The advantage of the new design was the cunning angling of the fly to ease the

Figure 6.6 'I lovable you': underwear as outerwear and the revival of corsetry.

Source: Advertisement for Lovable bras, *Cleo*, September 1992. (Reproduced by courtesy of Lovable.)

embarrassment of urinating in public (that is, for modesty). This design was revolutionary because it drew attention to the male genitals by virtue of the seaming. Its very convenience proved to be quite threatening to upper-class men, who continued to prefer drawers (subsequently known as boxer shorts). But other groups of men took to the new Y-fronts with enthusiasm. 'Sharper' men (that is, those with 'suspicious' morals) chose the more daring option of athletes' drawers (athletes'), bikini briefs, while some (especially sportsmen) chose 'slips' (jockstraps).

It was not until the 1960s that men's underwear was classified as fashion, a consequence of its convergence with swimwear. Men began to eschew drawers and Y-fronts and chose jocks (and their variants). Swimwear was associated with qualities of strength, muscularity, and sexiness – attributes of the new masculinity. 'Sports' clothing as underwear seemed appropriate. The new underwear was overtly promoted for its erotic connotations – 'as a prelude to sexual intimacy, the attraction of concealment, and the libido for looking (and touching)' (Steele 1989b: 56). This phase of men's underwear reflected new notions of the erotic and sexualised male body available for the female (and male) gaze. Implications of effeminacy, auto-eroticism and homosexual desire have intensified the sexualisation of the male body and the connotations of men's underwear.

In the early 1980s, androgyny influenced the promotion of underwear for men. Designs were streamlined and diverse, patterned fabrics replaced the uniform white cotton. But, most of all, the new underwear was advertised by young, tanned and muscled male models clad only in their knickers and striking provocative poses. When Calvin Klein launched his male underpants:

> Crazed fans broke the glass in dozens of New York bus-stop shelters to steal the poster: Klein installed a huge reproduction on a Times Square billboard so that he could view it from his car travelling to work.
>
> (Grant 1992: 20)

Sales of men's underwear have risen with its reclassification as 'sexy' fashion. Men now have a choice of styles in pants: jocks, tangas, boxer shorts and Y-fronts, each carefully marketed for its target consumer group (Carter and Brûlé 1992; Matura 1978: 3). Underpants are now ephemeral, sensual and desirable. Advertisements provoke controversy because the image of near-naked young men with skin-tight jocks is more suggestive than male nudes. Advertisements for underwear now display the garments 'as worn', thereby de-fetishising the abstract body, although the narrative (*mise en scène*) created around the garment and its 'real-life' model defines a new register of fetishism. This is especially so in advertisements which draw on the imagery or narratives of erotic photography and pornography. Advertisements for men's underwear stress 'sexual perception, appearance and experience' (Haug 1986: 83) by emphasising the body itself. Haug argues that: 'The purchase of underwear is provoked by emphasising the penis. Thus, after centuries of increasing prohibition, the penis is on public show as part of an image' (ibid.: 84). No longer do men's underpants merely encase the genitalia, now they are an index of masculinity and sexual potency.

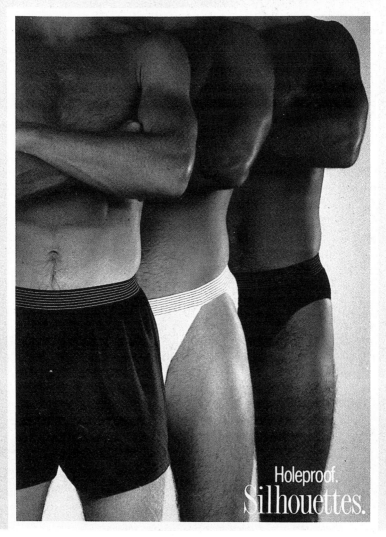

Figure 6.7 'Undercover exposé': the proliferation of men's underwear as up-front masculinity.

Source: Advertisement for Holeproof Silhouettes fashion underwear, Myer catalogue. (Reproduced by courtesy of Myer Stores Ltd.)

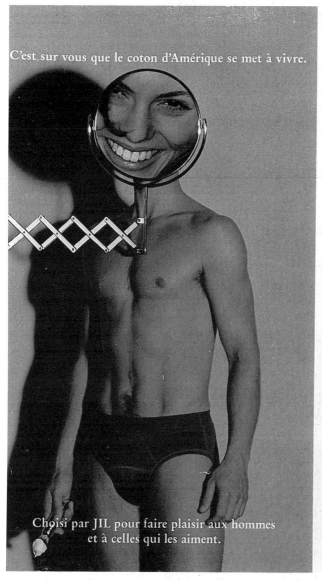

C'est sur vous que le coton d'Amérique se met à vivre.

Aujourd'hui, avec JIL, les hommes sont beaux parce qu'ils sont bien.

JIL a naturellement choisi un coton d'Amérique d'une exceptionnelle qualité pour un confort absolu.

C'est en le portant que vous apprécierez toute la

différence entre un sous-vêtement et un JIL en coton d'Amérique.

Aux Etats-Unis, nous n'avons eu de cesse de développer et de tester notre coton pour lui donner cette complicité avec la peau qu'aucun autre tissu ne peut

égaler: légèreté, fraîcheur, chaleur, solidité, beauté, douceur de ce coton. Et surtout, une délicieuse sensation de confort.

La prochaine fois, choisissez JIL et le Label Cotton USA. Vous apprécierez toute la différence.

Choisi par JIL pour faire plaisir aux hommes et à celles qui les aiment.

LE COTON D'EXCELLENCE.

Figure 6.8 The pleasures of underwear: not just for men.

Source: Advertisement for Jil underwear, *Marie-Claire*, May 1992.

Male underwear has been aligned with contemporary notions of male sexuality and sexual pleasure. Rather than playing down the male body as the site of sexual desire, underwear has incorporated the male body as a complex of sexualised attributes.

IN THE SWIM

There's no wrinkle, no bag, no sag, even under the most ruthless sun. No other human device can even approximate that utter freedom, that perfection of fit, at rest or in motion, that airy but strictly legal sense of wearing nothing at all. There is no substitute for this elastic yarn, which imparts lasting elasticity to any fabric.

(From a 1934 advertisement for lastex, quoted by Kidwell 1968: 31)

Swimwear is a specialised kind of clothing to suit occasions of bathing and swimming. Their design has had close connections with underwear because of their shared proximity to the body. The difference is that swimwear takes underwear into the public arena, and its history has therefore mapped body–habitus relations associated with moral concerns. As a piece of clothing, the swimsuit has become briefer over time, revealing more of the body. The contemporary swimsuit has social and practical attributes: to cling to the body, and reduce drag from the water. In aesthetic terms, modern swimsuits highlight bodily features associated with the display of fit and healthy bodies. Current codes of modesty are acknowledged by covering genitalia, yet simultaneously drawing attention to them by the cut and line of swimsuits. The ongoing skirmish between protocols of modesty and sexual attributes in the history of the swimsuit correlates with the changing shape to the social body. The swimsuit constitutes a barometer of standards of sexual and social morality.

As with the subject of lingerie, swimwear has only recently attracted analytic attention, mostly in the form of histories of its design (Kidwell 1968; Rutt 1990; Yarwood 1982: 26–9; Byrde 1987; Schreier 1989: 116–20; Silmon 1986; Martin and Koda 1990: and Probert 1981). These studies have shown that the development of men's swimwear has entailed a struggle between nudity and modesty, while the history of women's swimwear occurred against sustained attempts to cover and disguise the sexual attributes of the female body. The different histories of men's and women's swimwear highlight the gender politics of the history of clothing more generally. Because swimwear is a form of underclothing worn in public, swimwear has epitomised problematic attitudes to the body that have emerged in western culture. The sight and site of the body as revealed or alluded to by clothing, has prompted waves of public outrage and virtual hysteria over 'modesty and immodesty' (Schreier 1989: 116).

Historically, swimming and bathing were commonplace activities. There was little concern about wearing appropriate attire. Usually men swam naked. So did women, although sometimes they wore a loose chemise or shift. In medieval

Figure 6.9 Knitted swimwear: revealing limbs but retaining a modesty skirt and belt for respectability. (Mother and son, Petaho Beach 1930.)

Europe, according to Elias, people of both sexes undressed at home and ran naked through the streets to the bathhouse:

'How often', says an observer, 'the father, wearing nothing but his breeches, with his naked wife and children, runs through the streets from his house to the baths . . . How many times have I seen girls of ten, twelve, fourteen, sixteen, and eighteen years entirely naked except for a short smock, often torn at the feet and with their hands held decorously behind them, running from their houses through the long streets at midday to the baths. How many completely naked boys of ten, twelve, fourteen, and sixteen run beside them.'

(Elias 1978: 164)

This attitude to bathing and swimming as unremarkable did not last. In Europe, the situation began to change once notions of modesty and shame informed codes of dress conduct. In the eighteenth century, men continued to bathe naked although they wore clothes (jacket or vest and trousers or drawers) on the beach. Not until the mid-nineteenth century did men come under considerable pressure to bathe clothed. The design of the approved bathing attire shows why men resisted exhortations about modesty so strongly, for the early costumes were like shorts made of heavy serge. Lacking elasticised waists, they had a tendency to drag, or worse, to drop to the ankles in the water! Not surprisingly, men's swimsuits were not popular among those who were pressured to wear them. When they could get away with it, men continued to swim naked.

By the mid-nineteenth century, public concerns about 'public decency' reached fever pitch, and the pressure on men to wear bathing clothes was compelling. The obsession with modesty also influenced the design of bathing clothes. No longer could men get away with a pair of shorts for bathing. Men's swimsuits became a heavy one-piece design which covered not just the torso but also the arms and thighs. The number of complaints made by men about 'the clammy clutch from shoulder to knee' (Rutt 1990: 71) suggests that male swimmers detested the new modesty in swimwear.

Despite the objections, five different kinds of men's bathing costumes emerged during the late nineteenth century: drawers, the bathing dress, athletes' drawers, the Regulation costume, and slips (Rutt 1990: 72–3). Drawers were the crude, knee-length shorts that have remained a staple (albeit modified and refined) of male swimwear. The bathing dress was either a two-piece or one-piece cotton knit garment with short sleeves and mid-thigh leggings. This became 'standard male bathing wear in mixed company until the end of the Edwardian period' (ibid.: 72). Athletes' drawers (or athletes') were bikini swimbriefs that were also popular among runners and circus performers. They were usually worn over tights (as late as the 1920s). In England, the Regulation costume was prescribed by the Amateur Swimming Association Rules from 1890. This modified version of the one-piece featured shoulder straps, modest scooped necklines, and legs extending within three inches of the knee. It formed the basis of men's costumes until the 1930s, with pieces being whittled away as concerns about

Figure 6.10 Singlet top and modest bathing shorts for men and boys. (Father and son, Wales 1931.)

modesty were allayed. The most revealing kinds of costume were skin-tight slips or under-drawers, composed of two triangular pieces and the sides fastened with tapes: 'in effect a pair of athletes' drawers made of very thin material' (ibid.: 73).

By the twentieth century, men's swimwear reflected the gradual relaxation of attitudes about modesty and the revelation of the body. In the early decades of the new century, the need for men's swimsuits to have sleeves, legs, tights and tops was challenged and ridiculed, although it was not until the 1930s that trunks and slips became acceptable wear.

Ingenious ways were devised for men to circumvent regulations about swimwear. For example, in 1934, Jantzen introduced its Topper model, a two-piece men's costume which featured a zip with which the top could be removed when inspectors were not around. More commonly, the one-piece was modified with the addition of a belt, and subsequently became a two-piece costume. The sleeves became shorter, eventually shrinking to mere straps (like a singlet). By the mid-1930s, topless swimsuits were grudgingly accepted (Schreier 1989: 118). Similarly, the length of the legs of men's costumes shortened until only a modesty 'skirt' covered the bulge of the genitals.

Over the same period – and partly helping to revolutionise attitudes to swimwear – came the introduction of special swimwear for racing. These costumes

Figure 6.11 Launch party: boned, corset-like swimwear for women, bathing shorts for men. (Coolangatta 1954.)

were a tailored, slimmed-down version of the one-piece. The advent of new fabrics – initially nylon – and the parallel changes taking place in women's swimwear gave an impetus to the production and popularisation of swimming briefs after World War II. Through the 1950s and 1960s, men's swimwear became more and more skimpy until it was reduced to the 'hipster' style popularised in the 1970s. According to Rutt, 'the waistline reached the lowest possible point in 1974 when the back of the briefs just cleared the coccyx' (Rutt 1990: 78). Racing briefs have become increasingly skin-tight while beach briefs have varied more in pattern and colour than in style. Trunks (Okinouis, board shorts or baggies) are sometimes worn over briefs (scants or scungies).

The development of elastane fibres, which could be knitted with other fibres (such as nylon or polyester), facilitated the production of light-weight, skin-tight swimwear with little water resistance. Another new fabric, 'seal-skin-style' neoprene, was used from the 1980s in competition swimming because it offered less water-resistance due to the polyurethane finish over the knitted fabric (Rutt 1990: 80).

Trends in swimwear have run parallel to fashions in underwear as well as with other sportswear such as bike pants. The development of men's swimwear featured a concern with modesty that interfered with practical techniques of swimming and, in so doing, sexualised a previously unremarkable garment by drawing attention to the sexual attributes of the body. The trend towards brevity may be an historical phase. In the 1990s, health concerns about skin cancer, and practical considerations about maintaining body warmth and protecting the body from injury, have prompted new designs in swimwear reminiscent of neck-to-knee. Surf lifesavers have been pressured to wear lycra singlet tops over their bathers – and pantyhose in areas affected by jellyfish and sea-wasps. Board riders prefer wetsuits (with high necks, sleeves, and legs to the knee), while a modified version has been designed for children in colourful lycra, as protection against the sun. Thus, the body is once again being re-written as the site of competing attributes.

In contrast to that of men's, the history of women's swimwear has had sex at the forefront of fashion and debate. From the middle ages, women were discouraged from swimming and even bathing, for a range of reasons. It was not until the seventeenth century that bathing for medicinal purposes (therapeutic cures and spa bathing) increased the opportunity for women to bathe. This was not always a welcome prospect due to the restrictions placed on bathing women. They were obliged to wear a voluminous ankle-length chemise or shift (plus a cap) that was designed to hide their shape and thereby preserve their modesty. When women emerged from the water, attendants wrapped them up in gowns to ensure that no-one saw their wet, shapeless forms. A 1687 description of bathing in Bath is the earliest known detailed account of women's swimwear:

> The Ladyes goes into the bath with Garments made of a fine yellow canvas, which is stiff and made large with great sleeves like a parsons gown; the water

Figure 6.12 Swimwear and surfing: practicality and youth culture. (North Cronulla 1956.)

fills it up so that its borne off that your shape is not seen, it does not cling close as other linning, which Lookes sadly in the poorer sort that go in their own linning . . . When you go out of the bath you go within a doore that leads to Steps which you ascend by degrees that are in the water, . . . still ascend severall more steps and let your Canvass drop by degrees into the water, which your woman guides take off, and the meane tyme your maides flings a garment of flannell made like a Nightgown with great sleeves over your head, and ye guides take ye taile and so pulls it on you Just as you rise ye steps, and yr other garment drops off so you are wrapped up in ye flannell and your nightgown on ye top, and your slippers and so you are set in Chaire, . . . then a Couple of men with staves takes and Carryes you to your lodging and sets you at yr bedside where you go to bed and lye and sweate some time as you please.

(Celia Fiennes, quoted by Byrde 1987: 48–9)

The elaborate ritual of bathing was justified in therapeutic terms, although contemporary critics regarded many spas and baths as distinct health hazards. It was also part of an elaborate social charade. Visitors to spa towns were caught up in a highly regimented social whirl of instruction, bathing, entertainment, and formal interactions. Bathing – the ostensible reason for the visit – was a cumbersome and embarrassing part of the schedule. Evidence suggests that many women hated bathing and avoided it when possible. Fashion-conscious women, in particular, resented the 'frightful unbecoming' bathing dresses (Byrde 1987: 51–2). The cumbersome and ugly garb continued into the nineteenth century although its impracticality became increasingly obvious as sea bathing, and bathing for pleasure, became popular pastimes. In 1822, a Dr Spry criticised the absurd conventions about women's bathing dress:

Dresses of any kind very much defeat the intention, by preventing the water from coming immediately in contact with those parts of the body which are situations of disease. If the patients could bathe without being encumbered with a dress at all, it would be most eligible; but if a dress must be worn, it should be as light and loose as possible; and the advantage of separate baths for men and women would greatly promote this intention.

(Quoted by Byrde 1987: 53)

Spry's first option was, of course, too radical for contemporary standards of morality, but his other advice mooted changes that were to follow. Segregated bathing was introduced. Men and women bathed and swam in separate baths, or at different times of the day. Sometimes, a beach was divided into two sections – part for men, and part for women. Sometimes the women's section was screened off in the hope of deterring male onlookers from watching the bedraggled women emerge from the sea.

The design of bathing dresses also changed. The shift was replaced by a knee-length belted dress worn over pantaloons and stockings, and completed with a bathing cap, and slippers that were secured with ribbons tied like those on ballet shoes. Considerable attention was given to trimmings and fabric in order to make the garments as 'feminine' as possible. This 'feminisation' of the modified bathing suit underlined the sexual attributes associated with the garment, and concerns about the need to constrain sexuality. The establishment of swimwear as 'feminine' and fashionable allowed it to become the object of public attention and accordingly, swimwear entered the pages of fashion magazines and store catalogues in the 1880s (Kidwell 1968: 20).

The new women's swimwear was more practical than the earlier designs. Women could 'frolic' in the water rather than being dunked as before. But the garments were still a hazard. In order to preserve feminine 'modesty', the skirts were full, measuring up to eight feet eight inches in circumference (Kidwell 1968: 18), and weighing up to thirty pounds when wet (Schreier 1989: 119). Encumbered by this 'voluminous bathing outfit' (ibid.: 119), women had great difficulty doing any actual swimming. Ironically, although designed to hide the female form, the bathing dresses clung to the body when wet, outlining the figure in the most pathetic and ludicrous way. In other words, in practice, such attire proved to be anything but modest. Even so, the European style of trousers and no skirt was 'objected to by many ladies as masculine and fast' (Kidwell 1968: 18). Women clung to their bathing gowns as tenaciously as the gowns clung to them.

For most women, the elaborate rituals surrounding swimming and bathing were a torture to be endured. Women bathers made a spectacle of themselves, but not in ways that they might have hoped or intended. The use of bathing machines designed to shield bathers from the stares of others (especially men) only drew attention to the women. Gradually, the design of the bathing skirt was modified and the amount of fabric reduced. Even so, in 1902, one male swimming instructor demonstrated the dangers of the costume by wearing one himself:

> Not until then did I rightly understand what a serious matter a few feet of superfluous cloth might become in water. The suit was amply large, yet pounds of apparently dead weight seemed to be pulling at me in every direction. In that gear a swim of 100 yards was as serious a task as a mile in my own suit. After that experience, I no longer wondered why so few women swim well, but rather that they are able to swim at all.
>
> (Quoted by Schreier 1989: 119–20)

These comments suggest that women's bathing wear had become a contentious issue and that the tide was turning in attitudes to appropriate dress. The period from 1870 to 1900 was the turning point since it was during this time that edicts about modesty reached their peak (Schreier 1989: 118). But as dress codes and concerns about femininity raged, at the same time women began to transcend the limitations by engaging in exercise and sport (Warner 1988). On the one hand, gender definitions and prescriptions on women's behaviour were at their most acute, while on the other hand, many women were active and visible in public.

As bathing and swimming grew in popularity, so the sight of the bathing dress decreased. The design remained much the same – just slimmed down – and corsets continued to be worn underneath (Kidwell 1968: 23). Women who wanted to swim (as opposed to frolicking or promenading) preferred the new swimming costume, a knitted one-piece garment featuring sleeves and leggings (like a child's sleeping suit). Kidwell suggests that they were worn by daring swimmers from the 1870s onward, though they were not accepted by the arbiters of fashion and 'good taste' until the 1920s. Those who opted for the practical advantages of the costume were condemned for 'flaunting' their bodies in public. Rigorous attempts were made to outlaw such 'indecent' garments through legislation that imposed proper dress standards on the beach. Regulations specified bathing dress that covered the wearer from neck to knee. Women were fined for not wearing stockings, beach shoes or long skirts (Martin and Koda 1990: 58, 60). Despite the penalties, the regulations were frequently ignored. In Sydney, for example, one woman, charged under the 1864 Act for the Reform and Regulation of Female Apparel, offered this spirited defence of her behaviour:

MAGISTRATE: You displayed yourself unclothed, in a public place.

DEFENDANT: I was bathing in the ocean, m'lord, in my under-garments.

MAGISTRATE: Precisely so, madam. What explanation can you offer?

DEFENDANT: The day was hot and the ocean along the seashore looked cool and inviting, m'lord.

MAGISTRATE: You claim to have been in your full senses? You were fully aware of your actions?

DEFENDANT: Oh, enjoyably so, m'lord.

MAGISTRATE: As this illustration of the photographic art bears witness, you were observed, unclothed. Consider, madam. If other women follow the example you have set, then to what overt acts of freedom might not such an example lead?

DEFENDANT: Quite, m'lord.

(Quoted by Martyn 1976: 7)

While few women bathers may have been as articulate as this defendant, many ignored the regulations and embraced swimming and bathing as a form of exercise and freedom from social conventions. While the popularity of bathing dresses persisted, the number of women wearing swimming costumes grew. The popularity of costumes received an impetus with the sanctioning of swimming as a competitive sport for women. Women's swimming was first included in the 1912 Olympics. The events were dominated by Fanny Durack, wearing a sleeveless one-piece knitted costume with legs extending to mid-thigh (Pollard 1963: 138).

Aware of her controversial garment, Durack wore a long towelling robe to the starting blocks and only disrobed moments before each race. Her costume was similar to that worn by Adeline Trapp when she became the first woman to swim the East River in New York in 1909 (Kidwell 1968: 25). Both costumes were derived from the English Regulation costumes discussed earlier. Trapp's employers, the Brooklyn School Board, were appalled by her scanty costume and, thereafter, she arranged to have a blanket wrapped around her as she emerged from the water (similar to the Bath bathing custom).

Australian-born swimmer Annette Kellerman also shook up prevailing conventions. In 1907, she was arrested in Boston for wearing a daring one-piece swimsuit. Kellerman was unmoved and began to experiment with the design of costumes to suit her needs. She combined swimming suits with the body stockings of vaudeville to create revealing costumes and extraordinary displays of athleticism (Fotheringham 1992: 56).

Kellerman's swimming and diving displays caused a sensation in England and America. She adapted her routines for Hollywood and sparked a series of watersports films between 1916 and 1952 (when her own life story was filmed starring Esther Williams). The centrality of sportswomen in these films created new images of active women as well as new conventions of 'the female body as spectacle' (Fotheringham 1992: 181). The design of swimming costumes reflected these developments. By the 1920s, the need for practical swimming costumes was recognised. Kellerman herself recommended close-fitting garments that just met legal requirements. In a book on swimming, she advised women to:

> get one-piece tights and wear over the tights the lightest garment you can get. It should be a loose sleeveless garment hung from the shoulders. Never have a tight waist band. It is a hindrance. Also on beaches where stockings are enforced your one-piece under-garment should have feet, so that the separate stocking and its attendant garter is abolished.
>
> (Quoted by Kidwell 1968: 28)

Despite the regulations about swimwear, knitted costumes gained acceptance. The similarities between underwear and swimwear were reinforced by close affiliations between the swimwear industry and the underwear industry, a link which persisted until the 1930s (Martin and Koda 1990: 58). Accordingly, the new 'body-hugging' costumes were associated with the production of 'fashionable' body silhouettes. But, in order to distinguish swimwear from underwear, designs also emphasised tailoring and accessories such as belt, buttons and buckles to reinforce the public respectability of swimming, and remove it from the private, erotic associations of lingerie (ibid.: 54). Moreover, swimwear was one case where popular endorsement and demand for the new garment overcame official and moral objections. In other words, contrary to the usual trickle-down argument about fashion, the swimming costume was a trickle-up phenomenon – adopted by ordinary women and only reluctantly and belatedly sanctioned by the arbiters of taste and conduct:

> This is a fashion that did not trickle down from the styles proposed by designers and worn first by the wealthy. On the contrary, this is a fashion that bubbled up as a result of popular demand. In 1920, before the high-fashion magazines had changed their prescription of what was fashionable, Sears was offering only the more abbreviated and functional style.
>
> (Kidwell 1989: 142)

Swimming became a popular pastime for women; they took swimming lessons, exercise classes and entered swimming competitions (Warner 1988: 54): 'Thus, by the 1920s the swimming suit prevailed, complementing the image of the newly emancipated "modern woman"' (Kidwell 1968: 30). With the new swim-wear came a new female body – or, rather, the female body was reconstructed to resemble a boyish body, lacking breasts and hips. Attributes of femininity were replaced by those of androgyny (Martin and Koda 1990: 60, 62).

From then on, the bathing dress faded away while a new industry of design and production was born. Knitting mills experienced a bonanza as companies like Jantzen and Speedo streamlined designs and began advertising campaigns to promote the new costumes. In 1929, Speedo introduced 'racing costumes' which were developed for the Australian Olympic team and were subsequently adopted by other teams (J. Robinson 1986: 28). Since then, Speedo has become one of the leading international manufacturers of swimwear, specialising in racing costumes. In 1991, in the United States, Speedo accounted for 65 per cent of the competitive swimwear market. At the Barcelona Olympics in 1992, twenty swimming teams wore Speedo, confirming their domination of this market. In recent years, the company has been the subject of raids by international companies. For example, in 1991, Speedo was bought by Stephen Rubin (of Pentland) from the Linter Group. Rubin, who used to own Reebok (the sports shoe company) hoped to expand the range of Speedo products from swimwear to other sportswear, including scuba-diving gear, leisure clothes and waterproof watches (Huck 1991: 36).

While the body-hugging costume remained popular in the 1930s, non-racing costumes began to undergo an engineering revolution, similar to that in under-wear. Straps replaced sleeves, legs became shorter and necklines were lowered. The fashionability of the suntan from the 1930s onwards contributed to these modifications in order to expose the skin and avoid strap marks. The vestigial modesty skirt, covering the crotch, however, remained until the 1960s. Lastex, acetate and rayon provided new possibilities for producing fitted designs. By the 1940s, costumes were designed to mould the figure and constrain the body. The bust was enhanced in moulded wire bra components while the hips were encased in a girdle-like sheath.

The most radical innovation in women's swimwear was the bikini. Although there had been some two-piece designs in the 1930s – usually belted to appear like a one-piece – they permitted only a glimpse of a few inches of flesh at the most! In 1935, *Vogue* featured a two-piece for the first time. But it was the creation of a French engineer, Louis Reard, in 1946, that caused an uproar. Reard designed an exceedingly brief, halter-neck two-piece, out of fabric resembling four triangles of newsprint, and fastened merely by strings at the sides and the back. He named his creation 'the bikini', thinking it a bombshell in swimwear design analogous to the recently exploded atomic bomb on Bikini Atoll. Despite the controversy that raged about the new design, the bikini gained rapid acceptance in France among 'naughty girls who decorate our sun-drenched beaches' (Silmon 1986: 10). Other countries were more prudish and resisted the

Figure 6.13 Revelation and relaxation: the bikini revolution. (Cronulla 1962.)

bikini. Even Hollywood refused to acknowledge the bikini until it had become well established. Australian designer Paula Stafford introduced the bikini to the Gold Coast in 1952:

> It caused an uproar. Beach Inspector John Moffat lost no time in swooping down on a model caught in one of Paula's abbreviated creations. 'Too brief', he cried with a strangled sound as he escorted her off the beach. Paula was undeterred. She organised five more girls to wear her bikinis, told the papers, and invited the mayor, a priest and the chief of police. Nothing happened, but the publicity was unbelievable.

> (Joel 1984: 141)

Once the initial furore died down, the potential of the bikini became the catalyst for an entirely new approach to swimwear design (Silmon 1986). Bikinis soon eclipsed one-piece costumes as beach wear and swimwear. The sculptured looks of the 1940s and 1950s were replaced by softer, 'natural' lines of the 1960s. The temptation was always there to remove the top altogether. Actress Simona Silva caused a scandal at the 1954 Cannes Film Festival by posing topless.

The first official topless swimsuit was designed by Rudi Gernreich in 1964 and modelled by his wife, Peggy Moffat. The photograph became a celebrated document of the extremism of 1960s design. The importance of the topless swimsuit, also known as the 'monokini', was its influence on the design of one-pieces and bikinis more generally because it drew attention to the breasts and created new body vectors. Designers abandoned bra cups, favoured backless cuts, and generally experimented 'to do what bones and girdling could not' (*Time*, 31 December 1965: 29), namely, to highlight the contours of the female body and to emphasise the nipple. These costumes simultaneously concealed and revealed, playing off modesty with display.

It was not until the 1960s that the corset-like structure of swimming costumes was modified. The new designs allowed the contours of the body to fill out the swimsuit. The cut of costumes began to emphasise features of the torso through cut-out panels, backless costumes, extended armholes and higher-cut legs. Rather than encasing the body and imposing the desirable body shape, the post-1960s costumes highlighted the female attributes of the body, thus attracting new controversies about modesty and morality.

They were followed by the unstructured designs of the 1970s and 1980s, with costumes that covered genitalia but little else. Topless and nude bathing became more acceptable internationally, although they are still in the minority (Keenan 1977: 164–5; Batterberry and Batterberry 1982: 383–5).

The process of streamlining the cut and fit of one-piece costumes continued through the 1970s and 1980s, with the help of new fibres that had body-hugging characteristics. The costumes themselves revealed more and more of the torso, a trend most evident in the high-cut legs of the mid-1980s. As designs have become as brief as possible to cover the genitalia, designers have begun to return to some of the features of earlier costumes, incorporating modified corsetry, covering more of the body, and combining old fabrics and features with the new fibres. Critics have spoken of the return of glamour swimwear and a revival of Holly-wood influences in design. In addition to overt connotations of erotic underwear and glamorous icons, swimwear also became elided with sports photography and fitness. Bodies were reconstructed as exercise machines, sites of power, and icons of the spectacular. Swimwear and sportswear converged in design principles in accordance with these associations (Martin and Koda 1990: 131–2).

The 1990s heralded a return to more 'discreet' looks, with costumes that covered more of the body and have reintroduced strategic seaming and moulding. Model Jerry Hall introduced a range of swimwear in 1989 aimed at 'putting the "bums" back into women's bathers' (D. Williams 1989: 42). Her swimwear

**Prints by Ken Done. Designed by Judy Done. Made in Australia.
Only at the Done Art and Design shops.**

The Rocks, Darling Harbour, Skygarden, Queen Victoria Building, Mosman,
Surfers Paradise, Broadbeach, Cairns, Melbourne and Perth. Also in the U.S.A., Japan, Caribbean and Mexico City.
Enquiries (02) 698 8555. Or send for our free catalogue: 17 Thurlow Street, Redfern, NSW 2016.

Figure 6.14 The art of fashion: the body as canvas and swimwear as sculpture.

Source: Advertisement for Ken Done swimwear. (Reproduced by courtesy of Ken Done Art and Design.)

Right: Wendy Heather black lycra maillot with lace-up front, $94. Enquiries (02) 356 3766.
Centre: Moontide black and white gingham check maillot, $90. Enquiries (02) 360 9963.
Far right: Jets black and white spot lace-up maillot, $85. Enquiries (02) 698 4888.

Curves are the focus for spring with sculptured bodylines defined by basic black and white. Reminiscent of the glamorous Esther Williams era, the accent is on elegance; classics are racier. Gingham checks, polka dots and underwiring lend a lingerie look, and individual pieces can be worn alone or teamed with the latest long skirts and short shorts.

Staying in one pieces

36 THE AUSTRALIAN MAGAZINE

Figure 6.15 'Staying in one pieces': the return of sculptured swimwear.

Source: *The Australian Magazine*, 19–20 September 1992. (Reproduced by courtesy of photographer, Andrew Rankin, and *The Australian Magazine*.)

echoed Hollywood designs of the 1940s by emphasising full cuts and glamorous features. Decrying the skimpy cuts of most women's swimwear, Hall commented: 'All my girls have hourglass figures – big boobs, tiny waist, big hips. You know how most designers draw stick figures. Mine are real currrvy' (quoted by Mansfield 1992: 2).

Swimwear has become high fashion, with differentiated categories from racing to glamour wear, as concerns about modesty have changed. As this chapter has shown, the emergence of underclothing and swimwear as distinct genres of fashion has mirrored changing definitions of gender roles and social conventions. The advent of new styles has been accompanied by controversies about modesty, morality and sexuality. Dominant ideas about femininity and masculinity have been graphically challenged by new designs. The proximity of these clothes to the body, and the ways in which the clothes draw attention to sexual characteristics, have imbued swimwear with sexual tension (or frisson). Yet clothes that reveal more and more do not automatically indicate sexual 'freedom'. Rather, revealing clothes articulate new forms of public restraint on sexual behaviour, and new norms of sexual conduct. Sexuality is produced through the technical body and highlighted by lingerie and swimwear that complements the social body. Above all, underwear and lingerie have produced a variety of bodies for specific circumstances and practical techniques: the under-clothed body is a moving target.

Chapter 7

Cosmetic attributes
Techniques of make-up and perfume

BODY DECORATION

> The grey-haired lady had just flown in from Sydney . . . to attend the South
> Pacific's greatest 'sing-sing', featuring 60,000 grotesquely painted tribesmen
> in a two-day extravaganza of sound and colour.
>
> The lady adjusted her bifocals as she confronted a dozen half-naked
> highlanders wearing brilliant headdresses of bird-of-paradise plumes. Their
> bulging muscles glistened with pig grease.
>
> 'Goodness me!' my companion exclaimed. 'They certainly do look
> primitive, don't they?'
>
> Not understanding her words or resenting her stare, they stared right back
> with equal fascination.
>
> (Kirk 1969: 148)

Decorating the body, whether temporarily through paint, ornaments, or scents, or
permanently through pierced ears, tattooing, scarification, or lip plugs, occurs in
all cultures but practices are specific to particular relations between body and
habitus (cf. Cordwell 1979; Brain 1979; Ebin 1979). This chapter explores some
practices of body decoration found in western and non-western cultures. On the
one hand, techniques of body decoration are compared and contrasted as techniques of composing the social body within different conducts of life. Body
decoration is viewed, then, as historically specific, and culturally variable. On the
other hand, body decoration is also considered in terms of explanations and
interpretations proposed to account for such practices. This dual approach has
been adopted because body decoration is almost exclusively considered as a
process of inscribing meaning on the body, as a 'semiotics' of the body.

This emphasis, plus the distinction made between the western use of
'cosmetics' and non-western 'body decoration', has generally excluded their
consideration as simply different kinds of body techniques. Generally speaking,
body decorations in non-western cultures are interpreted in terms of group
identification, while western cosmetics are explained in terms of the assertion of
individuality (e.g. Corson 1972). Whereas body decoration is regarded as active
and purposeful behaviour, the use of make-up and cosmetics is interpreted as

passive and trivial behaviour. The theme of this chapter is that all techniques of body decoration concern the relationship between the self and the social body.

The interpretation of body decoration in non-western cultures is posed in terms of signifying characteristics such as group membership, fertility, sexual availability, strength, religious affiliation, status and power. These characteristics relate to the collective nature of the social group, rather than to the individual projection of 'identity'. Body decoration constitutes 'the imposition of a second, social "skin" . . . of culturally standardized patterns' (T. Turner 1969: 70). However, it is also possible to examine non-western body decoration in terms of habitus, the practical circumstances of the social body. In these terms, body decoration does not replace the old skin but sets up a play between the exterior public self (the decorated skin) and the relationship between the self and habitus. In other words, body decoration constitutes 'the visible exterior of an invisible interior' (O'Hanlon 1983: 332).

The first part of this chapter questions dominant accounts of non-western body decoration, especially the idea that individual practices construct group identity. Some detailed ethnographic evidence shows that body decoration constructs the self by drawing on group codes and conventions (O'Hanlon 1983). Body decorations are judged by peers in terms of their effectiveness and their plausibility (ibid.: 331; M. Strathern 1979: 248–52; A. Strathern 1987: 17; Lévi-Strauss 1969, 1976: 232–55):

> The art of concealment is related to the concept of bringing things outside . . . There should be a fit between the decorations and the man . . . Cover does not imply covering up an undesirable state.
>
> (M. Strathern 1979: 249)

In other words, attributes of self are constituted by the appearance achieved through body decoration. Mauss proposed that European culture witnessed a transition 'from a mere masquerade to the mask, from a role to a person, to an individual' (Mauss 1979: 90). Body decoration created a persona expressive of the 'inner self'. The notion of individuality constructed by Christianity has produced an *explanatory* rationale for western body decoration in terms of constructing a 'unique' identity. This creates what Marilyn Strathern (1979: 243) has called the cosmetic paradox (see Chapter 2). While body decoration creates the persona, the organisation of decorative techniques in terms of rules and conventions of selection and application means that, in practice, body decoration 'can draw attention away from the person'. While non-western cultures consciously exploit the paradox, decorative techniques in western culture embody a tension between individual projection and group membership.

As Marilyn Strathern (1979: 246) argues, people use body decoration as a means of 'draping' qualities and attributes of their achievements about their persons. In other words, bodies are 'worn' through the attributes of the person. This argument draws on the analysis of Marilyn and Andrew Strathern of the headdresses and body decoration of the New Guinea Highlanders, the Hageners.

Marilyn Strathern contrasts western and non-western body decoration in the following way:

> Cosmetics, for us, enhance the outer skin, deliberately attending to personal physical features. This leads to the possibility of an antithesis between the body so decorated and the inner or whole person. Formal decorations in Hagen . . . also rest on a contrast between an inner and outer self, but the operation supposes a continuity between these elements. Ornaments are hung about the body, yet the attention of spectators should be directed not to the body itself but to the decorations as a separate entity. They are meant to be attractive in themselves; far from a costume or regalia the actor dons, they are symbols of himself turned inside out.
>
> (M. Strathern 1979: 254)

Whereas western body decoration disguises the 'inner self' in order to project a public (outer) self, the Hageners use decoration to explicitly refer to inner qualities which are put on show for all to see. Rather than seeing the individual dancer as an 'individual', spectators appreciate the display of qualities possessed by the dancer through the decorations. Accordingly, dancers are 'decorated to the point of disguise . . . a dancer recognised at once has decorated himself poorly' (M. Strathern 1979: 243). Hageners both acknowledge and exploit the cosmetic paradox; by avoiding immediate recognition, they highlight the Hagen sense of the inner self and the qualities attached to the person of the individual dancer.

Hagen body decorations specify attributes of role and status; representations of emotions and attitudes; images of welfare (health, fecundity and prosperity); and indications of power (M. Strathern 1979: 245–6). Body decoration constitutes a kind of 'stock-taking' of Hagen society by elaborating codes for special ritual events and displays, rather than being a feature of everyday life. Individual dancers balance their own sense of decoration with the status of the group to whom they belong. The ritual of decoration and dance allows groups to vie for political position on the basis of how plausibly they portray the well-being of their group. Hagen body decoration serves to 'idealize rather than transform the person' (ibid.: 256). Yet Hageners resist offering explanations for their decorative rituals, insisting that 'it is just decoration' (A. Strathern 1987: 13). The practices and conventions are normalised into everyday life so they are 'unremarkable'. Hageners only wear body decoration for special occasions:

> And yet it is we who think of the people in New Guinea as practising face painting or body painting and consider this exotic! Seen from a Mount Hagen viewpoint, our assumption that women, not men, should walk around all the time with cosmetics on is the practice that is exotic and in need of explanation.
>
> (A. Strathern 1987: 17)

In other words, body decoration is a technique for producing a social body that is perfected for the practical habituses of particular cultures. Codes of body decoration vary according to circumstances, and the sense of 'self' actualised through body decoration will depend on the body–habitus relations specific to that social group. There is no fundamental distinction between western and non-western forms of body decoration, although western techniques have an historically specific rationale relating to the emergence of European 'civil' society.

MAKING UP THE SELF

> The theatrical face if not painted (made up), it is written . . . *to paint* is never anything but *to inscribe*.
>
> (Barthes 1982: 88)

In semiotic terms, body decoration is an act of writing. The traditional Japanese use of make-up constructs a 'face' by painting the surface white in order to fabricate a face 'rinsed of meaning' (Barthes 1982: 91). This 'inexpressive surface' is then used to write specific statements and signify certain emotions, thereby constructing the character of the face. The painted face denotes inner qualities, characteristics and reactions. For the Japanese, the face, body and regimes of gesture are used as surfaces to be inscribed with statements about the person though never revealing, or substituting for, the person. The written face constitutes a speech about the person and sets the rules of social interaction. It is equally possible to discuss Japanese body decoration as a set of techniques for constructing a social body through these written codes. The social body exists through its decoration. Lévi-Strauss observed that:

> Decoration is actually created for the face, since it is only by means of decoration that the face receives its social dignity and mystical significance. Decoration is conceived for the face, but the face itself only exists through decoration.
>
> (Lévi-Strauss 1969: 261)

The social body is composed of characteristics and qualities of personhood to be explicitly signified, depending on the occasion. Different social bodies draw on culturally specific techniques. Whereas the Japanese face is a minimalist form of decoration, it is equivalent to the elaborate, highly individualised headdresses of the Hageners, the intricate body paintings of the Caduveo in South America, and the unique expressivity of western cosmetics. Each produces the social body in culturally specific ways.

Lévi-Strauss (1976: 239–41) recorded hundreds of Caduveo face paintings which, in many cases, were identical to those drawn by a missionary two centuries earlier (suggesting that both the decorations and European traditions of art were stable). The designs consisted of 'a network of asymmetrical arabesques, alternating with delicate geometrical patterns' (ibid.: 239). Whereas these designs had once been done as tattoos, they were now usually painted on. This was interesting in several respects. First, Caduveo face painting was gender-specific, painted by women on other women. Second, when asked to draw the designs on paper, the women drew the faces as a flattened, bulbous, two-dimensional surface, not as a contoured, three-dimensional shape, as in western art. This representational convention indicated that the body was seen as a surface to be decorated and not as a contoured form in need of highlighting. Third, the Caduveo offered no explanations of why they painted, nor what the designs meant. They claimed 'either not to know, or to have forgotten' (Lévi-Strauss 1976: 243). In other words, as with the Hageners, there was no conscious explanatory process associated with the practice. Rather, face painting was a life conduct associated with the social body.

Lévi-Strauss proposed a structuralist explanation of face painting as a reflection of the social structure of Caduveo society. He argued that the decorative theme of dualism paralleled the dualism in codes concerning gender relations, spatial organisation, rules of marriage and heredity, and artistic styles (cf. Lévi-Strauss 1969: 261). The Caduveo wore their attributes of personhood on their bodies. The Caduveo responded to European clothing as being a similar technique of body decoration. When, for example, a European warship sailed up the Paraguay River in 1857:

> the sailors noted the next day that their bodies were covered with anchor-shaped motifs; one Indian even had an officer's uniform painted in great detail all over his torso – with buttons and stripes, and the sword-belt over the coat-tails.

> (Lévi-Strauss 1976: 245)

While the social body of the sailors was worn, in part, through their clothes, the Caduveo incorporated clothing and decoration into the one technique. Conversely, the Europeans interpreted the absence of clothing and the elaborate body decoration as a technique of the sexual body. Even Lévi-Strauss (1976: 244) argued that contemporary Caduveo women painted their faces and bodies for 'erotic motives' to make them 'delightfully alluring' to westerners. In each case, a process of prestigious imitation specific to each culture was conflated with the practical consequences of body decoration. European body decoration incorporated 'individualism' as a highly specialised form of self-conduct that grounded attributes of gender, status and the social body.

Western culture posits a dichotomy between mind and body, subject and object, and between male and female (M. Strathern 1979: 242; A. Strathern 1987: 17). The idea of the person is a psychological construction in which 'the "person" (personne) equals the "self" (moi) equals consciousness' (Mauss 1985: 21). Body decoration is the technique of self-actualisation of personhood and habitus. Western techniques of body decoration are also gender-specific, primarily denoting attributes of femininity. In sum, practices of body decoration can be seen as techniques for composing the social body, but those practices vary culturally and historically.

THE FACE OF FEMININITY

> Are you using yesterday's makeup for today's face? Introducing Lucidity Light-Diffusing Makeup SPF 8
>
> It's that rarest of things – a true breakthrough. A makeup that covers flawlessly . . . yet looks natural. A makeup that moisturizes and protects your skin, every minute you're wearing it. Estée Lauder Research has found a way for the colour to skim the surface of your skin so smoothly, it reflects light away from lines and shadows – makes them seem to disappear. You don't see the makeup . . . you see perfection. Wear it with Lucidity loose or pressed powder. Lucidity. Today's makeup. Only from Estée Lauder.
>
> (Estée Lauder advertisement 1991)

The dominant western technique of body decoration is achieved with cosmetics, or make-up. As a rhetoric, make-up promises transformations. Surface blemishes are hidden, youth is regained, skin becomes smooth, but, above all, the make-up should not be visible in its component parts, only its transformative impression. Make-up is a woman's secret projection of her desired self-image. In western cultures, it has become an integral step to realising femininity as an achieved set of characteristics (Craik 1989). The body is equipped with attributes through masking and manipulation. As a body technique, make-up constructs sexual attributes (hence the use of signifiers of sexual arousal such as red lips, dilated eyes and reddened cheeks), in addition to attributes of selfhood and status. Make-up inscribes the attributes of personality onto the social body. Beauty is the achievement of make-up as a positive declaration of the self. As with other body techniques, the application of make-up is ritualised and routinised.

The history of western cosmetics was bound up with European courtly culture and conduct (Elias 1983). Different make-up techniques were practised by the elite and non-elite groups. Moral attributes were associated with certain practices until the nineteenth century (Corson 1972: 393). Although skincare preparations and face powder were in common use, visible make-up (especially colourful applications on the lips and eyes) was confined to theatrical uses and to ladies of 'ill-repute'. The ambivalence which marked the use of cosmetics (such as rouge, nail polish and lipstick) declined as the marketing and availability of cosmetics transformed it from a home craft and family tradition to industrial manufacture and consumer distribution. Brand name cosmetics, such as the three dominant companies named after their respective matriarchs, Helena Rubinstein, Estée Lauder and Elizabeth Arden, changed the possibilities for cosmetics. Rubinstein declared in her promotional material that her name stood 'for beauty – beauty awakened, developed, constant, triumphant, not camouflaged' (Corson 1972: 457). Her products emphasised skincare, diet and exercise, and only belatedly did she introduce cosmetics. She recalled her campaign to extend the use of cosmetics to new milieus:

> Makeup was used exclusively for stage purposes, and actresses were the only women who knew anything of the art or who would dare to be seen in public

Figure 7.1 'Redefining beautiful': making up the self.

Source: Advertisement for Cover Girl Extension Mascara. (Cover Girl is a trademark of Proctor & Gamble. Reproduced by kind permission.)

wearing anything but the lightest film of rice powder . . . But makeup as it was to develop was unheard of outside the world of the theatre, although I experimented privately and learned many valuable lessons from stage personalities, which in turn I taught to a few of my more daring clients. They spread the word, and I knew that another beauty barrier would soon be toppled.

(H. Rubinstein 1972: 41)

As Rubinstein's empire grew through her salons and, subsequently, through distribution in department stores using trained consultants, so the popularity of cosmetics grew. The turning point in the acceptance of colourful cosmetics was Hollywood's manufacture of female screen stars. In 1917, Theda Bara came to Rubinstein to find a way to emphasise her eyes, which looked like black holes with the new camera techniques:

Eye makeup of any kind was unknown in America. Mascara had been used only in France by a few stage personalities, and not always well . . . For Theda Bara I made a mascara which drew attention to her lovely eyes so that they dominated her whole face – and the mascara did not streak! I also added a touch of colour to her eyelids. The effect was tremendously dramatic. It was a sensation reported in every newspaper and magazine – only less of a sensation than when Theda Bara first painted her toenails!

(H. Rubinstein 1972: 61)

Other actresses relied on the skills of Max Factor, a Russian wig maker who was employed by Hollywood filmmakers. His knowledge of Russian techniques of make-up for the stage was adapted in order to circumvent the hideous distortions of light and dark created by colour film. His success as a make-up artist quickly became prodigious. Factor was sought out by actresses to construct a special 'look'. He was regarded as a 'magician' who could conjure images in his beauty salons. Factor treated make-up as a 'science' both in creating products and adapting them to facial types. For example, he invented a calibration machine which gave precise measurements of the facial contours of clients. Cosmetics were then applied to overcome imbalances in shape, size or angle and to disguise 'defects'. His salon featured consulting rooms (rather like laboratories) which were decorated in four different shades designed to best enhance natural skin tones – blue for blondes, dusky pink for brunettes, mint green for redheads, and apricot for brunettes. He began to produce commodities especially for the film world, such as greasepaint (the forerunner of foundation cream), lip gloss (previously actresses had licked their lips between each take), eyeshadows, mascara, eye pencils and false eyelashes (Keenan 1977: 75). The demand for the 'looks' created for actresses was such that Max Factor began to sell his cosmetics commercially, under the respectable label of 'Society Make-up' 'so that women would not be scared off by too unladylike and showbiz an image' (ibid.: 80).

Through the 1930s, cosmetics became an accepted part of women's 'beauty' routines as a technique of self-presentation and prestigious imitation. Consumers had an insatiable appetite for beauty hints and make-up advice. Max Factor's development of water-soluble pancake in 1938 was a major turning point in the acceptability of make-up and colourful make-up, such as that inspired by Schiaparelli's outrageous shades of pink (Corson 1972: 516). Products were promoted with the promise of attaining the glamour of Hollywood 'so that YOUR lips will appear as perfect and as beautiful as those you see on the screen' (ibid.: 516). Corson suggested that this created 'problems in etiquette' because of moral attributes still associated with colourful make-up. Gradually, the wearing of make-up became tolerated in public, although there were still exhortations not to apply it in public! (ibid.: 516–17).

The cosmetics industry boomed. Max Factor cosmetics were the first to venture into mass marketing by creating promotions using film stars to project particular kinds of appeal (specific attributes of femininity). Consumers sought to imitate the 'looks' of their favourite stars. Despite Factor's early death, the company grew steadily and became the model for other cosmetic firms. The industry experienced spectacular growth. In 1941, Rubinstein offered 629 cosmetic items (Corson 1972: 519), while between 1940 and 1946, despite wartime rationing, the sale of cosmetics in the US rose by 65 per cent (ibid.: 528). Since the 1960s, the beauty industry has been one of the few growth industries in western economies, although in the 1980s the industry 'matured' and growth plateaued out.

The most significant post-war change was the extension of the use of cosmetics to teenage girls (Corson 1972: 535). Until then, make-up was associated with adult women and the attributes of mature femininity. Techniques were routinised and stabilised in cosmetic lines. Reducing the age threshold re-defined feminine attributes and re-vamped cosmetic techniques. Teenagers were adventurous and their tastes changed quickly.

Producers had to respond to the demand for new cosmetic ideas. One of the most successful companies to capitalise on this new market was Revlon. Vice-President Martin Revson argued that cosmetics gave women an escape from their dull and quietly desperate lives (Corson 1972: 538). Revlon's advertising played on this with campaigns such as the 1952 Fire-and-Ice promotion which tapped into that dissatisfaction with everyday life, and offered a way to transcend it with a range of lipsticks and nail polishes in 'passionate' reds. Revlon claimed that 'Every woman is made of Fire and Ice, though too many of them don't realize it. It is up to us to make every woman know it' (ibid.). The campaign was judged to be 'one of the most effective advertisements in cosmetics history, combining "dignity, class, and glamour"' (ibid.: 536). During the 1950s and 1960s, cosmetics were elaborated as a body technique to construct a range of attributes associated with the self, gender, sexuality, roles and prestigious imitation. By incorporating the rhetoric of individualism, cosmetics were identified with the ideal of the modern western woman.

The nature of cosmetics advertisements changed accordingly. Companies went for explicitly sensual and sexual appeals which overlayed the conventional transformative properties of the products. Products were updated and new ranges introduced that aimed to appeal to the prevailing mood of popular culture and its current idols and icons. In the 1960s, the products and protocols of application changed dramatically. The desire to achieve a look of sophistication and elegance was eschewed by the arbiters of popular culture. Youth, energy and irreverence were the new themes of fashion.

New kinds of make-up were developed and marketed which created the new look. For example, designer Mary Quant introduced her own line of cosmetics out of frustration with available products. Not only were the products inappropriate for the look of her clothes, they were also expensive and sold by rather snobby specialist staff. Quant's cosmetics were cheap and available in boutiques alongside the clothes. They were designed to complement the high-street fashion and created new facial looks, especially emphasising the eyes in new ways (Quant 1967: 161). Quant's cosmetics constructed attributes of youth, changing gender relations, and established new codes of prestigious imitation.

The history of modern cosmetics also reveals an emphasis on applying 'scientific' principles and protocol to the development, manufacture and selling of products while simultaneously promoting products as magical amulets. Thus, whereas body decoration was woven into rituals of cultural maintenance and affirmation in exotic societies, cosmetics were packaged in quasi-scientific formulae in western societies. The production and promotion of modern cosmetics adopted the technology of scientific research, technical procedures, pseudo-scientific names or symbols, and practical routines. Accordingly, new lines in make-up were developed in *laboratories* by white-coated *technicians* and delivered to *clients* in beauty clinics by trained *consultants* also in white coats: the use of scientific and medical analogies have been integral to the construction of the 'magic' of make-up (Radner 1989).

Techniques for promotion and sales have been elaborated in accordance with the technical interests and knowledge of consumers. New cosmetic products are developed, packaged and marketed to specific target groups by matching the attributes of the consumers with the transformative properties of the products. At a more basic level, cosmetics are targeted to particular fractions of the market as defined by demographic characteristics. There are three main groups: luxury and elite; middle of the road; and mass markets (Haug 1986: 77). Cross-cutting these groups is an appeal to age, in particular 'youth' and 'eternal beauty'. The sales of cosmetics are differentiated in terms of consumer groups by establishing a range of selling techniques – mail order, door-to-door, self-service, specialist counters and consultants. Brand-name differentiation is reinforced by separate counters and uniformed consultants. From the consumer's point of view, buying cosmetics is a process of matching the attributes of products with the ideal self (persona), according to practical circumstances of habitus. Frequently, known models are used to create associations of the product with particular qualities of femininity and personhood. Consumers choose the product whose model offers an 'imago' with which the consumer identifies (Radner 1989: 307). Make-up constructs attributes of the person on the surface of the body, especially characteristics associated with consumer ideas of femininity.

Research into prospective market niches may exceed the time taken to develop the cosmetic products. Further research goes into appropriate packaging designed to appeal to the targeted group. Consumers pay for the prestigious imitation associated with the packaging, not the cost of the ingredients. Cosmetics have a high profit margin despite the costs of product development. Mark-ups on some products are as high as 900 per cent (Corson 1972: 548). As little as '8 cents of the cosmetics sales dollar goes to pay for ingredients' (Goldman 1987: 697). The remainder is spent on researching the intended market, choosing a name and image, designing the packaging, training consultants and promotion. Advertising, for example, generally accounts for 25 per cent of sales revenue (ibid.: 722). For department stores, this is good news: 'Cosmetics on the ground floor is basic, it's your hard-core, prime-space traffic generator . . . unlike food with high costs and low margins' (quoted by Lawson 1990: 33). Cosmetics are a significant body technique in western consumer culture.

In the process, cosmetics have become a major international industry with four main players emerging in the 1980s: Unilever (whose companies include Ponds, Fabergé, Elizabeth Arden, Rimmel, and Calvin Klein), L'Oréal (Lancôme, Cacharel, Helena Rubinstein), Shiseido, and Proctor and Gamble (Oil of Ulay, Cover Girl) (Lawson 1990: 31). Other companies remain independent, including Estée Lauder, Avon, Mary Kay, and smaller brands. Competition is cut-throat and takeovers common. Intense effort is put into developing new products and, more importantly, new images and appeals, that is, into selling 'dreams and hopes in a bottle' (ibid.: 32).

Much of the promotional appeal of cosmetics depends on the visibility of the product on the wearer. The most visible cosmetic, lipstick, is used by 95 per cent of women, compared with only a third who regularly use nail varnish or eye shadow. Yet there is some evidence that cosmetic techniques are changing, with less emphasis on visible attributes and more on attributes associated with health and hygiene. During the 1980s, sales of decorative cosmetics have slowed down while the demand for skincare products has increased. Adapting to this emphasis, make-up is also being promoted in terms of having deep penetrating qualities below the skin. The development of the skincare market has extended the ritualistic possibilities of cosmetics routines. Skincare has been elaborated as a preliminary technique to make-up and routinised into three stages of cleansing, toning, and moisturising (Radner 1989: 305). Techniques of skincare are recommended as a regular and regulated discipline.

The ritualised application of cosmetics is repeated in the application of make-up. First, the facial surface is treated with base, concealer, highlighter, and blusher; next, the eyes are highlighted with shadow, pencil, eyeliner, and mascara; and finally the mouth is emphasised with lip liner, lipstick, and lip gloss (Radner 1989: 306). Part of the development of make-up routines is the specification of different protocols to achieve particular 'looks', chosen to create the face appropriate for the occasion, and for the impression a wearer wishes to project. Mary Quant, for example, divides make-up into four categories: natural; classical; party; and fantasy (Quant 1986: n.p.). The choice of make-up composes different attributes of femininity. The social body is customised for the occasions required within its habituses (cf. Synnott 1990: 62).

PERFUMED DESIRE

The fragrance that dresses a dream
(Caroline Herrera perfume advertisement 1991)

While make-up is based on visual techniques, perfume is a technique of smell. Make-up lends itself to promotional techniques whereas perfume cannot advertise its essential attribute directly. And yet perfume is a huge international business, worth $30 billion annually. With such huge profits to be made, about 300 new perfumes come onto the market each year. Perfume advertisements specify the attributes associated with the wearer of a particular scent. Slogans manufacture dreams and desire, and perfumers sell hope (Goldman 1987: 696). From the earliest civilisations perfume names like Tabu, Poison, Opium, Primitif, Obsession and Eternity evoke desired transformations and promise eroticism and romance. Advertisements establish attributes and role models attached to each perfume, emphasising the relationship between the scent, the human senses (alluding to the role of smell in sensuality and sexuality), and the wearing of identity (social body). Thus, women's perfumes promise to: 'Heighten your senses. Nothing is so personal as one's choice of fragrance . . . yet so telling' (United Airlines 1992: 3).

The use of perfumes is a well-established body technique (Kennett 1975: 9). From the earliest civilisations perfumers distilled the essence of flowers which were combined with natural substances (spices and musks) like myrrh, musk, ambergris, sandalwood and civet (Genders 1972). Perfumes had been used to deodorise rooms and bodies, so strong was the stench of everyday life (Corbin 1986). Since most scents did not last for long, elaborate rituals were developed to constantly replenish perfumes in circumstances where they were used. Developments in the nineteenth century enabled perfumers to stabilise the scent and prolong its life (De Long and Bye 1990: 81). This gave new possibilities for perfume manufacture and for conventions of use. It also extended the cultural milieus and specialised habituses in which perfume was used.

Processes of mass production and chemical analysis and re-constitution were the catalysts for the commercialisation of perfume and democratisation of its usage. Particular scents were associated either with the aristocracy or with qualities and lifecycle stages which were popularised through the European courts:

Over the decades, the aesthetics of the sense of smell became commonplace; the moderate price of perfumed soaps, the industrial manufacture of eau de cologne, the expansion of the network of drapers who distributed the products of perfumery enlarged the range of clientele. Flasks began to adorn the shelves of doctors and minor provincial notables. Even before toilet soap came into general use, the downward social mobility of eau de cologne was evidence that the poor man too had joined the battle against the putrid odour of his secretions.

(Corbin 1986: 199)

During the 1850s, techiques were developed to manufacture synthetic perfumes. This was cheaper than using natural extracts, and enabled the production of scents to be repeated. This provided the impetus for the growth of perfumeries and the standardisation of fragrances (Kennett 1975: 174, 181). As with cosmetics, perfume gradually relinquished its associations with dubious morals. Whereas perfume had traditionally been associated with prostitution, the new perfumes used delicate scents and were promoted to appeal to the new and delicate sensibilities of the middle-class Victorian woman: 'the discreet use of perfume became part of a complex system of visual, moral, and aesthetic perception' (De Long and Bye 1990: 81–2), that was, part of her habitus. Typical of the new approaches to perfume was the company, Guerlain. Established in 1828, Guerlain has produced a string of successful and enduring perfumes, starting with Jicky in 1889 (and still manufactured). This is often regarded as the first modern fragrance because it 'incorporated the then new, synthetic aromatic notes to add originality and new character to the beauty of natural essences' (Upton 1989: 150). Jicky was promoted in terms of the attributes of emancipated women, epitomised by the Gibson Girl (see Chapter 4). The promotion of early perfumes contrasted 'purity' as an attribute of Victorian femininity with 'sensibility' as that of post-Victorian femininity (De Long and Bye 1990: 82).

As well as companies devoted to perfumes, such as Guerlain, Coty, Rochas, Carven, Cacherel, Nina Ricci, Estée Lauder and Charles Revson (Revlon), couture designers also diversified into perfumes. Paul Poiret was the first with his 1912 perfume, Rosine (White 1973: 111). He was followed by Madame Lanvin with Arpege (1923); Coco Chanel with Chanel No. 5 (1925); and Jean Patou with Joy (1926) – reputedly the most expensive scent in the world (Etherington-Smith 1983: 95–7). Although modern perfumes are synthetic distillations using artificial essences of natural scents, they are still promoted in terms of the natural ingredients they mimic. For example, Jean Patou's Joy is described as 'an extremely concentrated floral scent, the equivalent of 2500 jasmine flowers fill each bottle' (United Airlines 1992: 4).

Other successful designer perfumes have included Shocking by Elsa Schiaparelli (1937); Christian Dior's Miss Dior (1947); Fidgi by Guy Larouche (1966); Rive Gauche by Yves Saint Laurent (1971); Osca de la Renta's namesake scent (1976); Chloe by Elizabeth Arden and Karl Lagerfeld's namesake (1975); Obsession by Calvin Klein (1985); and Romeo Gigli's signature perfume (1991). Perfume has become a lucrative sideline for designers because it provides a

Figure 7.2 'Perfumed desire': marketing scent by associated attributes.

Source: Advertisement for Samsara perfume by Guerlain. (Reproduced by courtesy of Guerlain Perfumes.)

marketable and affordable signature of the designer which reaches a wider, international market. While few women can afford designer clothes, many can afford to purchase an attribute of a designer in the form of a signature perfume. The associations attached to the designer and his or her clothes are translated into the qualities and reputed transformative properties of the scent. Consumers can establish an interest and a discipline of the self through the use of designer perfume.

The most successful designer perfume has been Chanel No. 5 by Coco Chanel. She disliked the floral scents which were the basis of most perfumes and experimented with a range of other scents. Her aim was to produce a perfume which was indefinable but irresistible. The result was a scent which featured a floral base of jasmine, rose, iris, ylang-ylang, amber and patchouli:

> There are some eighty ingredients in No. 5, and although it may smell as fresh as a garden, it is nothing like any garden you were ever in. It was in this way that she was making perfume history: No. 5 had the arresting quality of an abstract creation.
>
> (Charles-Roux 1989: 202)

The secret of the success of Chanel No. 5 was the image created around the new scent. Chanel discarded the fancy names and packaging favoured by other perfumers, instead opting for 'trim graphics' and 'stark harmony of presentation which relied solely on the contrast of black and white' (ibid.: 204):

> The noteworthy feature of the sharp-cornered cube Gabrielle put on the market was that it transferred the imagination to a different dimension. It was no longer the container that aroused desire, but its contents. It was no longer the object that decided the sale; the emphasis shifted to the one faculty really concerned: the sense of smell, brought into confrontation with this golden fluid imprisoned in a crystal cube and made visible in order to be desired.
>
> (Charles-Roux 1989: 203–4)

Chanel created a new aesthetics for fashion and established a new tradition at the same time. Her perfume was enduring despite the whims of couture. She established a link between changing fashions, the mood of the time, and assertive femininity. Perfumers began to respond to changing consumer orientations, changing representations of women, and to the eternal pursuit of new products and appeals. As De Long and Bye (1990) have shown, from the 1920s the ingredients and packaging of new perfumes have reflected the preoccupations of each decade. Even long-lasting scents have changed their promotional appeal and packaging over time.

Between the 1950s and the 1980s, the number of advertisements in fashion magazines doubled (De Long and Bye 1990: 83). More and more, the success of perfumes has depended on strategic naming, packaging and promotion to match product attributes with consumers. Whereas perfumes had traditionally been associated with Parisian sophistication, the expansion of the fashion and cosmetics industry in America was crucial to the expansion of the perfume industry.

Estée Lauder, in particular, exemplified the American approach to creating fashionable fragrances for middle-class women, and making them available through department stores (Upton 1989: 151). The first Lauder perfume was Youth Dew which was introduced in 1952. It quickly became a best-seller and secured a new market of consumers who did not normally buy perfume. It was a highly concentrated scent which outraged traditional perfumers but set new standards for consumers. Subsequently, many new fragrances opted for stronger concentrations. Perfumes overwhelmed the wearer and admirer alike. In other words, new ideas about the attributes of perfumes and their body–habitus relations, prompted different approaches to the manufacture of new kinds of scents.

Since then, the number of perfumes on the market has escalated and the number of appeals has multiplied. Perfumes are marketed for a range of markets differentiated by wealth, status, age and lifestyle. Given the competition between brands, perfumers constantly update their products to reflect new preoccupations and changing attributes of femininity. Goldman cites the example of Charles Revson's Revlon brand. In 1973, he inaugurated a new generation of perfumes in Charlie. This perfume was aimed at young women and drew on the current images (and rhetoric) of 'liberated' and career-oriented women (qualities reflected in the 'unisex' or tomboyish name). Like Chanel No. 5 before it, Charlie established new attributes of perfume: 'It sold sheer pleasure and enjoyment. It had a vision so fresh, so different, that it suddenly persuaded women all over the world to buy perfume' (Upton 1989: 151).

Charlie was explicitly designed to create a new market niche of young women who were disdainful of the classic fragrances. Charlie signified 'a youthful, carefree, independent, individual, confident and insouciant lifestyle' (Goldman 1987: 708). An elaborate marketing campaign was used to capture and groom this group. As the orientations of Charlie women changed, so too did the promotional appeal. In other words, the perfume was modified according to new historical circumstances. A 1982 campaign reflected more traditional orientations of young women towards marriage and family (ibid.: 699). Revlon subsequently developed a new fragrance to appeal to Charlie girls who had grown up. These women were, in marketing terms, 'past the aspiration state (that is, she is not Charlie). She has reached one level of success and expects to be at another level in the near future' (ibid.: 723). Revlon spent three years choosing the name, Scoundrel, which was believed to capture the spirit of this group (ibid.: 699). As the Charlie example suggests, perfume is a flexible body technique, customised by different attributes of self and habitus.

The choice of perfume name is crucial to establishing the qualities of the perfume or desirable associations for the wearer. Perfumers choose a name which invests 'the fragrance with the human qualities evoked by their positioning concept. Perfume and cologne ads typically anthropomorphize their fragrance' (Goldman 1987: 709). Focusing on the ingredients of perfumes is one way to allude to the scent – although such descriptions are rarely used in media advertising. Ingredients of 'patchouli, frankincense, vanilla, bergamot and iris' make up Guerlain's Shalimar, while Estée Lauder's Beautiful is described as a 'floral blend, brightened with citrus and warmed with woods and spices' (United Airlines 1992: 3–4). Descriptions contrast the top notes (often floral, spices or wood) with the bottom notes (smoky, musk, leather, chypre).

Perfumes require a 'distinctive personality' (Goldman 1987: 700) and packaging to match. This is achieved by extensively researching the characteristics of the intended consumer group in terms of demographic variables (age, income, occupation) and 'psychological characteristics' (moods, attitudes and composite consumption patterns) (ibid.: 698). Potential consumers select the packaging qualities with which they identify. Romeo Gigli, for example, has combined luxury and fantasy in the design of the bottle – an Aladdin's lamp with a crystal ribbon as a stopper – with utility. Rejecting the customary elaborate packaging, Gigli has chosen a brown paper box in which to present his perfume (Gerrie 1992: 36)! The launch of a new perfume, such as L'Oréal's Paloma Picasso or Guerlain's Samsara, can cost up to $50 million (Lawson 1990: 30). As one perfume marketer said: 'We sell an image and we will use any vehicle to emphasize it. It's all done by design' (Goldman 1987: 697). Gimmicks such as free gifts bearing the brand logo (tote bags, umbrellas, product samples) have become an effective way to create consumer loyalty because they 'encourage consumers to participate – insofar as they now share an immediate interest in the sign's respectability – in promoting recognition of the logo as a signifier-signified of status' (ibid.: 721).

De Long and Bye (1990: 84–6) have identified five themes in advertisements: traditional, romantic, casual, intellectual and seductive/sensual. These themes are encapsulated in the names of heroines, ideal imagos or exotic temptresses (for example, Carmen, Tosca, Chloe, Loulou, Charlie, Mitsouko); designer names and signature perfumes (Vanderbilt, Oscar de la Renta, Miss Dior); attributes of femininity (Panache, Lace, White Satin); exotic locations or themes (Xanadu, Sikkim, Fidgi, Paris); signifiers of seduction or passion (Opium, Tabu, Poison, Obsession, Vol de Nuit, Primitif); and signifiers of romance or classicism (Chanel No. 5, 4711, Arpege, Tweed, Je Reviens). Traditional themes have, by far, dominated perfume advertising appeals although seductive, romantic and intellectual themes have become more common in the 1980s (De Long and Bye 1990: 87–8). Women are offered 'a vast scenario of romance conducted on an epic scale' (Gell 1977: 37).

Perfumes invoke a 'misplaced literalism' which 'we must suppress if we are to respond as intended' (Gell 1977: 36). Ultimately, perfume enables us to transcend 'the sweet life' in name alone (ibid.: 37). Typical characterisations of perfumes reiterate phrases such as these: 'a timeless fragrance with a touch of the Orient' (Shalimar), 'feminine yet contemporary' (Lancôme's Tresur), 'a modern, floral fragrance' (Cacharel's Anais Anais), 'a totally original, artistic fragrance' (Nina Ricci's L'Air du Temps) (United Airlines 1992: 3–8). In a more extreme form of anthropomorphisation, Giorgio's Giorgio is described as: 'The best-selling fragrance in Beverley Hills, it has a totally feminine, floral scent. Many precious natural oils make up its sensuous personality' (ibid.: 5).

Figure 7.3 'Sheer sensuality': perfume names have attracted controversy by alluding to cultural instabilities and sexuality.

Source: Advertisement for Opium perfume by Yves Saint Laurent. (Reproduced by courtesy of Yves Saint Laurent Perfumes.)

As a practical technique, perfumes are constructed as the site of sexual desire in the trained body, as a means to produce and intensify desire. Perfume is a regulated expression of desire. This accounts for the excessive and 'explicit' names of perfumes, like Joy, Shocking, Opium, Poison and Obsession, which have attracted controversy on their release.

Calvin Klein's Obsession was the most controversial new perfume in the 1980s. Not only did the name disturb commentators – seeming to reflect the proclivities of the designer himself as well as his relationship with his clients – Calvin Klein deliberately employed erotic associations in advertisements for the product. This guaranteed the success of the scent. Subsequent advertisements have continued this explicit imagery, including one which shows a naked couple swinging face to face on a swing, 'their swaying bodies pressed together from the waist down. The effect is a gorgeous Y-shaped sculpture that suggests ecstasy and love' (Grant 1992: 20). The Obsession campaign marked a particular construction of gender and sexuality, addressing its attributes to both men and women. The cultural milieu of the 1990s suggests that perfume advertisements will offer very different qualities.

Signature scents, named after famous personalities, have created even more tangible sets of associations (and reactive paranoia). These include Cher's Uninhibited, Elizabeth Taylor's Passion, Joan Collins's Spectacular, Catherine Deneuve's Deneuve, Mikhail's Misha, Coty's Sophia and Linda Evans's Krystal. The success of celebrity perfumes depends not simply on finding 'a pleasing "juice"' (McLean 1991: 2), but on combining a popular image of a star with an emotional response in the consumer, and sufficient promotion including in-store appearances by the celebrity. The emergence of signature perfumes has extended the association of scents and qualities to identifications with stars and role models. This strategy has not ensured success. There is a tension between marketing perfume to mass markets and promoting it in terms of the qualities of an individual star. Few 'star' perfumes have flourished.

Perfume is now available to a wide range of groups in western consumer cultures. Perfumers and their marketers make fine distinctions between niche markets. For example, perfumes aimed at elite markets tend to use advertisements featuring the name and associations alone, while perfumes aimed at mass markets feature pictorial images and explicit messages (Goldman 1987: 723). These strategies reflect different competencies of reading and interpretation, as well as constructing distinct attributes for different consumer groups. With this extension and differentiation of the market for perfume, manufacturers have realised that perfumes can be created for every occasion. They are no longer a luxury for theatre, and for seduction or only for special occasions. There are perfumes for the office, for sport, for informal occasions, and even for staying at home (De Long and Bye 1990: 87). Accordingly, descriptions of perfumes key into the occasions for which they are worn.

From the mid-1960s, when the female market was saturated with products, cosmetics companies turned their attention to marketing cosmetics for men.

Women had achieved the elaboration of techniques of body decoration as an integral part of self-formation. Men employed other techniques to constitute attributes of masculinity. Although a few cosmetic products for men had been marketed earlier (first in the 1930s and then again in the 1960s), they had never taken off. Manufacturers concluded that men held 'particularly strong, traditionally deep-rooted, inhibitions' about 'effeminate' products (Haug 1986: 78). Male attitudes to cosmetics are, of course, culturally specific, and whereas men have used forms of body decoration liberally, Victorian men eschewed these techniques of femininity. They avoided fragrances other than those that could be construed as aiding health or cleanliness, such as bland toilet waters and after-shave preparations.

The growth of men's cosmetics was initially established as a medico-hygienic technique. Despite resistance to the idea of male cosmetics, sales have risen steadily through the 1970s and 1980s. By adding cosmetic treatments and products to the lines in barber shops, men have extended their definition of grooming to include moisturisers, mousse, lip gloss and sometimes foundation creams or concealers. Most effort has gone into developing skincare products, deodorants and haircare products, although the scent market is potentially the most lucrative. The medico-hygienic attributes were subsequently joined by attributes of masculinity associated with the body, self-presentation and discipline.

Generally, due to greater pressures for men to enhance their looks, the stigma attached to cosmetics has diminished as male role models have adopted these products. Beauty (or 'grooming') salons for men have become more numerous (de Muth 1992: 20). While the emphasis has been on facials, hair removal, shaving, massage and skincare, salons also offer hair perms, eyelash tinting, and make-up. Salons tend to be staffed by women because 'men don't generally like to be touched by other men' (except in contact sport)! Salon workers find male clients less demanding than women:

> Women expect you to miraculously transform them into someone younger and more beautiful. With men it's different . . . they really enjoy the treatments and at the end they're generally surprised and grateful for any improvement.
>
> (Quoted by de Muth 1992: 20)

In other words, women are more competent and confident as consumers. If men are coy about skincare and indulge in make-up only if it is invisible, they have been slowly weaned onto the idea of men's scents. In the 1970s, the marketers tried again, this time concentrating on establishing new conducts of rite. Male cosmetics were promoted in terms of strong attributes of masculinity (aggression, activity, macho icons). Once these were established, a vast new market opened up. Since the 1980s, and coinciding with a decline in the market for women's cosmetics, sales of men's perfumes have grown strongly. New products stressed active masculinity (macho strength), through appeals structured around narcissism and the cult of youth.

More recently, other men's perfumes have been aimed at appealing to 'a man of the world' (United Airlines 1992: 1). Scents such as Lagerfeld's Photo, Ralph Lauren's Polo, and Nick Faldo's Golf Club Cologne (packaged in a container shaped like a golf club head), reflect themes of contemporary masculinity (creative professions, elite sports, typical men's leisure activities). These perfumes share a construction of attributes of action, status and male preoccupations, which contrast sharply with the attributes of women's perfumes.

The majority of men's scents appeal to traditional notions of masculinity. Names evoking conquerors, legends and explorers dominate male perfumes (Storace 1991: 42) including Aramis, Top Brass, Kouros, Antaeus, Sybaris, Eau Sauvage, Jaguar, Boss, Samarkand, Jamaica, Iquitos and, of course, the best-known men's perfume, Brut. If women are offered romance on an epic scale, men are offered adventure on an equally awesome scale.

Whereas women's perfumes create the feminine attributes of the body, men's perfumes are promoted as 'classic, subtle scents that enhance rather than overwhelm a man's individual aura' (United Airlines 1992: 1). They are targeted towards three lifestyle demographic groups: 'the contemporary man' (for example, Giorgio Armani's Armani), 'confident sophisticated and enduring' men (Gucci's Gucci for Men), and sexy men. In the latter vein, Karl Lagerfeld's Photo is characterised as: 'This sexy men's fragrance has a flash of grapefruit and mandarin, exotic spices, jasmine and geranium . . . with a warm finish of rich woods and leather' (ibid.: 2). The descriptions of men's perfumes emphasise the non-floral ingredients such as herbs (for example, basil, chamomile), citrus, spices, woods, leather and tobacco. Generally, the base notes of these perfumes are more pronounced than in women's perfumes.

Other perfumes emphasise their male market niche with an extraordinary literalism. Names like L'Homme, Uomo, Pour Homme, Pour Lui and Passion for Men act 'as a powerful reassurance' that these perfumes are for sophisticated, western men with experience and authority (Storace 1991: 42). The packaging confirms this appeal to uncompromising masculinity with 'massive X-rated bottles, chunky tops, and generally, shall we say, uncircumcised look' (ibid.: 42). The growth of men's perfume has accompanied the re-working of attributes of masculinity and male sexuality, and their translation into marketing techniques. Over time, ingredients, names and appeals of perfumes have provided an index of changing attributes of gender and the social body.

In other words, perfumes are a form of clothing. A fragrance 'wardrobe' consists of a range of 'alternating' scents to be worn as appropriate to specific occasions (Upton 1989: 206), whether it be 'a light scent to symbolize the carefree ingenue or a musk to enhance the sensual moments in one's life' (De Long and Bye 1990: 87). This has included scents designed to disguise 'natural' odours, namely, 'intimate deodorants'. These are packaged as 'defences against one's own body smells', especially those associated with sexual functions and activities (Haug 1986: 77). As Haug has observed, the campaign against natural smells has been highly effective. In Germany, for example, 43 per cent of 16- to 60-year-olds and 87 per cent of 19-year-olds use intimate deodorants (ibid.: 77).

Figure 7.4 'Pour L'homme': emphasising masculinity is a feature of men's
            perfume names and packaging.

Source: Advertisement for Pour L'homme Eau de Toilette by Cacharel. (Reproduced by
courtesy of Austrabelle.)

Perfumes and cosmetics constitute a body map of cultural preoccupations, representations of gender, codes of sexuality and qualities of personhood. Above all, perfumes and cosmetics work on the body in a regulated disciplined way to produce the social body. This chapter has considered cosmetics and perfume as techniques of body decoration, arguing that these techniques construct attributes of personhood on the surface of the body.

Chapter 8

Fashioning masculinity
Dressed for comfort or style

FASHIONLESS MEN

> Men's bodies have never simply stood for sex; consequently, their clothes
> never have either. Pity the poor man who wants to look attractive and well
> dressed, but who feels that by doing so he runs the risk of looking unmanly.
>
> (Steele 1989b: 61)

Women are fashionable but men are not. This lament is common in western
cultures. Indicatively, most studies of contemporary fashion emphasise female
fashion and marginalise attention to male dress. Yet the equation of fashion with
women and the exclusion of men is historically and culturally specific, stemming
from nineteenth-century Victorian and European notions of etiquette, gender
relations, and sexuality. In particular, these ideas proposed a radical split between
genders and assigned each of them specific roles and locations. An index of this
order of sexual division was the continuous recreation of dress codes. Within this
process women were gradually assigned the role of the fashionable gender of the
species.

Accordingly, the rhetoric of men's fashion takes the form of a set of denials
that include the following propositions: that there is no men's fashion; that men
dress for fit and comfort, rather than for style; that women dress men and buy
clothes for men; that men who dress up are peculiar (one way or another); that
men do not notice clothes; and that most men have not been duped into the
endless pursuit of seasonal fads. In other words, there is a tendency to underplay
if not deny the phenomenon of men's fashion. Yet, pushed a little, people hold
very strong and diverse views about men and clothing: commonsense clichés
about men's fashions disguise passionate opinions. Men's fashion relates to, but
is distinct from, the codes of women's fashion. Whereas contemporary codes of
women's fashion have revolved around achieving 'a look' as an image to be
admired (spectacle), men's appearance has been calculated to enhance their
active roles (especially occupation and social status).

Historically and cross-culturally, the clothing of men and women has been
subject to trends in styles and fashions. From the eighteenth century, in western
Europe male fashion has received less attention than women's. This chapter

Figure 8.1 Status and formality: derivations of the suit in men's working clothes.
(Crew of Welsh steamer circa 1920.)

examines both the un-fashioning of western men and the post-1960s reassertion of male fashion and male bodies. This revival is explained in terms of changing power relations associated with gender relations, specifically in terms of challenges to male-dominated practices of post-industrial societies. As men's power is questioned by women's involvement in the workplace and in assuming responsibilities in the public sphere, men have adopted new codes of clothing conduct, modifying attributes of respectability and authority by incorporating frivolous and narcissistic elements.

During the 1980s and 1990s, there has been considerable debate about the invention of men's fashion: the main claim has been that men have abandoned their studied lack of interest in clothes and devoured the images and looks offered by a spate of designers and fashion stores. A common refrain has been that men have awakened from a fashionless stupor and 'rediscovered' clothes. Yet an examination of earlier generations and centuries – not to mention cross-cultural comparisons – makes this account questionable. Not only is there a history of men's fashion, but codes of wearing and sanctions for ignoring or subverting those codes have, if anything, been stronger for men than for women.

Within European culture, cycles of changes in men's dress have been longer and less dramatic, especially since the eighteenth century. Men's fashions typically have used a smaller range of fashion garments, with a basic wardrobe consisting of shirt, trousers and jacket. Within this range, there has been a narrower degree of adaptation – for example, in the choice of tie (Finkelstein 1991: 107–29), socks or sweater. One analyst (D. Robinson 1976) has even argued that the barometer of men's fashions can be found in the shaving and trimming of beards! Between 1840 and 1970, beards (a composite measure of sideburns, moustaches and beards) appeared in regular cycles of fashionableness that corresponded to fluctuations in width of skirts. The heyday of the beard was between 1875 and 1895 when the fashion for wide skirts was also at its fullest. Robinson argues that these cycles in 'style preferences' resisted manipulation:

> The remarkable regularity of our wavelike fluctuations suggests a large measure of independence from outside historical events. The innovation of the safety razor and the wars which occurred during the period studied appear to have had negligible effects on the time series. King C. Gillette's patented safety razor began its meteoric sales rise in 1905. But by that year beard-lessness had already been on the rise for more than 30 years, and its rate of expansion seems not to have augmented appreciably afterward. Far from initiating a great style wave, Mr. Gillette rode on one to fame and fortune.
>
> (D. Robinson 1976: 1138)

Not only is it possible to identify cycles in men's fashions but they run parallel to those in women's fashions. Arguably, from the nineteenth century, however, men's fashions have offered fewer choices at any one moment and therefore acted to impose conformity on those adhering to fashion. Normative men have either resisted fashion or conformed to mainstream elements. Conversely, expressive (individualistic or idiosyncratic) male fashion has been confined to particular groups and 'subcultures', such as 'gentlemen', gays, popular entertainers, ethnic groups, and popular subcultural groups (see Almond 1988; Cosgrove 1989; Kohn 1989; D. Lloyd 1988). The implication is that these groups are not normative, but articulate non-mainstream forms of masculinity reflected by, and coded in, their choice of clothes. These other 'masculinities' have pivoted around heterosexuality but frequently have invoked parodies of mainstream male mores. As Pumphrey (1989) has argued, definitions of masculinity are coded through clothes and the associated politics of style. He suggests that the Western (as history, novel and film) has offered one enduring style from which men's fashions and group identities have derived. Even so, the way in which the Western has figured is ambivalent:

> The heterosexual norm exemplified in the Western has always been satirised and parodied within gay cultures and, drawing directly on that tradition of resistance, style politics does offer heterosexual men new ways of conceptualising and acting out masculinity – not least because at the immediate level of everyday social life it ridicules the coercive homophobia that has so fundamentally shaped the processes by which masculinity has traditionally been maintained, and offers new ways in which these men can relate to each other.
>
> (Pumphrey 1989: 97)

Underpinning Pumphrey's argument is a sense of ambivalence towards the relation between male style and male sexual identity. Contemporary men struggle to articulate the image of male sexuality appropriate to their circumstances. For some, this has an overwhelming importance; for others, little at all – or so it seems. The very act of decorating and displaying the male body in twentieth-century Europe has been fraught with partially spoken – and often competing – desires and fears. The myth of the 'undecorated' male effectively suppresses ambivalence about this process of forming the male social body. In industrialising Europe, men became consumed by employment which could secure status and power. In a conscious move, men disassociated themselves with the idleness and extravagance of aristocratic codes of dress and behaviour. Men dressed to confirm their involvement in the new industrial order. While men competed in the tough world of politics and economics, women were allocated the role of decorating and complementing the public status of men through their clothes and demeanour.

As indicated in earlier chapters (especially Chapters 2 and 7), decoration and dress has frequently been a major feature of masculinity in other cultures. New Guinea headdresses are primarily the province of men; body decoration is as much a male as a female pursuit in most non-European societies (such as Africa, South America, Australian Aborigines, North American indigenous peoples, Polynesia); splendid Polynesian capes are worn primarily by men; and so on (see R. Rubinstein 1985). But, in European culture, the emergence of our form of civility has involved a fundamental disquiet about male decoration. The presentation of the body and practices of etiquette were central to the formative character of civil society. The sumptuary laws which lasted from the thirteenth to the seventeenth centuries are the most commonly cited example of the attempt to regulate fashion and codify display. These laws specified appropriate clothing according to occupation and social status. In particular, they imposed restrictions on eligibility to wear certain kinds of garments, fabrics and accessories – especially fur, gold, silk and jewels. Since the rules were set by the court, they sought to enhance the status of the aristocracy through sartorial distinctiveness.

Sumptuary laws also had implications for commerce. By prescribing consumer habits precisely, the laws regulated 'the acquisition and exchange of valuable goods' (Finkelstein 1991: 138). Overall, they eschewed excessive display for its own sake. But, as with any regulatory code, the act of suppression and articulation of permissible limits, both codified status and created an alternative set of rules and codes. Despite the laws, which were frequently flaunted, especially by the upwardly mobile merchant class, neither fashion nor consumerism was eradicated. Rather, the laws enshrined the significance of clothing and appearance as signs of economic and social position. Clothes were an inherent component of persona. As Elias (1983) has shown, a reaction to this legislative imposition from the court was the formation of dress codes among ordinary people, especially wealthy business classes. This gave rise to the phenomenon of 'town fashions'. Thus, it is somewhat misleading to interpret surviving court fashions as indicative of mainstream dress norms of the time.

THE CIVILISING IMPERATIVE

The history of European court society of the Renaissance reveals that fashion flourished at that time. Indeed, it functioned as a major determinant of position within the court. Although the consumption of clothing had been a preoccupation for centuries (Lemire 1990), court society turned consumerism into an art form. The most extravagant monarch was Louis XIV who has been called 'the consumer king' (R. Williams 1982: 26). Not only did he himself display an obscene indulgence in lavish and opulent clothing, ornamentation, housing, furnishings, parties and fetes, he set impossible standards for his nobles and those who wished to curry favour. Once admitted to court society, the nobles 'had to spend ruinously to stay there' (ibid.: 28), running up huge bills and indebtedness to the king:

> State spending increased astronomically. In return for this expenditure, the monarchy gained a dependent nobility which gathered at court because royal power was concentrated there, only to find themselves committed to a level of consumption which further enhanced that power.
>
> (R. Williams 1982: 29)

It was a vicious circle. By preying on their vanity, Louis XIV created a circle of 'insatiable consumers' who spent huge sums of money in order to remain in favour with the king, and supported the regime in order to keep their creditors at bay (ibid.: 30). In the end, the court became a self-perpetuating world out of touch with society at large and wider political forces. Foreigners were 'astounded' by the splendour and excessive extravagances of the French court (de Marly 1987: 122).

Over time the rigid grand habit of the court was regarded as unfashionable and conservative by the fashionable classes in the towns and by the younger members of the court. Often they ignored the requirements of the *habit de cour* or incorporated elements from town fashion, thereby incurring the wrath of Louis XIV (de Marly 1987: 64, 129). But the end of the king's reign did not mean the end of consumerism. Citizens had been exposed to glimpses of unimagined possibilities and the power of money. The social structure of European societies had already changed significantly and was continuing to do so. Subsequent developments of a bourgeois class and an urbanised population embodied the desire for material goods and conspicuous consumption. The bourgeoisie wanted to live 'nobly' by acquiring goods 'that imitated aristocratic styles from the past' (R. Williams 1982: 50). This desire to emulate aristocratic elements was a mere affectation confined to a small group and occurred alongside the emergence of explicit codes of fashion and etiquette in civil society.

Trends in clothing and cycles of fashion demonstrated this. Costume collections show that men's clothing – at least for the wealthy – was elaborate and extravagant. For example, seventeenth-century men's dress was based on doublet, breeches and cloak. When resources permitted, these garments were heavily embroidered, sometimes trimmed with silver or gold thread, edged with satin, and featured lace collars (A. Hart 1984: 50–5). According to Hart (1984: 52), printing and embroidering motifs (what she calls 'decorative abuse of expensive textiles') became fashionable from the late sixteenth century. When the expensive fabric could not be afforded: 'Calicos and cottons were treated to look like silk, while wallpaper with gold floral patterns and chairs upholstered in "Pompadour" style were made for the salons of the middle bourgeoisie' (R. Williams 1982: 50).

Although the influence of court society declined, the desire to decorate the male body did not. However, the aristocratic influence waned. In contrast to the elaborate tops and leggings (breeches, pantaloons, stockings) preferred by the court, in the eighteenth century, the basis of men's wardrobes became the suit, although the jackets were still very full with coat skirts, and the trousers were knee-length breeches. This trend was a trickle-up phenomenon, since it was based on the clothing of working-class men but gradually became the standard dress for men of all classes (Steele 1989c: 78). The cut and preferred fabric of the coat (embroidered or woven patterned silk or wool) changed each season (A. Hart 1984: 55). In the 1740s, the suit became somewhat plainer and the waistcoat – visible underneath – became the extravagant fashion statement. By the late eighteenth century, these garments were becoming more standardised though still elaborate. A preference for dark colours was also evident. The nineteenth century was a turning point. Changes in tailoring techniques 'concentrated on fit rather than style' (ibid.: 62) by creating waist seams, underarm seams, and introducing Cossack trousers. There were enormous variations in the style of coats and experimentation with different kinds of trousers. But, over time, men's dress became less elaborate, less decorative, and less variable.

Yet despite the trend towards more standardised dress, there were still seasonal fashions and precise rules of dress etiquette. The trend towards plainness occurred against periodic campaigns in favour of extreme decorative male dress. These included the phenomena of the beau (early eighteenth century), Macaroni fashion (1760s to 1770s) and the dandy (early nineteenth century) and the aesthete of the late nineteenth century. These are usually contrasted with subsequent plain fashions for men, which are explained in terms of political and economic upheavals, in particular, the French Revolution. Steele (1985b), however, argues that the trend towards plainer clothes was under way much earlier alongside the moments of excess in men's fashions. In fact, she suggests, these fads triggered the trend.

Steele (1985b: 99) argues that there was a battle between men's fashions that accompanied the growth of civil society and the gradual erosion of aristocratic power and prestige in Europe. The Macaronis appeared during 'the peak of aristocratic power' (ibid.: 99). They epitomised the desire of aristocrats to distinguish themselves from the growing bourgeoisie and minor gentry through their clothes. They drew on images from the French and Italian courts to emphasise that difference and create an impression of solidarity with their European counterparts. This occurred against a background of emerging political awareness among newly empowered groups in England. Inevitably, the tensions between the groups spilt over into vicious attacks on the character and appearances of each. Macaroni fashion became the rich butt of caricatures and satire in anti-aristocratic literature produced by those who despised the values held by the Macaronis:

> the image of the Macaroni was used to attack the perceived vanity, irresponsibility, effeminacy, and lack of patriotism of the aristocracy, especially (but not exclusively) the Court elite. Elaborate and modish male dress was perceived as symptomatic of corruption, tyranny and foreign attitudes, while plainer male dress was heralded as an emblem of liberty, parliamentary democracy, enterprise, virtue, manliness, and patriotism.
>
> (Steele 1985b: 98–9)

Typical items of clothing attracting scorn included the Macaronis' shoes with buckles or bows, light silk stockings, accessories, nosegays, neckchiefs tied in a bow, decorative buttons, tasselled canes, watches, trinkets and baubles. Above all, in contempt for the declining fashion for wigs, the Macaronis wore elaborate headdresses:

> But the Macaroni wig was both new and Frenchified, and it paralleled the current fashion in women's wigs, which, since the late 1760s, had been worn ever higher. Apparently, it was bad enough that 'female macaronis' be subject

to the arts of the French *friseur*, but it was utterly contemptible that men should copy them. Many critics suggested that the Macaroni had 'a good quantity of hair . . . for his head produces nothing else', but one writer used a more devastating image that associated external appearance with internal corruption: 'Their toupees imitate their high elevated thoughts, which, teeming with maggots of various kinds, display to the world their humour'.

(Steele 1985b: 102)

Through caricature and denunciations like these, the Macaronis were implicated in a style war between traditional elite arbiters of taste and new groups of cultural nationalists. The mercantile and bourgeois classes in Britain were in the process of consolidating their social identity and distinguishing it from what had gone before at the same time as the elite tried to insist on their superiority and assert their vestimentary distinction. Although there was not yet a clear sense of British civil fashion, the new groups preferred simplicity and drew on images of military, sport and country life (Steele 1985b: 96). Clearly, the antithesis between the 'country' associations of this code and the court associations of Macaroni fashion was underpinned by deep-seated hostility. Yet despite the strident denunciations of the Macaronis' aristocratic dress, there was also a desire to imitate certain aspects of it (ibid.: 101). The tensions between the desire to imitate and the impulse to reject aristocratic ways embodied the dominant themes of contemporary political, economic and moral life:

The fashion in men's attire changed as more and more people came to perceive sober male dress as being a reflection of patriotism (versus aristocratic cosmopolitanism), liberty (versus tyranny), country and city (versus Court), Parliament and Constitution (versus Royal prerogative and corruption), virtue (versus libertinism), enterprise (versus gambling, frivolity, and dissipation), and manliness (versus a fribbling, degenerate exotic effeminacy).

(Steele 1985b: 108)

By the 1780s, the values associated with Macaroni dress had been discredited and rejected. As a consequence, men's dress became plainer. Moreover, it was interpreted as a sign of British patriotism, cultural dominance and economic success. But while clothing became simpler, it did not mean that men's fashion or codes of dress disappeared. Rather, they became more subtle and internalised. Subsequent moments of excess in men's dress were thus posed against this plain backdrop, and were widely resisted precisely because they articulated the values and association that the fashion system tried to keep invisible.

The emergence of consumerism and the growth of bureaucratic and civil society heralded other more accessible sources and conduits of fashion. Success in public life depended as much on the successful management of appearances as it did on economic clout (Finkelstein 1991: 115). The extension of industrialism and urbanism created new possibilities for fashion. Individuals could buy the qualities they desired and wished to project:

With a plentiful supply of material goods, the individual's right to possessions, be they gold adornments, furs, silk clothes or heeled shoes, took on a
different meaning. Now, the ownership and display of goods became evidence
of an individual's accomplishments and attributes. Ownership made an individual appear wealthy, socially mobile, in possession of refined sensibilities
and tastes.

(Finkelstein 1991: 115)

Central to the new possibilities opened up by consumerism was the manipulation
of appearances. People had greater access to clothes, a new awareness of fashion
and fads, and the possibility of buying the look they desired. Accordingly,
appearance, complemented by 'artifice and performance', combined in new
registers of social etiquette and measures of achievement:

a shift in sensibility took place when the age of consumerism was expanding,
in the early nineteenth century, and a new balance was being struck in which
the external appearance, particularly of men, was becoming a significant
index of political and social interests. At the time, a man could demonstrate
his thorough disinterest in the struggles for power and his distance or removal
from ancestral wealth in the style of clothes and the mien he adopted.

(Finkelstein 1991: 112)

A new attention to appearance and calculated display heralded the emergence of
conspicuous consumption organised around the body. For men, this involved
restraint rather more than excess. Social success was predicated on respectability
which was gauged by conveying an impression of a serious (business-like)
demeanour created by wearing sombre clothes.

In contrast, 'society' fashion adapted these norms in an extreme way,
epitomised by the figure of the dandy. The socialite Beau Brummell became
synonymous with dandyism. During the early years of the nineteenth century,
Brummell was socially ambitious and used his appearance to gain favour with
high society. He abhorred the ostentatious display conveyed by the extravagant
frippery of the nobility and chose instead simple, understated clothes, and wanted
to create 'a new kind of aristocrat' based on 'a purely subjective influence over
society' (R. Williams 1982: 111). To this end, he 'concentrated on the body and
used his clothing to bring attention to and enhance the human frame' such that
'his social identity was fashioned from his appearance' (Finkelstein 1991: 113).

Brummell created a style of dress that was 'more austere, manly and dignified
than any before or since' (Moers 1960: 31). He chose to wear a well-tailored coat
with a tight waist and knee-length skirt, over waistcoat, shirt and cravat, and
pantaloons. Although apparently plain, Brummell's clothes were the product of
highly skilled tailoring and painstaking care with his toilet. According to Moers:
'Brummell's major contribution to history was his highly original advocacy of
cleanliness. It was a matter of pride with him that he did not need perfume: he did
not smell' (ibid.: 32).

Through the judicious choice of well-cut suits and fresh, starched linen neck-cloths and shirts, Brummell imposed a new restrained code of men's dress: 'the fashion ideal of understated elegance' (R. Williams 1982: 112). This became the language of dress for the modern man and 'the forerunner of the modern business suit and the necktie' (Finkelstein 1991: 113). These clothes 'were suitable for all classes and occupations' that, in the long-term, 'would clothe democracy' (Moers 1960: 33):

> By making simplicity the fashion, Brummell established a style suitable for any man, king or commoner, who aspired after the distinction of gentleman. Without sacrificing elegance or grace, he invented a costume that was indubitably masculine.
>
> (Moers 1960: 35–6)

The secret of men's dress was a standardised sober suit enlivened by choice of tie and accoutrements. Items like the necktie allowed individual interpretations; indeed, it was Brummell's favourite item. But mostly clothing codes entailed more subtle conventions concerning the cut, fabric and mode of wearing. Even the business suit, the apparent leveller of men's dress, invokes complex and almost imperceptible 'esoteria of fabric, fibre, tailoring and aesthetics' for the cognoscenti (Finkelstein 1991: 110). Above all, taste was costly. Modish consumers were locked into patronising the most expensive purveyors. Thus, an elite consumer group developed alongside a democratic one. While the elite group thought they could transcend banal taste and everyday life, the democratic group 'wanted to rescue everyday consumption from banality by raising it to the level of a political and social statement' (R. Williams 1982: 110). The tensions between these two groups marked the character of nineteenth-century male consumer culture.

The irony of the era of the dandy was that this elitism and desire to distinguish themselves from ordinary people by 'spiritual superiority all depended on the vulgar act of shopping' (R. Williams 1982: 119). It was very expensive (ruinous in Brummell's case) to acquire the appropriate dress, furnishings, possessions and lifestyle of the dandy:

> In consequence, the dandy ideal was not only dragged down to the level of materiality – an unavoidable fall for any human ideal . . . but it was dragged down more specifically, and less necessarily, to the level of the marketplace. The dandy expressed himself as a consumer; dandyism was inherently tainted by commercialism.
>
> (R. Williams 1982: 119–20)

But dandyism was an important moment in European men's dress because it established new sets of relations between trend-setters and fashionable groups, and secured new sartorial codes for men in industrialised societies. The dandy combined vestiges of the peacock with rules for the plain man.

SUITED FOR RESPECTABILITY

Despite the activities of the dandies, most people were constrained by financial and practical circumstances as well as by more conservative aesthetic considerations. Generally, the nineteenth century was characterised by conservatism in men's dress and resistance to change. This was maintained by successive campaigns against excess in men's dress. According to Paoletti (1985), these campaigns were conducted by endorsing positive role models and ridiculing undesirable tendencies. Specialist shops in the form of gentlemen's outfitters catered for the new male mode and became authoritative sources about men's dress. Male fashion advice came from tailors, columns in men's magazines and etiquette books which described 'the perfect gentleman' (ibid.: 121).

The 1880s man dressed in a way that was 'inconspicuous to the casual observer, but perfect in its attention to quality, fit and correctness' (Paoletti 1985: 121). There was more concern with men's involvement in the workplace, which required a suitably serious and practical outlook and appearance. 'Conformity and conservatism in dress indicated reliability' (Kidwell 1989: 129). But, in the space of a decade, the well-dressed man became a pale reflection of his earlier self. Now he bought ready-to-wear clothes from department stores and men's clothiers, and primarily wore suits – for work, sport, and leisure. He was 'neat but casual, clean but not fussily immaculate, and versatile, not occasion-specific' (Paoletti 1985: 121).

So, what led to this rapid change in the wardrobe and the image of the fashionable man? According to Paoletti (1985), men became subject to a number of pressures both in the workplace and at home. Attitudes were changing. More men worked in sedentary occupations, especially in office jobs. These required different kinds of clothing, hence the growing popularity of the business suit as a practical, multi-purpose garment and the basis of the wardrobe for the white-collar workplace. In some occupations, such as the police force, the military and medical workers (doctors and surgeons), uniforms were introduced in order to indicate professional authority (Steele 1989c: 64–91). In blue-collar jobs, overalls, dungarees and boilersuits gradually replaced suits as functional and conformist clothing more suitable for the job. These practical garments were colour-coded by occupation: white for laboratory and manual work, blue for engineering, and khaki for operational tasks (ibid.: 82).

As a fashion garment, the suit was invested with sexual attributes of the new masculinity of the 1890s. This stylistic rhetoric of conversion was accompanied by denunciations of clothes and adornment which threatened 'traditional masculinity or masculine values' and sustained 'ridicule of occasion-specific styles such as the frock coat' (Paoletti 1985: 124). By the late nineteenth century, there was a relentless trend towards plain dress characterised by the uniform choice of colour, style and fabric (Finkelstein 1991: 133). Men's suits retained considerable padding throughout the garment to enhance the shoulders and the hips. By tailoring the jacket to feature a nipped-in waist, a rounded effect was

Figure 8.2 Discipline and punish: boys' school uniforms. (Wales circa 1900.)

achieved which complemented the hourglass figure of the fashionable woman (Kidwell 1989: 126–9). Some men wore corsets (made of rows of stretched springs) while others wore pantaloons made with rows of drawstrings at the waist which created a full-hipped look. The impression created was one of substantial bulk. Kidwell has noted how the similarity between the nineteenth-century male and female ideal silhouette is often misunderstood and misinterpreted:

> Even what was similar in men's and women's dress was perceived differently. When contemporary writers made reference to the shape of a fashionable man's body, they most often described wide shoulders, while reporters of feminine fashions focused on narrow waists. Any reference to the apparent width of the shoulders in women's dresses was in terms of how this feature

showed off in contrast a small waist. Thus the optical illusion created by the V angle of the lapels on a man's coat and the V angle of the gathers on a woman's bodice were interpreted differently.

(Kidwell 1989: 129)

From the 1890s, the rounded male physique gave way to a new look. Suits were tailored in an angular, square mode using stiff, sturdy and durable material allowing freedom of movement. By using a limited range of dark colours and discreet, subtle patterns, the suit became the perfect multi-occasion garment. Complemented by white or pastel shirts, the dour suit was relieved only by the choice of tie or cravat. Ornamentation was viewed with suspicion. The overall impression conveyed the serious disposition of men locked into the industrialising economy. As Finkelstein (1991: 133) has noted, the severity of men's dress was reinforced by its contrast with women's fashions. These were made in softer fabrics in light colours, and cut to exaggerate curves and flowing lines which drew attention to the contours of the female body. Not only did these fashions restrict movement and allow only minimal physical exertion, the excessive use of jewellery and accessories underlined the ephemeral interests and frivolous image of nineteenth-century women.

In earlier chapters, we have discussed the rhetoric of the New Woman that accompanied significant changes to the circumstances of women in the late nineteenth and early twentieth centuries. There was also a complementary rhetoric about the New Man. But whereas the New Woman was heralded as a symbol of the new age, her male counterpart came in for heavy criticism:

Numerous cartoons depicted a topsy-turvy world of the future populated by strong, domineering women and passive, domesticated men. The challenge to young men of the turn of the century was not only to adapt successfully to the pressures of modern urban life, but to adjust to these changing standards of femininity.

(Paoletti 1985: 126)

The ideal of masculinity was no longer the mannered, passive, leisure-seeking 'Gentleman', but a young man filled with ambition and courage: 'energetic, athletic, ambitious and less concerned with style than action' (Paoletti 1985: 126). In accordance with this ideal, the 'Coming Man' spent little time on his clothes and appearance. His wardrobe was based on the business suit with a sack-style jacket: 'Neatness was desirable, but not really expected, as it seems to have been believed to have run contrary to masculine nature' (ibid.: 127). The new look was advocated in etiquette books as well as through popular magazines and cartoons. Paoletti argues that ridicule of what was deemed to be inappropriate men's dress, especially the Perfect Gentleman as well as unmanly and effeminate looks, was a strong and effective feature of this period. The term 'dandy' was revived and applied to the positive role models associated with the new dress codes – the American equivalent was 'the dude' (ibid.: 129). These fashions were often uncomfortable and comical (ibid.: 124). In the 1890s, the Dude was replaced by a companion to the Gibson Girl, the Gibson Man, who was well-dressed but casual, athletic and possessed a cool, square-jaw (ibid.: 132). This ambitious young man was popularised in advertising campaigns which extolled his modern outlook and business-like mode of dress.

The suit has remained the basis of the male wardrobe throughout the twentieth century. There have been some attempts to challenge the narrow range of men's fashions, notably from the British Men's Dress Reform Party which lasted from 1929 to 1937 and similar groups in other countries, including New Zealand, India, China, Australia, South Africa, Egypt, Costa Rica, Austria, the USA, and Canada (Burman and Leventon 1987). The reform movement aimed to rid men's dress of unhealthy and restrictive clothes by replacing the uniform of suit and shirt. In particular, they targeted the collar and tie, recommending a Byron collar instead. The shirt should be replaced by a decorative blouse making the jacket an optional extra. Breeches or shorts were recommended in the place of tight trousers, and sandals instead of shoes. The movement actively promoted its views in pamphlets and newsletters, fashion parades and competitions. Generally, the reaction was one of ridicule in magazines like *Punch*, and scorn from the general public. One letter to the *Daily Sketch* warned: 'In my experience of life – nearly eighty years – unconventional dress leads to unconventional manners and a lower standard of society' (quoted by Burman and Leventon 1987: 80). The Reform Movement also reflected the shifting locus of fashion influence from Europe to the New World. No longer did London and Paris dominate ideas of male dress. Different climatic and working conditions in other countries required different ways of dressing. In addition, mail-order, catalogues, and ready-to-wear became the main forms of selling clothes. The challenge to Europe was especially strong in America which slowly became the main influence on everyday men's clothing as opposed to high fashion.

Although the Men's Dress Reform movement was short-lived, it had a lasting impact on men's swimwear and on outdoor leisure and sports wear – though it is difficult to conclude whether these changes were in the air already or precipitated by the movement. In relation to swimwear, the movement opposed the heavy full costumes in favour of swimming naked or simply wearing slips. It also recommended the use of artificial silk instead of wool in manufacturing swimwear on the grounds that it was lighter and did not become water-logged because it had much greater water resistance. These changes were eventually taken up. The movement also advocated lighter and looser clothing for leisure wear, such as shorts and short-sleeved shirts for tennis. This was a radical innovation. American tennis player Bunny Austin overcame considerable self-consciousness when he first wore shorts at the 1932 United States Men's National Championship:

> I myself took over two years to summon up enough courage to wear shorts, although for years I had known how much more healthy, comfortable and reasonable they were for tennis. I hovered in my bedroom . . . putting them on,

taking them off, putting them on again, wrestling with the problem of Hamlet
– 'To be or not to be'. At last I summoned up all my courage, put and kept
them on, and wearing an overcoat to conceal them as much as possible, went
out of the hotel to play. My bare legs protruded beneath the coat and I slunk
through the lounge self-consciously. As I passed through the door an agitated
porter followed me. 'Excuse me, Mr. Austin', he whispered diffidently, 'but I
think you've forgotten your trousers'.

(Quoted by Schreier 1989: 115–16)

After some controversy and resistance to the exposure of men's knees and hairy
legs, these daring garments gradually gained acceptance. One enduring variant of
the suit, shorts and military uniform was the 'safari suit' which was made in
light-weight fabrics suitable for sub-tropical and tropical climates. Distinctive as
it is, with its military-styled jacket and shorts, the safari suit has retained a loyal
following in many post-colonial societies. More generally, innovations like these
acted as a catalyst for the manufacture of specialised sports and leisure wear.

But the movement had less effect on business clothing. Despite the practicality
of its recommendations, Burman and Leventon (1987: 85) argue that 'loose, soft
cloths, shortened arms and legs, and unstructured necklines of reform clothes'
failed to denote the 'visible authority' associated with tailored suits, stiff collars
and formal ties. In other words, by now, a rounded male silhouette was deemed
inappropriate for the serious disposition of working men denoted by the rectangu-
lar look of the suit.

The dominance of the suit as the appropriate dress for white-collar occupations
remained unchallenged. The basis of the modern man's wardrobe was set. Apart
from minor deviations and variations, twentieth-century American and European
men have been clad in shirt, trousers, and jacket. Fashion commentators have
consistently stressed the functional basis of men's clothes. For example, Elizabeth
Ewing argues that the development of the motor car led to more protective outer coats
for men and women to cope with the breezy ride (quoted by A. Hart 1984: 67–8).
Equally, the car (and motorised forms of public transport) induced a preference for
streamlined clothes which did not drag or get caught up when entering and alighting
from these vehicles. Also in line with increased mobility, sweaters were popularised
in the 1920s, enabling the expression of individual taste and giving an impetus to the
home-knitting industry.

The necktie generally replaced the cravat and the bow-tie, allowing men to exploit
its decorative value as 'an assertion of identity and social status' (Finkelstein 1991:
127). There have also been suggestions that the necktie 'links together the physical
symbols of virility' (from the larynx to the male sex organ), 'through the desire to
enhance the sexual attractiveness of the wearer and to draw attention to the genital
organs of the body' (ibid.: 121–2). Seen in this light, the infinite variety of the necktie
has been interpreted as a potent sign of male sexual identity.

The suit itself has also undergone various modifications in design during the
twentieth century (Kidwell 1989: 130–41). In the early years of the century,

men's suits created an oval shape with relatively narrow shoulders, flared coat, wide hips and tapered trouser legs: 'It took a series of revisions in specifications starting in 1926 with a change in the collar, to transform this oval outline to a roughly inverted-triangle silhouette by 1939' (ibid.: 130). Gradually the shoulders became the focus of the cut while simultaneously minimising the width of the hips. But although the trade magazines advocated the new line from 1926, the majority of men resisted the look until the late 1930s (ibid.: 132). Hollywood was an important catalyst for popularising the big-shouldered look which lasted through to the 1960s and was revived in the 1980s.

From the 1930s, there were attempts to define men's fashions in consumer categories. The American department store Sears, for example, distinguished the snappy dresser, the university or fashion-conscious man, the business man, and the conservative dresser (Kidwell 1989: 141). Minor variations in styles and details were targeted towards these groups.

Restrictions imposed in World War II on clothing had lasting effects through the 1950s and early 1960s on men's fashion. Nonetheless, there were some rearguard responses to these edicts. When, in 1942, the President of the British Board of Trade, Hugh Dalton, introduced measures insisting on single-breasted jackets, minimising the use of pockets and buttons, and limiting trousers to nineteen-inch wide legs, there was a mass objection to a further restriction on turn-ups (cuffs). Despite a plea to parliament by the nation's tailors, Dalton did not budge, responding: 'There can be no equality of sacrifice in this war. Some must lose lives and limbs; others only the turn-ups on their trousers' (quoted by A. Hart 1984: 70). The pared-down suit remained popular after the war though elaborated in other respects. But apart from various male style subcultures, such as the 1940s American 'zoot suit' subculture (Cosgrove 1989), the 1950s British Edwardian look and the Teddy boys, 1950s Australian bodgies, men were incontrovertibly conservative in their choice of clothing.

Pumphrey (1989: 96) recalls how older men in the 1950s and 1960s took pride in resolutely 'refusing to take notice of fashion'. Not only were there pressures for men to conform to conservative norms of dress, but there was 'an aggressive indifference to dress and a silent avoidance of bodily display' (ibid.: 96). By choosing to wear 'doggedly characterless dark suits', men demonstrably rejected 'the frivolous, superficial, ephemeral and trivial' (ibid.: 97).

Accompanying this display of uncompromising masculinity was a 'pronounced homophobia' (Chapman 1988: 233). Any indication of attention to dress or decoration by a man was looked on with suspicion. Yet, while aggressive masculinity and homophobic paranoia characterised codes of male dress and social etiquette, different attitudes graced 'the sports field, gym, running-track and beach . . . where momentarily those sanctions broke down – where the body could be rubbed, oiled, shown off' (Pumphrey 1989: 96). Sporting activities not only gave a licence to the display of the body but deliberately transformed the body into disciplined musculature. The male sporting body internalised a 'regimen of discipline, punctuality, obedience and attentiveness' (Miller 1990:

78) in order that the trained body could be displayed and admired. In contrast to male dress codes, the codes of sporting behaviour valorised exhibitionism, physical contact between men, and the display of physical attributes. Sport celebrated male muscularity which in turn was 'the *sign* of power – natural, achieved, phallic' (Dyer 1989: 205).

Perversely, normatively homophobic sportsmen have engaged in blatantly homoerotic activities (touching, embracing, kissing, cuddling) which elsewhere they would denounce. In other words, sport has been 'the privileged space of the legitimate gaze of male upon male' (Miller 1990: 82). Out of the sporting arena, however, the men have continued to eschew signs of masculinity and sexuality. Insofar as clothes articulate masculinity, they display attributes of strength and power rather than male sexual desire and homoeroticism.

The history of sports clothes demonstrates the slow acceptance of pragmatic requirements of physical exertion over a concern with decorum. It was not until the late nineteenth century that sportsmen exchanged their jackets and flannel trousers (modified forms of the business suit) for customised wear for sports such as football, gymnastics, basketball, baseball, tennis, swimming, riding and cycling (Schreier 1989: 92–120). Outfits like the jerseys, knickers and bright-red stockings adopted by the Cincinnati Red Stockings in 1867 were highly controversial at the time, since the freedom of movement they permitted was achieved by figure-hugging garments condemned as 'positively indecent' (Quoted by Schreier 1989: 104).

Not only have men been reluctant to wear clothes that exude sexuality but they have also been loathe to indulge in other behaviour associated with sexual display, including shopping (Pumphrey 1989: 97). By rejecting consumerism and other activities involving the projection of ideal transformations (through window shopping, romance reading, window displays, fashion parades, and fashion magazines), men have reiterated their serious, materialistic concerns and rejected effeminate wiles.

This situation began to change in the 1960s once some designers decided to take an interest in men's clothes as fashion. It was the start of a process that wrested male clothing design away from tailors, chain stores and wholesale manufacturers (A. Hart 1984: 71). The suit itself changed with the Nehru look, the Mao look and the use of outrageous fabrics. More generally, there was a 'movement towards light-weight, unstructured styles and the popularity of separates and casual clothes' (ibid.: 73). No longer was the suit the basis of the whole wardrobe. A separate set of leisure garments evolved. A distinction between the fashion of the workplace and the fashion of everyday wear became an important element of men's clothing. From the excesses of the 1960s – at least among some young men – men in general became a little more adventurous in the 1970s and 1980s. They experimented with a wider range of colours than before and were more adventurous in choice of garment and cut.

Recognition of this has come in the growth of men's fashion magazines such as *Vogue Men*, *Uomo*, *Cosmo Man*, *GQ*, *The Face*, *i-D* and *Arena* (Mort 1988;

Figure 8.3 Leisure wear and youth culture: trousers, jackets, jumpers and casual shirts. (Apprentice bricklayers in Berlin 1959.)

Rutherford 1988). Other magazines have incorporated special inserts or produced special issues for men. Not only do such magazines promote fashions but a range of other products for the contemporary man. Such strategies have not always been successful and numerous male-oriented fashion and lifestyle magazines have failed. One magazine, *The Hit*, published in the UK, was aimed at 15- to 19-year-old men, but failed after just six issues. Research suggested that the concept was fine, but that:

> unlike girls of the same age (and women in general) who identify strongly with a community of women, young men baulked at being spoken to as a community of men: 'they might like BMX bikes, waterskiing and the Jesus and Mary Chain, but they don't like magazines to suggest that other men

within their age group feel the same way as them'. In other words, speaking to young men as men is a risky business, because it targets men in gendered terms rather than the norm which defines everything else. Masculinity's best-kept secret is broken open.

(Mort 1988: 212)

The 1980s witnessed a sustained effort by advertisers to capture the male market. Of course, men are not a homogeneous market and advertisers have been at great pains to distinguish different demographic, lifestyle and consumer groups among men. At stake was 'the hyper-cultivation of the male body' (Mort 1988: 204) around new codes of masculinity, physicality, and dressability.

In order to appeal to male consumers, advertisers and marketers have to play on traditional associations of masculinity, such as individuality, competitiveness, mateship and aggression, while attempting to wean men into consumer identifications and relations. Garments like jeans proved to be useful vehicles for this transformation of men into consumers with dress sense and stylistic aspirations (Goldman 1992: 175–200).

Scheuring (1989) has examined the way in which the humble pair of jeans was transformed from practical, rural and blue-collar work-clothes into a fashion garment synonymous with youth. The break came in the 1950s when middle-class, white rock singers and film stars (such as Elvis Presley, Eddie Cochran, Gene Vincent, Marlon Brando and James Dean) adopted the Levi Strauss 501 style (with buttoned flies) and black leather jackets to convey a 'tough, rugged, youth-rebel appearance' (ibid.: 227). Their working-class and black counterparts, on the other hand, wore anything but jeans which were a reminder of their poor roots. Jeans were a symbol of middle-class revolt from the strictures of respectability and conformity. Parents frowned on their jean-clad offspring, some American colleges banned them from being worn on campus, and places like restaurants displayed signs prohibiting customers in jeans.

Perhaps more than any other object, jeans epitomised the values of 1960s youth culture. The success of Levi's meant that young men escaped the pressures of the male fashion industry and clung to this basic garment with minimal variations. Although Levi Strauss has remained a market leader, many other brands of fashion jeans (notably Lee and Wrangler) benefited from this growing sector. The fashion industry was desperate to turn jeans into a fashion commodity, subject to regular variation and stylistic change.

The popularisation of flares (trousers which flared out from the knee) provided new opportunities for jeans manufacturers who produced a range of designs and massively increased sales: 'now changes could be calculated and influenced' (Scheuring 1989: 229). By the mid-1970s, the wearing of jeans was no longer confined to workers and young men. New designs were produced for middle-aged 'swingers' who were young at heart but wide in girth (often with open-fronted shirts and gold neck chains). As the economic well-being of wearers of jeans increased, the fashion industry saw yet more possibilities.

Designer jeans were born. As well as carrying the designer logo and name, these exclusive jeans were cut to suit the particular proportions of the clients of designers. American designer Calvin Klein was the first to market signature jeans. When he introduced his 'refitted, well-cut' Calvin's in 1978, 200,000 pairs sold in the first week, even though they cost 50 per cent more than leading brands like Levi's (Grant 1992: 20). Klein capitalised on the exclusive associations of designer jeans, and promoted his clothes through explicitly sexual imagery. His best-known advertisement featured actor Brooke Shields, murmuring, 'You know what comes between me and my Calvin's? Nothing'. It was denounced as 'pornographic' but was highly successful (Grant 1992: 18). His success has been attributed to a combination of recognising women's desire to wear casual, com-fortable clothes; drawing on androgynous images and designing 'unisex' clothes for women and men; sexualising the image of designer labels; and adding the exclusiveness of a designer signature to the ubiquitous pair of jeans.

Sales of Calvin's jeans reached about $400 million world-wide in 1984. After a slump of several years, Calvin Klein attempted to revive sales in the early 1990s, partly through his use of provocative promotions. An advertising supple-ment for his denim collection was shot by radical photographer Bruce Weber for an issue of *Vanity Fair* (October 1991) around the theme of 'denim and skin' against images of a rock concert:

> The collection of sexually ambiguous images features male band members in jeans and leather jackets fondling nude, semi-nude and fully clad women, then undressing themselves and their dates. Included in the narrative are sculpted poses of male and female limbs entwined in bed, and a hunk in a shower engaging in what some interpret as masturbation.
>
> (Grant 1992: 20)

Although the advertisement created a storm, sales of his jeans rose by 30 per cent the following month, though this momentum was not maintained and Klein's empire remained shaky. Other designers have also jumped onto the designer-jeans bandwagon, though not always successfully. The best known include Gloria Vanderbilt, Liz Clairbourne, Versace, Guess, Donna Karan, and The Gap. In the United Kingdom, the label Joe Bloggs has taken 'an intrinsically American product', adapted it with 'embroidery and graphic detail', experimented with a range of colours, and attached very prominent signature labels, thus creating a parody of the signature but a highly distinctive (and therefore marketable) range of jeans.

As a result, jeans have become respectable dress, not only for leisure but for a casual, dressed-up look. While they have remained the mainstay of workers and youth, the latter constantly seek ways to mark out their choice of jeans as different from those of the fashion industry. While young people may tear, rip, appliqué, or tie-dye their jeans, designers produce 'sporty formal' denim suitable for more bourgeois lifestyles. Upwardly mobile men and women can look 'acceptably shabby'. The success of jeans as a ubiquitous fashion and a symbol

Figure 8.4 'Jeans couture': from hard labour to high fashion.

Source: Advertisement for Versace Jeans Couture, *Elle* (UK), April 1992. (Reproduced by courtesy of Versace UK.)

of youth testifies to the adaptability and opportunism of the fashion industry and to the mercurial tastes of the fashionable classes.

In sum, what is often regarded as the norm of men's clothing – namely, the lack of fashion and the lack of interest by men – is questionable. At most, this has been a recent historical and cultural aberration. While it is true that men's clothing in Europe has become plainer since the eighteenth century, it has still been subject to cycles of fashion in terms of preferred garments, style and cut, choice of fabric, colours, and modes of wearing.

What has marked out changes in men's fashion has been the association with the workplace. Clothes were the index of professional character. In particular, the business suit was associated with authority and status. In the corporate world, the suit was also associated with seriousness in so far as 'a similitude exists between the appearance of the individual and the demeanour, even personal character-istics, which s/he can be expected to possess' (Finkelstein 1991: 109). This aura of similitude also extended to moral qualities associated with the position adopted by the wearer. By treating clothes as an index of social and moral qualities, recent male fashions have celebrated the body itself and played down the decorative attributes of clothing and body decoration. The emphasis on the display of masculine attributes constitutes a profound challenge to western conventions of morality.

NEW MALE MODES

> The new man is many things – a humanist ideal, a triumph of style over content, a legitimation of consumption, a ruse to persuade those that called for change that it has already occurred.
>
> (Chapman 1988: 247)

Over the past decade, a new term has entered discussions of men and clothing – the New Man. The idea of the New Man has an implied counterpoint – the old-fashioned man. This man seems to be derived from several masculine types: 'the gentleman' who is 'styled and stereotyped as the strong and silent type' (Gentle 1988: 98); the action man who is 'virile, strong, independent and anomic' (Logan 1992: 88) and denoted by the cowboy, war hero and Marlboro Man; the slob who is functional but uninterested in speed and style; and the chauvinist who is authoritative and ambitious (but equally ruthless and a misogynist). While all may be recognisable, these types conflict and refer to different cultural attributes of masculinity. The new man is a contradictory composite: 'one who is becoming more self-conscious of what it is to be a man, and one who sees through the farce of masculinity and all the entrappings that accompany it' (Gentle 1988: 98).

The emergence of the New Man has been as much a reaction to the impact of feminism and changing opportunities for women as it has been a reassessment of masculinity itself. One outcome of feminism has been the characterisation of men in negative ways and attacks on 'macho' notions of masculinity. Alternatively, attributes of narcissism and nurturing have been added to codes of masculinity. Marketers have capitalised on these attributes by emphasising lifestyle marketing rather than simply product marketing (Chapman 1988: 228). The marketers' version of the New Man placed the male body at the centre of identity and sexuality. Appearance, and therefore narcissism, were central to this construction of masculinity. The New Man was not only aware of fashion but an active consumer in the pursuit of his sense of self.

The early 1980s British advertisement for Pure New Wool has been cited as epitomising new approaches to marketing the New Man (Imrie 1986). Instead of advertising comfortable cardigans for middle-aged men, the wool marketers developed the 'Beware a Wolf in Sheep's Clothing' campaign which was targeted at younger men who would not read the conventional wool advertisements because wool and fashion were thought effeminate. The advertisers 'developed the idea of the urban animal – a guy on the prowl . . . a loner who had no need of peer approval. It was a strategy to slowly persuade men into a new frame of mind regarding fashion' (quoted by Rutherford 1988: 33). The images and text undermined traditional ideas of masculinity and modes of representing masculinity while at the same time establishing new codes and re-establishing the power of the male gaze. In contrast to the usual spectacle of the female body, this advertisement offered viewers the sight of the male body:

> The model in the advert snarls his unease and disapproval, caught in a feminised image that strips him of his masculine power. His snarl, and the title of the ad, both warn the viewer (woman) that he still retains that animal predatory sexuality that is proof of his manhood. It's an image that confronts the insecurities of a masculine identity in doubt. The model disavows his passivity through his aggressive look, though demonstrating that he still has control over definitions of who he is.
>
> (Rutherford 1988: 32)

The advertisement was extremely successful in capturing the new image of a softer masculinity and in establishing reversed codes of voyeurism. A few years later, the advertisers launched another campaign, 'Wool Talks Your Language', which reflected the uptake of the new masculinity. This presented men as 'fashionable, stylish and emotional' and portrayed wool as 'an emotional fabric' (Rutherford 1988: 33). The two-stage campaign not only reflected constructions and representations of changing codes of masculinity, but demonstrated the new attributes required of 1980s masculinity.

Part of this new awareness entailed remodelling men's bodies and their clothes in terms of goods and images, and personal appearance, as well as behaving in 'less aggressive and less stereotyped' ways (Gentle 1988: 99). The new male fashions were unlikely to be worn by normative men and, indeed, Gentle concluded that the use of the term, the New Man, had more to do with changing roles of women than with changing codes of masculinity. The New Man conflated the emergence of a new male consciousness of being male and living up to the expectations of masculinity (cf. Seidler 1989; Hoch 1979) with the emergence of erotic fashion for men. Part of this process involved 'the emergence of another "new woman", in as far as these eroticised male garments were training women to sexually objectify men' (Gentle 1988: 99).

Changing codes of depicting men have been central to the New Man phenomenon. Traditionally, the female gaze was indirect – furtive glances from viewers and averted, demure gazes towards the camera. The male gaze, by contrast, was direct, dominating and castrating (Dyer 1989: 200). The structure of both gazes has been changing. Although male models still tend to look 'either off or up' or through the camera and spectator, the number of images directed at either male or female viewers and consumers has increased. As the nature of the male gaze has become more complex, conventional viewing relations have changed (ibid.: 201). The male body has been sexualised by dissection into fetishised objects of desire.

The New Man has prompted the fashion industry to distinguish different male markets in terms of lifestyles composed of attributes of personality, roles and prestigious imitation. Types include: the quiet family man (self-sufficient and family-oriented); the traditionalist (conservative, conventional, ordered); the discontented man (dissatisfied with his lot, suspicious, wanting a change); the ethical highbrow (aesthete, sensitive, ascetic, discriminating); the pleasure-oriented man (macho, hedonistic, impulsive); the achiever (forceful, ambitious, status-conscious); the he-man (action man, dominant, thrill-seeker); and the sophisticated man (intellectual, socially aware, cosmopolitan) (Bachmann 1978: 7–9). These types translate into three kinds of clothing groups: non-fashion basics, fashion basics, and high fashion.

Segmentation enables marketers to target particular demographic groups while taking account of lifestyle and patterns of consumer behaviour. Advertisers have found print to be the most effective advertising medium. Moreover, advertising is not restricted to male-oriented magazines. They are 'equally effective in "dual readership" magazines and woman-oriented magazines [such as] *Cosmo*' (Bachmann 1978: 9). Department stores, such as Bloomingdale's, cater for the range of male consumers by establishing different physical sales areas with names like Europa, Peterborough Row, The Traditionalist, The Sportsman, The Polo Man, and Saturday's Generation (Cohen 1978: 25). Through such strategies, marketers have developed a significant market for men's fashion products. According to Mort (1988: 194), a 'new bricolage of masculinity is the noise coming from the fashion house, the marketplace and the street'.

Throughout the 1980s, media and popular culture have anticipated the emergence of the rejuvenated peacock, a man who is aware of his body not just as a machine but as an object of sexual attraction enhanced by his choice of clothes and ways of wearing them. The New Man rhetoric has accompanied the intensified production of male fashions, and cosmetics. In the 1990s, two new kinds of masculinity were identified: the New Lad and Iron John. While the New Man has aged into a contented family-oriented lifestyle, the new boys are more outgoing

(Carter and Brûlé 1992: 49). The New Lad acknowledged the attitudes of the New Man but was more interested in a hedonistic lifestyle and male pastimes. Iron John was something of a throwback to the chauvinistic male. According to Carter and Brûlé, the three types could be distinguished in fashion terms. While Iron John dressed in practical, casual, non-designer clothes with boxer shorts for underwear, the New Lad preferred Versace, Montana and Calvin Klein – with Y-fronts underneath. The New Man chose Romeo Gigli, The Gap, Agnes B., and Nicole Farhi, with Paul Smith tropical boxer briefs as underpants. In short, the New Man has spawned variants of masculinity which exhibited distinct fashion statements.

As a result of these changes, men's fashion has become a growth industry. The length of fashion cycles of men's clothes has reduced as seasonal collections have become the norm. While the clothes are still more conservative and less extreme than women's, that is, still based on shirt, jacket, trousers and the suit, much greater variety of cut, colour and fabric has become possible. Male fashion also includes distinct categories of leisurewear, underwear, and specialist fashion wear. To accompany these developments, men's fashion boutiques have challenged the monopoly of gentlemen's outfitters, department stores and chain stores. A variety of composite looks have been achieved by adapting classical looks to contemporary images of youth. Not only are more collections of men's clothes available, but men have entered the modelling industry in significant numbers. The change has been reflected in the fashion magazines which regularly feature advertisements and specials composed of images of masculinity and male body parts.

Designers such as Jean Paul Gaultier, Giorgio Armani, John Galliano, Kenzo, Rei Kawakubo, and Yohji Yamamoto have deliberately pushed the limits of men's fashion by proposing new radical looks. Many have swapped the unisex themes of the 1960s and 1970s for androgyny and cross-dressing (Garber 1992), using softer fabrics, and flowing lines, for example, in shirts and trousers.

Meanwhile, women have taken to wearing men's shirts and modified men's suits, as well as 'His Pants for Her' underwear. Designer Romeo Gigli, acknowledging that many women prefer to wear trousers and men's shirts, has explicitly designed clothes for the androgynous couple, who share a wardrobe (Gerrie 1992: 39). At the more extreme end of high fashion, Gaultier has, for example, used 'feminine' fabrics like lace and silk, sexualised leather garments, and experimented with men's skirts (Gentle 1988: 99). His collections have created controversy because they question and undermine definitions of masculinity by creating clothes that are effeminate. Yet frequently Gaultier's ideas have had an impact on male fashion in subsequent modified versions. His early 1980s skirt, for example, was revived in the early 1990s as the 'skuit' (a mid-calf-length 'skirt' tailored in suit cloth), and promoted not as high fashion, but as a practical and comfortable alternative to trousers (Tredre 1992a: 8). Rather than being an aberrant form of male dress, versions of the skirt have been common historically and cross-culturally (for example, among the ancient Romans, among Arabs, Greek Imperial Guards, the Scottish kilt, sarong, kimono, shepherd's smock, and

Figure 8.5 'Tropical connections': customising the suit for the new masculinity and new lifestyles.

Source: Cover for Van Gils catalogue. (Reproduced by courtesy of Van Gils.)

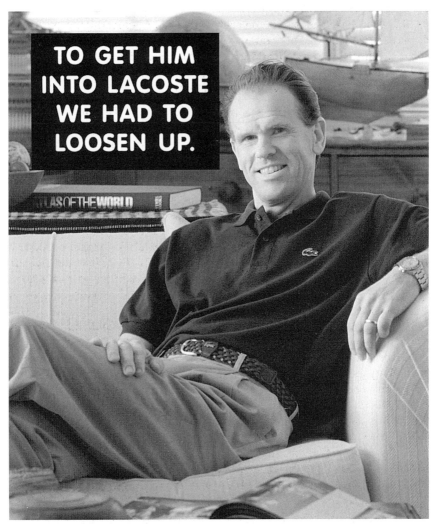

TO GET HIM INTO LACOSTE WE HAD TO LOOSEN UP.

Peter Hillary, Antarctic explorer and mountaineer, regularly gets into tight spots at work. Which is why he's very comfortable in our new loose fit polo. And with a choice of summer colours, we're sure there's one you'll feel at home in, too. The **new loose fit Lacoste polo** is available at Myer, Grace Bros., Aherns, Daimaru, David Jones, John Martins, Hanna's and Lacoste boutiques.

DDB Needham LAC 049

Figure 8.6 'Loosen up': the casualisation of men's fashion.

Source: Advertisement for Lacoste polo shirt. (Reproduced by courtesy of Peter Hillary, Lacoste and Sportscraft.)

so on). Religious and military garb has frequently incorporated 'female' items of clothing (see Garber 1992: 210–33).

Male models, too, make eye contact with the viewer, adopt sultry expressions, display their best masculine features, and allow their bodies to be dissected by the camera. Garber has shown that dress codes have established the boundaries of self through rules concerning status and gender, and the 'anxieties' associated with them. Calculated cross-dress (transvestism):

> was located at the juncture of 'class' and 'gender' . . . To transgress against one set of boundaries was to call into question the inviolability of both, and of the sex of social codes – already demonstrably under attack – by which such boundaries were policed and maintained.

(Garber 1992: 32)

Thus, codes of clothing conduct detailed the particular circumstances where 'transgressive' dressing was sanctioned, although even these circumstances were invested with ambivalence and anxiety. In western cultures, the popularisation of 'women's' dress for men, via a garment such as the 'skuit', would constitute a significant re-alignment of categories of gender and clothing. It would escalate changing conducts of masculinity, prompted by the relaxation of men's dress codes away from garments associated with authority and formality towards a greater range of outfits denoting informality and leisure.

Changing conventions of men's fashion have entailed re-worked attributes of masculinity that have transformed male bodies into objects of the gaze, of display and decoration. This radically undercuts the Victorian and post-Victorian idea of masculinity as the display of restraint in a disciplined body. The re-writing of male dress codes may have other implications. Finkelstein (1991: 134) has argued that the more frivolous, casual look of men, and their overt concern with their bodies and their looks, may reflect the changing status of men. No longer are they the sole representative of social power, or the primary worker dressed in 'business-like' clothes, but many men now share jobs or home duties, are students or, increasingly, are unemployed. Men's dress codes have been modified in accordance with these changed life circumstances. The growing acceptance of 'casual' wear for men has also modified the working wardrobe, with the 'leisure suit' and a range of jackets, slacks and shirts challenging the dominance of the formal suit, business shirt and tie. Once again, a process of 'trickle up' has allowed clothes not previously associated with the workplace and social elites to revise clothing codes for men. Conversely, as women move into careers, professions and high-status arenas, their wardrobes are incorporating aspects of traditional male dress. Even so, the differences between the clothing conduct of the middle classes and wealthy elites does not epitomise the fashion behaviour of other groups. Rules maintaining status and gender distinctions persist. A significant proportion of men and women have resisted overt decoration and display of the male body. The revival of the peacock may be some way off yet.

Chapter 9

Conclusion
Nothing to wear

FORMATIONS OF FASHION

> From what is taken by scholars to be the beginnings of an institutionalized fashion cycle in the West, namely fourteenth-century Burgundian court life, up to the present, fashion has repeatedly, if not exclusively, drawn upon certain recurrent instabilities in the social identities of Western men and women.
>
> (Davis 1985: 24)

The expression, 'nothing to wear', stems from the impulse to match clothes with a particular occasion in order to compose the appropriate social body. The phrase also expresses unease with one's vestimentary competence and uncertainty about one's composure. Techniques of dress are invested with tensions which Davis (1985: 24–5) relates to the instabilities on which fashion systems are based. A recurrent pattern of 'fashion-susceptible instabilities' has informed practices of western fashion, including:

> youth versus age, masculinity versus femininity, androgyny versus singularity, inclusiveness versus exclusiveness, work versus play, domesticity versus worldliness, revelation versus concealment, licence versus restraint, and conformity versus rebellion.

These oppositions map the extreme tensions in western culture concerning status, gender, occasion, the body and social regulation. The specificity of western fashion has been the inflection of these instabilities by the *scope* of consumerism. Different clothing codes can be seen as legitimate systems of fashion alongside western consumer fashion. However, other fashion systems have also played on instabilities inflected by other forces, including inchoate forms of consumerism and other modes of acquisition. In all cases, fashion systems establish technologies of self-formation through techniques of dress, decoration and gesture which attempt to regulate tensions, conflict and ambiguity. As Garber (1992: 27) has observed: 'Clothing – and the changeability of fashion – is an index of destabilisation'. This chapter explores three aspects of the specificity of western consumer fashion: characteristics and commonalities with precursors; consumer techniques of fashion that show how everyday fashion has become the dominant system; and the development of work and leisure fashion as major sub-systems.

Fashion and fashionable behaviour can be identified in many cultures and historical periods which predate 'consumerism'. For example, Foley (1973: 161) cites evidence of 'annual changes in smart stuffs and colours' and the attendant textile trade in ancient Greece. By the fourteenth century, fashion was an important element of European societies, as indicated by the imposition of sumptuary laws to prevent lower classes emulating or creating fashions; rapid fluctuations that turned master-tailors into labourers within a year; and the popularity of fashion dolls (or *Mademoiselles*):

> Before the end of the fourteenth century change in tastes had become frequent and extensive. The frequent denunciations of contemporary writers, who saw all class distinctions waning in the imitative scramble after new modes of dress, point to permanence and stability as rather the ideals of the few than the habit and tendency of the many, and reveal also the influence of changing taste on the conditions of production.
>
> (Foley 1973: 161)

In fifteenth-century France, the hold of fashion was such that Charles VII was petitioned to establish a ministry of fashion (Foley 1973: 167). The pace and orbit of fashion accelerated during the sixteenth century to the point where it was seen as undermining the authority of the court. Louis XIV and Charles II both attempted to impose dress codes in order to maintain the exclusiveness of the court and prevent the *nouveaux riches* from displaying their wealth (ibid.: 161; Minchinton 1982: 223). Similar processes occurred in England between the fourteenth and seventeenth centuries 'to ensure social legibility and enforce social hierarchy' (Garber 1992: 26). These were elaborated in most detail by Elizabeth I. One of the consequences of regulation was unintended. Rather than confining people to their designated rank, the laws provoked an intense interest in fashion and a desire to transgress the codes, both in a process of prestigious imitation and as an act of rebellion. The updating of laws supports the proposition that people frequently flouted the laws or found ways to get around them. Moreover, the quest for fashionable clothes was not confined to the rich, but 'infected all levels of society from the aristocracy down to the very labourers' (Lemire 1990: 255):

> Long before industrial production filled shops throughout the nation, the English were charged with an appetite for the current modes which transcended rank. Such general aspirations appalled moralists. Yet, high relative income was not as universal as the desire to have the semblance of style.
>
> (Lemire 1990: 256)

To obtain clothes they could not afford to buy, the fashion-conscious rented outfits, wore fakes, bought second-hand clothes, or stole garments. Theft of clothes was a major problem throughout the seventeenth and eighteenth centuries and soon was associated with a thriving black market organised by gangs of professionals:

> Thieves relied on public demand, so that whatever they stole would find a buyer; but the best profit would likely be made from the sale of good quality, fashionable clothing.
>
> (Lemire 1990: 261)

Lemire concluded that the spirit of consumerism was alive and well during this period, fanned by the popularisation of fashions in style. Already looking fashionable 'was central to the public presentation of the individual. Clothing was the apparent making of the man or woman – by all public calculations at any rate' (Lemire 1990: 257). This applied to all classes, not just the aristocracy. Although the rich could easily afford to look fashionable, lack of money was no obstacle to emulating fashions by other means. Indeed, 'prostitutes and mistresses were commonly said to be the most fashionably dressed and were sometimes innovators of fashion' (Minchinton 1982: 223).

By the nineteenth century, differences between the quality of clothes worn by different groups began to narrow. Economic expansion led to the growth of the middle class and increased disposable income among a wider strata of society. The circulation of fashion was enhanced by developments in textile and manufacturing technologies, and techniques of mass production and distribution (Kidwell and Christman 1974: 15–17). As it became possible to produce more goods more quickly, especially with the aid of machines for cutting, sewing and pressing, stores and salons expanded to cater for new markets. By the late nineteenth century, it was possible to distinguish elite fashion and its consumers (whose clothes were custom-made by dressmakers and couturiers) from a broader system of fashion among other social groups. The most significant changes to fashion occurred within this system. As the circulation of fashion magazines increased, and the development of paper patterns made it possible to make replicas of stylish modes at home, trends in fashion emanated from non-elite groups in competition with elite fashion.

The specific character of western consumer fashion was the size and reach of fashion products, and the accelerated rate of stylistic change, rather than consumerism *per se*. A range of commercial practices was adapted to the requirements of the fashion industry, including techniques of advertising and promotion, mass production, increased product range, multiplication and differentiation of markets, as well as new techniques of selling. These techniques underpinned the fashion process and shaped associated body techniques. Fashion became a tool of prestigious imitation among most social groups, the specific character of which was flavoured by techniques of gender; fashion and consumer knowledges, competences and habits; and by the circumstances of different lifestyles. Clothes were a key to the modern consumer's sense of identity.

CONSUMERISM UNLIMITED

Fashion provides for an orderly march from the immediate past to the proxi-
mate future. It is a reflection of a common sensitivity and taste. Fashion then
is the epiphenomenon of convention, the disciplining force of consumer
choices in the face of an expanding market of alternative goods.

(Minchinton 1982: 222)

The emergence of consumerism has already been discussed in previous chapters.
In relation to fashion, new techniques of selling were profoundly significant. The
hallmarks of fashionability were not simply extended to non-elite groups, but
became their lifeforce. Fashion became a vehicle of conspicuous consumption
and upward mobility: qualities of personhood were conveyed through the
fashioned body. Consumerism became a technique of self-formation requisite to
new conducts of life. Lang and Lang (1965: 341) concluded that 'the middle
classes are least resistant to the demands of fashion'. New modes have been
publicised through advertising and department stores more than through any
other medium.

One of the most interesting developments was the American innovation of
mail-order shopping, which extended the reach of fashion by creating new
consumer groups which boosted the market significantly. Mail order was a
convenient 'manual' of fashion because it enabled far-flung potential consumers
to follow fashion trends, select appropriate garments, and place an order for
ready-made, standardised clothes. At first, mail-order catalogues were
distributed among populations distant from urban shops. The mail-order firms
recognised the interests of their rural clientele by including farm supplies and
household goods along with clothing and fashion lines. In America, the first
company was Ward's (1872), followed by other major companies such as May,
Stern and Company (1882), and Sears, Roebuck and Co. (1893) (Kidwell and
Christman 1974: 161–4). The popularity of mail order soared. Department stores
also introduced mail-order departments, thereby supplementing their retail
activities and offering shoppers a choice between personal and distance shopping. The attraction was that a customer could be completely outfitted by the
stores without leaving home:

They acted as 'personal shopper', fulfilling ambiguous requests and
suggesting additional merchandise. Sears could send out five size-38 union
suits as promptly, and probably more cheaply, than John Wanamaker, but only
Wanamaker's would try to select a waist suitable for an elderly, dark-haired
woman. Some customers placed themselves entirely in the hands of their
favourite store: Filene's Personal Service Bureau chose every garment –
except for three dresses bought in Paris – in an Illinois woman's wardrobe.

(Benson 1986: 88)

Over ten million Americans were mail-order shoppers by the early twentieth
century. To meet demand, the Sears catalogue grew from 321 pages in 1894 to

1,064 pages in 1921. Women's wear quickly came to dominate the catalogue. Catalogues not only offered convenience but were a source of recreation, education and pleasure. They were the perfect means of showing off the products of mass production and distribution by sketching perhaps hundreds of new modes and models, emphasising new fashion features, teaching consumers about ready-to-wear and fitting garments. It was proof of the democratisation of fashion offering everyone affordable, stylish goods: 'there were few Americans who did not have the means of dressing reasonably well, and at moderate cost, immediately at hand' (Kidwell and Christman 1974: 165). The catalogue secured the legitimacy of ready-to-wear fashion and accelerated fashion trends among ordinary consumers.

Despite the spread of chains of department stores, discount stores and specialist boutiques, the catalogue has remained popular throughout the twentieth century. Between 1972 and 1975, the sales value of mail order exceeded that of retail for clothing in Britain (Hay 1976: 41). One consequence of the success and longevity of mail-order fashion has been that the size and resilience of the non-elite fashion sector has been a significant factor in the development of fashion markets. Because of the lead-time in producing catalogues and sufficient quantities of merchandise, 'mail order companies must be able to distinguish the influential fashion trend from the gimmick' (ibid.: 19). In addition, because mail-order consumers are generally over-represented in the socio-economic classes C and D, potential shoppers are less persuaded by newness and nowness than a sound bargain and a reliable product. Catalogues have remained a major part of the fashion industry and a significant source of knowledge about products and stylistic change for consumers.

With the production of catalogues for personal shoppers as well, consumers can combine personal shopping with catalogue browsing, selection and complementary purchasing. In America, mail-order sales have exceeded those in discount stores and have grown 7 per cent annually since 1981. In 1989, Americans spent $77 billion on mail order (Anon 1990b: 70). A study of American and Canadian catalogue shoppers found that 'nonstore retail sales are growing at a rate 50 per cent faster than traditional store sales' and that 'catalogue shopping is one of the most popular forms of nonstore buying' (Gerht and Carter 1990: 220). These shoppers are motivated by convenience and/or recreation (the enjoyment of browsing through catalogues):

> While Canadian shoppers generally are attracted to catalogue shopping because of the convenience and the intriguing technology provided by such methods, U.S. shoppers view catalogue shopping as more of a recreational process.
>
> (Gerht and Carter 1990: 225)

Because of their effectiveness as a selling technique, and their popularity with consumers, catalogues have diversified their appeals, especially towards high fashion and niche fashion markets in urban areas. Sometimes, the target consumer is defined in very specific terms. For example, the Banana Republic chain of fashion boutiques targets 'a white woman, 25–44, college educated, single or married, one child at home, professional with an income of $30,000 or more' (Lester 1992: 82). The lifestyle associated with these attributes is busy and cosmopolitan, with an appreciation of *objets d'art*, exotic cultures, a desire for romance, and a penchant for travel. The 'adventurous' clothes and 'foreign' settings depicted in the catalogues complete the parameters of this consumer's habitus.

Yet, despite the centrality of catalogues to consumer fashion, there has been little academic research into the mail-order industry and consumer habits, such as how they form fashion competences, influence shopping and clothing practices, and form 'taste' (though see Lester 1992; Roderick 1992). In contrast, designer fashion has received attention far in excess of its influence on clothing conduct. As a result, studies of fashion have underestimated consumer discrimination and influences on the shape of the industry.

As noted in Chapter 3, the role of ordinary consumers in the formation of fashionable looks was also symbolised by the development of the paper-pattern industry which, from the 1850s, enabled people at home to adapt modes and styles to their own tastes and budgets (Walsh 1979). By the 1870s, the industry was enormous. Butterick's, the largest company, increased sales from over four million patterns in 1870 to over six million in 1871 (ibid.: 307). Initially, paper patterns were an American phenomenon that appealed to new settlers and immigrants seeking to improve their circumstances (Kidwell and Christman 1974: 15). Fashion was seen as something that emanated from Europe to America. The paper-pattern industry provided the opportunity to reverse the flow. European sales of paper patterns grew quickly, and although they did 'not match those at home, they pointed the direction for future exports of American consumer culture' (Walsh 1979: 313). In fashion terms, the growth of home sewing and the rise of department stores shifted the dynamics of fashion away from elite groups towards average consumers.

Techniques of consumerism have also inscribed attributes of gender in particular ways, such that femininity has become an achievement based, in part, on the mastery of consumer competencies. A consumer culture directed at women selling women an image of ideal selfhood was nurtured through advertising, shop windows, consumer tie-ins with Hollywood, and the images presented in women's magazines (Eckert 1978; Gaines and Herzog 1990; Reekie 1991). Techniques of market research combined with psychological theories of personality and the rhetoric of fashion coalesced in the new 'science' of selling. It was directed specifically towards women who were the major shoppers. Indeed shopping and 'instinctive' feminine qualities were explicitly associated and promoted:

> The sales experts' perception of women as instinctively concerned with the care of the home and family reveals an unspoken assumption that women were

naturally and biologically suited to mothering, and therefore to shopping. This form of biological determinism, in which men were perceived as producers and women as consumers, underpinned much of the new marketing psychology.

(Reekie 1991: 366)

The idea was also promoted that women 'were fickle' and attracted to anything new (Reekie 1991: 367), thereby legitimating the 'need' to constantly update fashions and introduce new styles in seasonal collections:

> Although clothing – ready-made, custom- and semicustom-made – was only one kind of merchandise displayed for all to see, the quantity and diversity of apparel offered surpassed the inventories of all but the very largest clothing speciality stores in major cities. Apparel for the entire family was shown under one roof, in an extensive series of salerooms and display areas, punctuated by garments arranged on headless figures and on plush or horsehair-covered stools, benches, divans, and settees.

(Kidwell and Christman 1974: 159)

Shopping became a popular pastime for women, offering them access to a public space, conviviality, fantasy and freedom. But it was a highly specialised activity, invoking particular competencies, habits and knowledges. The stores offered customers a wide range of services including telephones, checkrooms, lost and found services, free delivery, gift suggestion departments, mail- and telephone-order departments, barber shops, post offices, bus services, and shoe-shining stands (Benson 1986: 85). Department stores offered a full day's entertainment and pleasant surroundings. The significance of shops as a specifically female institution cannot be overestimated. Department stores were perhaps the only major public institution designed for women to emerge from industrialisation. Not only did they cater to 'feminine' tastes and habits, they purported to embody equality and democracy: 'The palace of consumption, with its myriad services, appeared to be a relatively democratic institution; the free-entry and one-price policies in theory guaranteed the same reception and treatment for all' (ibid.: 89). The appearance of openness softened the often rigid stratifications and differentiations between consumers that were at the core of the organisation of department stores. In addition to gender attributes, customers were specifically addressed in terms of wealth, lifestyle and 'fashionability', both between stores and within stores.

The growth of ready-to-wear and department stores radically impacted on the very idea of fashion. Exclusive high fashion became marginal to the expansion of the everyday fashion industry. Sales of ready-to-wear netted unimaginable profits. As the exclusiveness and viability of *haute couture* was threatened, designers turned to those larger, mass markets. The introduction of *prêt-à-porter* lines by the Paris couturiers was a recognition that everyday fashion was the dominant system despite the pretensions maintained by *haute couture* (Brenninkmeyer 1965: 270–2; Lang and Lang 1965: 323–5).

Yet the connections between high and everyday fashion were complex. Leopold

(1992) has argued that the emphasis on the narrow elite market and assumption of a trickle-down effect, has overlooked the characteristics of the supply-side of everyday fashion. It has been assumed that the one-off basis of *haute couture* was simply overwhelmed by techniques of mass production in the everyday fashion industry, and that associated techniques of mass distribution and consumption provided the means to popularise styles among wider markets. Instead, Leopold suggests that the organisation of high fashion around uniqueness, individual skill and stylistic change was reproduced in everyday fashion, and undermined the full application of mass production techniques:

> the seemingly anarchic and rapidly changing proliferation of style in women's clothes, a feature that has distinguished it not just from other industries but also from other branches of the clothing industry, has served as a substitute for technical innovation, arising not in response to a rise in incomes or to changes in consumer preferences or to the exhaustion of possibilities arising from early mass production, but rather from the industry's failure ever fully to embrace mass production techniques.
>
> (Leopold 1992: 102)

Thus, although fashion production was infected by the rhetoric of mass production, it has in fact resisted mechanisation and relied on the single sewing machine and hand-finishing techniques. Indeed, 80 per cent of a sewer's time is spent in 'garment handling' rather than sewing (Leopold 1992: 105). Where developments in aspects of production have occurred, they have perpetuated the use of individual labour. Innovations have included specialised machinery (for button-holing; blind-stitching, overedging, etc.); specialised workers organised into section work (doing just sleeves, collars or cuffs); and jobbers or middlemen who concentrate on selling styles to retailers, then subcontracting out production. These changes have further fragmented the industry, reduced profit margins and planning cycles, and eroded conditions in the industry. Leopold suggests that, because the industry has strived to achieve the look of hand-sewing and hand-finishing, its capacity to embrace true mass production techniques has been limited.

This tension has enabled *haute couture* to maintain and trade on its exclusive image of the hand-crafted garment, as well as the made-to-measure ethos of specialist firms or sections of department stores. Even the rise of 'line-for-line' copies of designer outfits for sale in department stores forced 'the dressmaking industry to adapt hand-sewn garments to machine production, i.e., to mimic the very techniques of manufacture it was designed to replace' (Leopold 1992: 110). At the other end of the market, the introduction of 'price lines' incorporated differences in quality and finish into products and 'acted as a further disincentive to both cheapening and standardising production' (ibid.: 112).

Greater changes came with the popularisation of the idea of 'separates'. Instead of buying complete outfits, demand increased for wearing jackets, trousers, sweaters and skirts which could be bought separately and incrementally (the forerunner of mix-and-match):

Each of these so-called 'little ticket' items was cheaper to produce – and to buy – than the 'big ticket' item which it replaced. Wardrobes could be infinitely extended by the incremental addition or substitution of relatively inexpensive individual garments. Items which quickly became unfashionable could be discarded without guilt. Small-scale clothing purchases could be made continuously.

By this means, clothing was transformed from a consumer durable to a non-durable good.

(Leopold 1992: 113)

The idea of obsolescence in fashion was suited to separates. The 'need' for seasonal updates of styles and lines complemented this trend. In other words, the mass market was driving the production of a number of different lines of goods, based on a fashion theme, and directed towards particular market shares. Rather than revolutionising the production techniques themselves, the impact of mass production in the textile industry (in terms of capital investment, concentration and scale) coupled with the development of cheaper synthetic fibres, provided the possibility for satisfying market fractions by producing a range of fashion apparel that varied in quality (and was priced accordingly). The beauty of this strategy was that limited numbers of each line preserved the illusion of exclusivity and quality:

Rather than cheapening its products, [the industry] has turned more to the custom-made end of the spectrum, relying more heavily on those aspects of design which increase the cost differentials between its own products and those mass-produced in the hinterlands. It has then exploited this reputation by using its top-of-the-line activity (which is largely unprofitable for most firms) as a loss leader for designer brand, ready-to-wear price lines pitched to lower income groups.

(Leopold 1992: 114)

In other words, high turnover was achieved by constantly updating styles and differentiating between product lines. The consequences have been that the apparel manufacturing industry has remained highly exploitative, fragmented and volatile, partly due to the practice of employing women in circumstances which impede industrial regulation (cf. Coleridge 1989: 104–16; Phizacklea 1990; Kidwell and Christman 1974; A. Taylor 1983; Goldstein 1988a, b; Anon 1990a, b). In recent years, the focus of the textile and apparel industries has steadily moved from European centres to Asian countries, where wages are lower and output is higher. The industry relies on small sweatshops (often employing twenty to thirty people) producing bulk orders to strict deadlines. By using unskilled labour drawn from disadvantaged groups (either using cheap labour in poor countries or immigrant women in western countries), it is difficult to regulate working conditions. Each workshop produces a specified quantity or contracts the work out to piece-workers at home. Garments that cost just $2 to make sell for $30 to $40 overseas (Coleridge 1989: 109). Profits are made by the jobbers and retailers.

The implications of the development of fashion for mass markets have been that the role of *haute couture* was undermined while new fashion systems were created by the structure of production processes within the industry. A trickle-up phenomenon has been a feature of this process as consumers have sought out higher-quality, more exclusive clothes and labels. The designer label was a guarantee of quality and a sense of timelessness that transcended the whims of the high street. Epitomised by Dior's New Look and Chanel's little suit, forward-looking designers capitalised on the shift from the '*atelier* to the global corporate conglomerate' (Steele 1992: 125). The popularity of *prêt-à-porter* collections enabled Paris fashion to revive in the post-war years (L. Taylor 1992: 127). Designer houses and post-war governments stressed the message that 'You cannot divorce trade and creative art' (ibid.: 137). Paris adopted the promotional and marketing techniques of the high street, especially appealing to new markets in Britain, the United States and South America. The French fashion industry regained its position in terms of setting trends in style, though increasingly it interacted with other centres of fashion – notably New York, London, Milan and Tokyo.

Not only were clothes now designed for mass markets, the licensing of designer names for a range of accessories and other consumer products soon proved to be far more profitable than the fashion side of the design business. The name of the designer was a lure in itself, a guarantee of quality and stylishness. So fetishised have certain designer labels become, that a profitable business in fakes and counterfeits has developed (Coleridge 1989: 283–90; Stead 1991: 34–41; Warneminde 1991: 36–41). Although registered labels are covered by intellectual property rights over copyright, design and trademark, it is difficult and expensive to prosecute counterfeiters. While some companies spend large amounts on exposing scams, others are flattered by the imitations. Counterfeits have become a commodity in themselves: 'the vogue is to wear not the genuine item but the fashionable facsimile' (Stead 1991: 41). Once again, counterfeit emphasises the distinction between the hand-finished and the mass-produced item, either elevating the status of the former or revealing little difference between the 'real' thing and the fake. Indeed, counterfeiting is merely an overt form of the practice of prestigious imitation on which the fashion industry is based – namely, the popularisation of a new style or idea by its modification and differentiation for different markets.

FASHIONING WORK AND PLAY

One of the biggest changes that has occurred to post-war fashion systems has been the multiplication of fashions for everyday wear. No longer is fashion confined to formal clothes for display purposes. Fashions have developed for leisure and work situations. While work clothes emphasise practicality,

Figure 9.1 Leisure and pleasure unlimited: moving high fashion into high-street markets.

Source: Advertisement for Emporio Armani, *Elle* (UK), April 1992.

discipline and professional competence, leisure clothes compose attributes of relaxation, pleasure and 'being at leisure'. Western consumer fashion has become imbued with the twin themes of work and leisure as the organising principles of codes of clothing and fashion habituses.

Jeans have epitomised the growth of leisure clothes. As outlined in Chapter 8, jeans have undergone a series of adaptations to new markets and occasions – including tough work-clothes, male youth anti-fashion, youth (male and female) high fashion, and elite designer fashion. Levi Strauss has even marketed the 'Dockers' range for ageing and expanding waist-lines (*The Economist*, 22 June 1991: 67). Since the average westerner owns between three and six pairs, jeans are a billion dollar industry (Filmer 1992: 43). But, despite the new fashion versions of jeans, the originals have become high status items. For example, the enduring popularity of Levi's 501 buttoned jean has countered the conventional wisdom that fashion always seeks newness. Public demand has forced the company to continue to manufacture original designs (Leopold 1992: 115), while original models have become status symbols. For example, pairs of Levi's which featured 'LEVI' in capitals on the famous red tab (they changed to using a small 'e' in 1971) have become a collector's item, worth up to $10,000 a pair (Hamilton 1992: 12; Filmer 1992: 45).

As a component of the fashion system, jeans have been adapted to different occasions, statuses and habituses. The humble origins of jeans reinforce the point that fashion does not automatically emanate from elite groups but may often reflect the establishment of distinct identities and lifestyles among everyday or subcultural groups. In the case of jeans, the process of prestigious imitation occurred last among elite groups, and, even then, amid resistance.

Like jeans, their usual complements – T-shirts, jackets and runners – also had humble beginnings. They, too, have become huge industries. The T-shirt evolved from the white under-vest worn beneath a shirt. By the 1950s, the under-vest could be worn without a shirt and became known as the T-shirt. Hardly a promising garment for fashion, the cotton T-shirt has surpassed all expectations. Variations in cut and colour, plus printed motifs and embroidery, have made the T-shirt a ubiquitous fashion item with endless variations, providing cheap, accessible, transient indices of style.

Leisure jackets were based on the suit jacket but tended to be less structured and softer. Alternatively, leather jackets, popularised by the airforce, Hollywood and biker culture, have had an enduring popularity.

Runners have also evolved from cheap, canvas or leather shoes specifically designed for running and sport, to become a fashion statement. Their elevation to fashion came about with the popularity of organised gym exercise and aerobics, which conflated the health connotations of sport with fashion – and prompted the production of high-fashion outfits in the form of leotards, tights, jock-straps and exercise boots. The other influence was American black street and music cultures which adopted runners as practical and comfortable footwear, then jazzed them up to be distinctive.

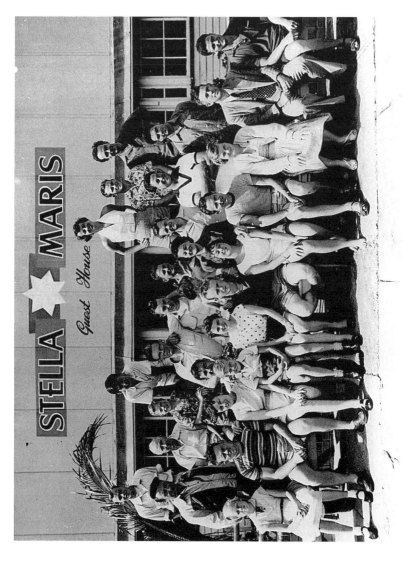

Figure 9.2 'Stella Maris': Everyday fashion on vacation. (Guests at Stella Maris guest house, Coolangatta 1954.)

Runners have become a multinational business, worth over $6 billion annually in America. They have come a long way from the basic functional shoe, offering a range of styles and special features (such as cushions, pumps and super-long tongues) to persuade consumers to update their wardrobes. Different coloured runners provide the possibility of colour coordinating shoes with clothes. As a result, 80 per cent of Reeboks are bought for panache, not performance (Anon 1992: 71).

In the case of each of these leisure fashions, the transformation of a garment into a fashion item has entailed a trickle-up process, and established imitative techniques based on particular, non-elite lifestyles and practices. These examples suggest that the fashion process is not only dynamic, but always under challenge from non-elite groups and forces that articulate certain instabilities in dominant western culture.

As the possibilities for variations on the theme of jeans have expanded, so too have other types of leisure wear. Stores are now dominated by fashions for more informal lifestyles and for occasions and activities associated with periods of non-work. The idea of leisure wear is perfectly suited to the built-in obsolescence of the fashion industry by offering the potential to create infinite variations on a theme or updating leisure looks. Chains of stores like The Gap, Benetton, and Esprit specialise in fashionable leisure wear for a slightly up-market clientele. Chain and department stores feature leisure wear as the major part of their apparel range.

Designers such as Calvin Klein, Katharine Hamnett, Norma Kamali and Ralph Lauren have also specialised in leisure clothes. Leisure is big business. From a consumer's point of view, leisure is also a conduct of life which must be regulated and managed. Leisure clothes compose the attributes of particular occasions and performances. The growth of leisure wear reflects the restructuring of consumer societies, and an increase in non-work modes of existence.

While leisure is relatively new for the majority of people, the specification of specialised clothes for work has a longer history. Some jobs have developed around a distinctive form of dress (for example, cooks, bakers, butlers, maids, gardeners, cleaners and nannies, religious and military officers), but the separation of workplaces from the home enhanced the idea of special work-clothes and uniforms.

While some work-clothes were designed as protective clothing, most 'function either as a badge of professional status or as an emblem of service' (Steele 1989c: 67). As well as combining characteristics relating to professional competencies, status and practical action, work-clothes also construct attributes of gender. Work-clothes for men have always been less extreme and less controversial than those for women.

As shown in Chapter 8, the suit has been the basis of male work-clothes and hence has standardised the range of possible variations and limited the number of radical changes. The suit is also the basis of school uniforms for boys, in the combination of shirts and trousers with tie and jacket (a variation on the suit).

Figure 9.3 Neither feminine nor masculine: the ubiquitous three-pleated girls' school uniform. (Class of St. Aloysius Girls' School, Sydney 1951.)

By contrast, girls' and women's uniforms have eschewed 'feminine' forms of dress, although they have retained the skirt as the basis of the uniform. Yet although trousers have been (and still are) resisted, female uniforms have incorporated features associated with masculine and military garments – such as epaulets, ties, blazers, and 'men's' shirts (Craik 1989: 18–19; Garber 1992: 21–5). On the one hand, they play down femininity and the female body shape, but, on the other, they problematise gender by rejecting equivalence with male uniforms. Garber (1992: 24–5) cites the problems faced by the United States military in designing uniforms for female cadets, which were neither too 'masculine' (trousers and short hair) nor too 'feminine' (revealing female contours). Adaptations to uniforms (in the United States and elsewhere) have entailed 'designing' a middle path, by 'feminising' masculine components and introducing 'feminised' ones (such as tailored slacks or skirt with a plain shirt), as well as encouraging women to wear make-up.

The military legacy is a feature of most uniforms. For example, police uniforms were explicitly modelled on army uniforms with the aim of conveying authority and distinguishing police from civilians. Thus, early New York policemen's uniforms featured great-coats, trousers, rows of buttons, shield and cap, elements of which still persist.

By contrast, policewomen wore long skirts, bodices with buttons, a badge – and carried a gun in a handbag (Steele 1989c: 67–71). Whereas the men's uniform was designed to be practical (that is, complementing the attributes of the work of police), the women's uniforms were strictly 'feminine' and restricted the duties they could perform, or, rather, determined that they could only perform duties that did not require extreme physical exertion. Hence, the duties of policewomen have centred on welfare, domestic incidents, public relations, and clerical work. It was not until the 1980s that trousers became an option for women police. Contemporary uniform manufacturers offer two styles: 'the law enforcement knockoff . . . and the "soft look" uniform – blazer and slacks – for the growing number of clients who prefer their security low-key' (ibid.: 72).

Gender differences were also incorporated in uniforms that offered protection. These first developed in blue-collar jobs where the day suit was inappropriate. Early innovations were jeans, the dungaree, and the boilersuit. These were worn by men; women in blue-collar jobs wore skirts, aprons and coveralls. Not until World War II did significant numbers of women wear trousers and boilersuits when they were employed as mechanics and in hard physical jobs.

A second kind of protective clothing was based on the laboratory coat. This was adopted by doctors (especially surgeons) in the 1890s, apparently to stress the scientific nature of medicine (rather than for reasons of hygiene as is often assumed). By contrast, doctors' assistants, nurses, acquired a very different kind of uniform, rather more like that of a maid (striped or gingham dress with bib and apron, cap, cuffs and collar) (Steele 1989c: 76). The role of the nurse was thus composed as one of service, caring and subordination. In other words, these medical uniforms reflected the gender attributes accorded to each occupation.

Figure 9.4 Naval influences: school uniform based on the sailor's suit with patterned skirt and silk stockings. (School girls in Shanghai circa 1920.)

Accordingly, changes to medical uniforms have only occurred since more women have entered medicine and more men have become nurses.

As these examples suggest, uniforms are a clothing genre that starkly highlights the differentiation of status, competence and gender. The idea of workclothes has drawn on indicators of authority and power, physical labour, and science. Since these correspond to attributes of masculinity, uniforms impose ambiguous identities on women. Where occupations have required other competencies – such as office work (specifically typing, clerical and personnel duties) – the possibilities for work-clothes for women have been greater, though again, clothes were designed to be practical and professional without looking ultra-feminine or ultra-masculine (Steele 1989c: 84). Tailored suits, office dresses, shirts and skirts worn with high heels became the basis of office wear. Trousers have remained on the fringes:

> a tailored suit with a skirt created an image that combined the supposedly practical, business-like uniformity of the man's suit with *a bland statement of female gender*. Such a costume said in effect: I am a business woman, not an imitation man; but while we are working, please treat me as a colleague.
>
> (Steele 1989c: 87)

While office dressing differs for secretaries, service staff and clerks from professionals, women in all jobs are admonished not to over-emphasise either feminine ('sexy') or masculine ('mannish') attributes – equal opportunity and sexual harassment provisions notwithstanding. A survey of jurors found that the credibility and authority of female lawyers was influenced by the choice of neckwear. Those wearing men's ties, bow-ties or ascot ties were judged less well than those wearing soft ties:

> The best tie was a long, narrow scarf tied in a flat knot and tucked inside the buttoned jacket – giving an 'effect similar to that of a man's tie, but with a softness that identifies the scarf as belonging to a woman . . . ' The second most positive response went to the traditional woman's bowed blouse – the floppy bow-tie.
>
> (Steele 1989c: 90)

As the gender-associations of uniforms and work-clothes have become less differentiated, the genre of clothes for the workplace has become increasingly specialised and elaborated into a distinct fashion system. For example, 'dressing for success' has accompanied the move of women into business and professions, necessitating a more formal, authoritative look based on – but distinct from – the men's business suit (Horin 1983; Norwood 1987):

> The professional woman's business outfit neither effaces femaleness nor exaggerates it. It seeks instead . . . to give businesswomen 'a look of authority'. The authoritative look for women's business wear is an attempt to isolate certain of the properties of male business clothing and incorporate them into female fashion. The object of this undertaking is to give businesswomen new credibility, presence, and authority in the business world.
>
> (McCracken 1985: 44)

The secret of successful dress was deemed to be 'the detail of cut, style, quality and authenticity' which denotes 'professionalism and credibility' (Norwood 1987: 36). High-fashion looks were eschewed in favour of classic fashion with just a dash of elan in the accessories: 'Jewellery is a woman's signature, so it is important it is tasteful and not cheap' (ibid.: 38). The overall look was composed of attributes of professional competence appropriate to the occupation and

Figure 9.5 'Things worth sharing': unisex wardrobes and leisured lifestyles.

Source: Cover of Country Road catalogue 1991. (Reproduced by courtesy of Country Road, Australia.)

workplace situation. The professional woman's wardrobe also signalled gender attributes by choosing skirts over trousers, despite the widespread preference for trousers among women. Even women politicians, for whom the equation of trousers with attributes of seriousness and competence might seem to be an advantage, typically wear skirts. As Soh noted in her study of Korean women politicians:

> skirts remain the only proper dress for women in certain occupations and social categories. Neither the Queen of England nor Margaret Thatcher as Prime Minister have ever been seen in trousers at official functions.
>
> (Soh 1992: 382)

As women's active incorporation into mainstream sections of employment has been acknowledged, an increasing number of companies and businesses have adopted a corporate wardrobe in order to project a collective image and offer employees good-quality and stylish clothes at a good price (Lees 1988; Cosic 1992). Designers produce mix-and-match ranges that can be purchased selectively by staff. Designs have to be classic because the clothes should not look dated and because they have to fit many different body shapes. Because of regular updating, corporate wardrobes are a barometer of the generalisation of new fashion trends, reflecting new fabrics, lines, lengths and shapes.

The emergence of work-clothes and corporate wardrobes – and their integration into the fashion system – can be attributed to the centrality of work to the articulation of the self through the demonstration of status, competence and gender – where the work-clothes are part of the habitus of the workplace and distinguished from other non-work environments.

Clothes for work and leisure have articulated the dominance of gender in the organisation of western fashion systems by constructing separate dress codes for men and women, based on an opposition between the active (practicality) and the passive (impracticality and display). Although this distinction has been modified, gender attributes continue to dominate fashion design and behaviour, even in so-called unisex fashion and cross-dressing (Garber 1992). Western techniques of articulating gender have over-determined characteristics of status and competence in the actualisation of the social body of the western consumer.

Western fashion systems are also predicated on their claiming of the domain of fashion as a mark of their civility and distinction from other cultures. The insistence on demonstrating civility is visible in the tension between revelation and concealment that runs through western fashion behaviour. The incorporation of elements of exoticism constantly reinforces the difference and distinction between western and other forms of dress. This book has suggested that the distinction is over-played and unhelpful, overlooking the character of fashion systems as purpose-built body techniques.

Trends in western fashion in recent decades suggest that fashion is a pervasive feature of everyday living, and certainly not confined to, or determined by, *haute couture* or elite socialites. Clothing the body is a technique of every social body

Figure 9.6 'True blue revolution': fashioning jeans through parody.

Source: Advertisement for Joe Bloggs jeans, *Elle* (UK), June 1992.

through which the physical body is actualised in its habituses. Body parts are highlighted, concealed and juxtaposed by clothes which determine or constrain certain gestural ranges. The attributes of the person are worn. In that sense, clothes create the parameters of a person's living environment. Elite western fashion is just one arrangement of fashion as a body technique.

The argument of *The Face of Fashion* has been that there are many competing fashion systems. In respect of western consumer fashion, it has been suggested that elite designer fashion does not constitute all fashion behaviour, nor uniformly determine other sets of arrangements. Indeed, it is possible to identify distinct systems of fashion within elite and everyday fashion. Often, conditions of everyday life impose vestimentary regulations or changes that percolate through to elite fashion. Generally, however, fashion behaviour invokes rules and codes of dress, adornment and gesture to articulate attributes of the social body. At a collective level, fashion maps social conduct and, in turn, is shaped by it. Fashion statements appear to mark a moment, but the fashioned body is never secure or fixed. The body is constantly re-clothed and re-fashioned in accordance with changing arrangements of the self.

Bibliography

Adams, P. and Cowie, E. (eds) (1990) *The Woman in Question*, London and New York: Verso.

Almond, K. (1988) 'Public image versus private self: the tragedy of camp dressing', in J. Ash and L. Wright (eds), *Components of Dress*, London: Routledge: 95–7.

Anon. (1965a) 'Furore over fashions: far-out photography', *Time*, 86, 3 December: 42.

—— (1965b) 'Less for sea than seeing', *Time*, 31 December: 24–9.

—— (1973) 'The Australian *Women's Weekly*: depression and war years: romance and reality', *Refractory Girl*, Winter: 9–13.

—— (1987) 'What fashion "look" do men like best?', *Cleo*, October: 125.

—— (1990a) 'Europe – a thread of hope for UK textiles', *Labour Research*, July: 19–20.

—— (1990b) 'Pile 'em high and go bust', *Economist*, 7 July: 70.

—— (1991a) 'A comfortable fit', *Economist*, 22 June: 67–8.

—— (1991b) 'Slaves of fashion', *Economist*, 7 December: 84, 86.

—— (1992) 'Reebok: pumping up', *Economist*, 15 February: 70–1.

Art Gallery of New South Wales (1987) *Yves Saint Laurent Retrospective*, Sydney: The Trustees of the Art Gallery of New South Wales.

Ash, J. and Wright, L. (eds) (1988) *Components of Dress*, London: Routledge.

Ash, J. and Wilson, E. (eds) (1992) *Chic Thrills: A Fashion Reader*, London: Pandora Press.

Australian National Gallery (1986) *The Glamour Show: Studio Photographs 1925–1955*, 10 May-14 September, catalogue, Canberra: ANG.

Bachmann, G. (1978) 'Marketing information systems for apparel manufacturers and retailers', in E. Richards and D. Rachman (eds), *Market Information and Research in Fashion Management*, Chicago: American Marketing Association: 5–9.

Back, K. (1985) 'Modernism and fashion: a social psychological interpretation', in M. Solomon (ed.), *The Psychology of Fashion*, Lexington, Mass.: Lexington Books: 3–14.

Bailey, A. (1988) *The Passion for Fashion*, Limpsfield, Surrey: Dragon's World.

Bailey, D. (1985) *Shots of Style*, London: Victoria & Albert Museum.

Ballaster, R., Beetham, M., Frazer, E. and Hebron, S. (1991) *Women's Worlds: Ideology, Femininity and the Woman's Magazine*, Basingstoke: Macmillan.

Barber, R. (1992) 'Jeff Banks', *Clothes Show Magazine*, March: 27–31.

Barthes, R. (1982) *Empire of Signs*, New York: Hill & Wang.

—— (1984) *The Fashion System*, New York: Hill & Wang.

Bartky, S. (1988) 'Foucault, femininity, and the modernisation of patriarchal power', in I. Diamond and L. Quinby (eds), *Feminism and Foucault: Reflections on Resistance*, Boston: Northeastern University Press.

Bath Museum of Costume (1980) *Museum of Costume, Assembly Rooms, Bath*, catalogue, Bath (Avon): Bath City Council.

Batterberry, M. and Batterberry, A. (1982) *Fashion: The Mirror of History*, Bromley, Kent: Colombus Books.

Baudelaire, C. (1972) 'The painter of modern life', in *Baudelaire: Selected Writings on Art and Artists*, trans. by P.E. Charvet, Cambridge: Cambridge University Press.

Bayley, S. (1991) 'Fashion: being and dressing', in *Taste: The Secret Meaning of Things*, New York: Pantheon Books: 142–72.

Benson, S.P. (1986) *Counter Cultures: Saleswomen, Managers and Customers in American Department Stores 1890–1940*, Urbana: University of Illinois Press.

Berger, J. (1972) *Ways of Seeing*, Harmondsworth: Penguin.

Bergler, E. (1955) *Fashion and the Unconscious*, New York: Basic Books.

Bernard, B. (1978) *Fashion in the 60's*, London: Academy Editions.

Betterton, R. (ed.) (1987) *Looking on: Images of Women in the Visual Arts and Media*, London: Pandora.

Billyboy (1987) *Barbie: Her Life and Times*, Toronto: Banton Books.

Blumer, H. (1968) 'Fashion', *Encyclopaedia of Social Sciences*, USA: Macmillan and Free Press: 341–5.

—— (1969) 'From class differentiation to collective selection', *Sociological Quarterly*, 10, 3: 275–91.

Bonfante, L. (1990) 'The naked Greek: the fashion of nudity in Ancient Greece', *Archaeology*, September/October: 29–35.

Bordo, S. (1988) 'Anorexia nervosa: psychopathology as the crystallisation of culture', in I. Diamond and L. Quinby (eds), *Feminism and Foucault: Reflections on Resistance*, Boston: Northeastern University Press.

—— (1989) 'The body and the reproduction of femininity: a feminist appropriation of Foucault', in A. Jaggar and S. Bordo (eds), *Gender/Body/Knowledge: Feminist Reconstructions of Being and Knowing*, New Brunswick and London: Rutger University Press.

—— (1990) 'Reading the slender body', in M. Jacobus, E. Fox Keller and S. Shuttleworth (eds), *Body/Politics: Women and the Discourses of Science*, New York and London: Routledge.

Bourdieu, P. (1984) 'Haute couture et haute culture', in *Questions de Sociologie*, Paris: Les Editions de Minuit: 196–206.

—— (1986) 'The biographical illusion', *Actes de la Recherche en Sciences Sociales*: 62–3, 69–72 (trans. by D. Saunders).

Braden, M. (1991) 'Women: special again', *Washington Journalism Review*, 13, 5, June: 30–2.

Brain, R. (1979) *The Decorated Body*, London: Hutchinson.

Brenninkmeyer, I. (1965) 'The diffusion of fashion', in M.E. Roach and J. Eicher (eds), *Dress, Adornment and the Social Order*, New York: John Wiley & Sons: 259–302.

Brookes, R. (1980) 'Fashion: double page spread', *Camerawork*, 17: 1–3.

—— (1989) 'Sighs and whispers in Bloomingdales: a review of a Bloomingdale mail-order catalogue for their lingerie department', in A. McRobbie (ed.), *Zoot Suits and Second-Hand Dresses*, Basingstoke, Hampshire: Macmillan: 183–8.

Burman, B. and Leventon, M. (1987) 'The men's dress reform party 1929–37', *Costume*, 21: 75–87.

Byrde, P. (1987) '"That frightful unbecoming dress": clothes for spa bathing at Bath', *Costume*, 21: 44–56.

Cameron, S. (1978) 'Shades of things to come', *Financial Times*, 20 June: 19.

Caputi, J. (1983) 'One size does *not* fit all: being beautiful, thin and female in America', in C. Geist and J. Nachbar (eds), *The Popular Culture Reader*, 3rd edn, Bowling Green, Ohio: Bowling Green University Popular Press: 186–204.

—— (1991) 'The metaphors of radiation', *Women's Studies International Forum*, 14, 5: 423–42.

Carrick, J. (1987) 'Turn of the century posters: representing women', *Arena*, 79: 108–18.

Carter, A. (1978) 'Fashion: a feminist view', *Sunday Times Magazine*, 1 October: 50–5.

—— (1982a) 'Notes for a theory of sixties style', in *Nothing Sacred*, London: Virago.

—— (1982b) *Nothing Sacred: Selected Writings*, London: Virago.

—— (1982c) 'Unbridled sweeties', in *Nothing Sacred*, London: Virago: 95–9.

—— (1982d) 'The wound in the face', in *Nothing Sacred*, London: Virago: 90–5.

Carter, E. (1984) 'Alice in consumer wonderland', in A. McRobbie and M. Nava (eds), *Gender and Generation*, London: Macmillan: 185–214.

—— (1991) 'Review: Jane Gaines and Charlotte Herzog (eds), *Fabrications: Costume and the Female Body*, New York and London: Routledge, 1990', *Screen*, 32, 4: Winter: 483–91.

Carter, M. (1987) 'Fashion photography – the long slow dissolve', *Photofile*, Autumn: 5–7.

Carter, M. and Brûlé, T. (1992) 'Of mice and men', *Elle* (UK), April: 49–50.

Chaney, D. (1983) 'The department store as a cultural form', *Theory, Culture and Society*, 1, 3: 22–31.

Chapman, R. (1988) 'The great pretender: variations on the new man theme', in R. Chapman and J. Rutherford (eds), *Male Order*, London: Lawrence & Wishart: 225–48.

Chapman, R. and Rutherford, J. (eds) (1988) *Male Order: Unwrapping Masculinity*, London: Lawrence & Wishart.

Charles-Roux, E. (1989) *Chanel*, London: Collins Harvill.

Clark, A.K. (1987) 'The girl: a rhetoric of desire', *Cultural Studies*, 2, May: 195–203.

Clark, R. (1982) 'Norman Parkinson: 50 years of portraits and fashion', *British Journal of Photography Annual*: 35–45.

Cocks, J. (1988) 'Issey, an essay', in I. Penn, *Issey Miyake: Photographs by Irving Penn*, Boston: A New York Graphic Society Book: n.p.

Cohen, A. (1975) *Sonia Delaunay*, New York: H.N. Abrams.

—— (1978) 'A New York retailer looks at fashion', in E. Richards and D. Rachman (eds), *Market Information and Research in Fashion Management*, Chicago: American Marketing Association: 24–6.

Coleridge, N. (1989) *The Fashion Conspiracy*, London: Mandarin.

Corbin, A. (1986) *The Foul and the Fragrant: Odor and the French Social Imagination*, Cambridge, Mass.: Harvard University Press.

Cordwell, J. (1979) 'The very human arts of transformation', in J. Cordwell and R. Schwarz (eds), *The Fabrics of Culture*, The Hague, Paris, New York: Mouton: 47–75.

Cordwell, J. and Schwarz, R. (eds) (1979) *The Fabrics of Culture: The Anthropology of Clothing and Adornment*, The Hague, Paris, New York: Mouton.

Corrigan, A. and Meredyth, D. (1992) 'The body politic', unpublished paper, Faculty of Humanities, Griffith University, Brisbane.

Corson, R. (1972) *Fashions in Make up*, London: Peter Owen.

Cosgrove, S. (1989) 'The zoot suit and style warfare', in A. McRobbie (ed.), *Zoot Suits and Second-Hand Dresses*, Basingstoke, Hampshire: Macmillan: 3–22.

Cosic, M. (1992) 'Suited to the job', *Australian Magazine*, 12–13 September: 26–9.

Coward, R. (1987) '"Sexual liberation" and the family', in R. Betterton (ed.) *Looking On: Images of Women in the Visual Arts*, London: Pandora: 53–7.

Craik, J. (1984) 'Fashion, clothes, sexuality', *Australian Journal of Cultural Studies*, 2, 1: 67–83.

—— (1989) '"I must put on my face": making up the body and marking out the feminine', *Cultural Studies*, 3, 1: 1–24.

—— (1991) 'The gloss wears off', *Australian Left Review*, 130: 16–19.

Crawley, E. (1965) 'Nudity and dress', in M.E. Roach and J. Eicher (eds), *Dress, Adornment and the Social Order*, New York: John Wiley & Sons: 46–9.

Cunnington, C.W. and Cunnington, P. (1981) *The History of Underclothes*, London: Faber & Faber.

Danger, E.P. (1973) 'Colour trends and consumer preference', in G. Wills and D. Midgley (eds), *Fashion Marketing*, London: Allen & Unwin: 477–84.

Davidoff, L. (1973) *The Best Circles: Society Etiquette and the Season*, London: Croom Helm.

Davies, M. (1982) 'Corsets and conceptions: fashion and demographic trends in the 19th century', *Comparative Studies in Society and History*, 24: 611–39.

Davis, F. (1985) 'Clothing and fashion as communication', in M. Solomon (ed.), *The Psychology of Fashion*, Lexington, Mass.: Lexington Books: 15–27.

De Kupsa, C. (1978) 'A national manufacturer looks at fashion management', in E. Richards and D. Rachmann (eds), *Market Information and Research in Fashion Management*, Chicago: American Marketing Association: 10–17.

De Long, M. and Bye, E. (1990) 'Apparel for the senses: the use and meaning of fragrances', *Journal of Popular Culture*, 24, 3, Winter: 81–8.

de Marly, D. (1980) *The History of Haute Couture 1850–1950*, London: Batsford.

—— (1987) *Louis XIV and Versailles*, London: Batsford.

de Muth, S. (1992) 'And then Andrew looked in the mirror', *The Independent*, 2 April: 20.

Del Renzio, T. (1976) 'The naked and the dressed', *Art and Artists*, 10 March: 34–41.

De Neve, R. (1976) 'The fashion photo: from cool to kinky and how it got there', *Print*, 30, July/August: 24–33.

Derfner, P. (1976) 'The privileges of alienation', *Art in America*, 64, March: 42–3.

Derrick, G. (1992) 'Unfashionable, but good for fashions', *Business Review Weekly*, 9 October: 76–7.

Di Grappa, C. (1980) *Fashion: Theory*, New York: Lustrum Press.

Dyer, R. (1989) 'Don't look now', in A. McRobbie (ed.), *Zoot Suits and Second-Hand Dresses*, Basingstoke, Hampshire: Macmillan: 198–207.

Ebin, V. (1979) *The Body Decorated*, London: Thames & Hudson.

Eckert, C. (1978) 'The Carole Lombard in Macy's window', *Quarterly Review of Film Studies*, 3, 1, Winter: 1–21.

Elias, N. (1978) *The Civilising Process: The History of Manners*, Oxford: Basil Blackwell.

—— (1983) *The Court Society*, Oxford: Basil Blackwell.

Emberley, J. (1987) 'The fashion apparatus and the deconstruction of postmodern subjectivity', in A. and M. Kroker (eds), *Body Invaders: Panic Sex in America*, New York: St Martins: 47–60.

Etherington-Smith, M. (1983) *Patou*, London: Hutchinson.

Evans, C. and Thornton, M. (1989) *Women and Fashion: A New Look*, London, New York: Quartet Books.

Ewen, E. (1980) 'City lights: immigrant women and the rise of the movies', *Signs*, 5, 3 Supplement: S45–65.

Ewing, E. (1974) *History of 20th Century Fashion*, London: Batsford.

—— (1978) *Dress and Undress: A History of Women's Underwear*, New York: Drama Book Specialists.

Faurschou, G. (1987) 'Fashion and the cultural logic of postmodernity', in A. and M. Kroker (eds), *Body Invaders: Panic Sex in America*, New York: St Martins: 78–93.

Featherstone, M. (1982) 'The body in consumer culture', *Theory, Culture and Society*, 1, 2, September: 18–33.

—— (1987) 'Lifestyle and consumer culture', *Theory, Culture and Society*, 4, 1: 55–70.

Ferris Motz, M. (1983) '"I want to be a Barbie doll when I grow up": the cultural significance of the Barbie doll', in C. Geist and J. Nachbar (eds), *The Popular Culture Reader*, 3rd edn, Bowling Green, Ohio: Bowling Green University Popular Press: 122–35.

Filmer, D. (1992) 'Jeans', *Clothes Show Magazine*, May: 42–7.

Finch, C. (1991) '"Hooked and buttoned together": Victorian underwear and representations of the female body', *Victorian Studies*, 34, 3: 337–63.

Finkelstein, J. (1991) *The Fashioned Self*, Oxford: Polity Press.

Flügel, J.C. (1930) *The Psychology of Clothes*, London: Hogarth Press and The Institute of Psycho-Analysis.

Foley, C. (1973) 'Consumer fashion', in G. Wills and D. Midgley (eds), *Fashion Marketing*, London: Allen & Unwin: 157–69.

Foote, S. (1989) 'Challenging gender symbols', in C. Kidwell and V. Steele (eds), *Men and Women: Dressing the Part*, Washington, DC: Smithsonian Institution Press: 144–57.

Fotheringham, R. (1992) *Sport in Australian Drama*, Cambridge: Cambridge University Press.

Foucault, M. (1984) *The History of Sexuality*, vol. 1, Ringwood: Penguin.

Fox-Genovese, E. (1978) 'Yves Saint Laurent's Peasant Revolution', *Marxist Perspectives*, 1, 2: 58–93.

—— (1987) 'The empress's new clothes: the politics of fashion', *Socialist Review*, 17, 1: 7–30.

Frank, A. (1990) 'Bringing bodies back in: a decade review', *Theory, Culture and Society*, 7, 1: 131–62.

Freadman, A. (1988) 'Of cats, and companions, and the name of George Sand', in S. Sheridan (ed.), *Grafts: Feminist Cultural Criticism*, London: Verso: 125–56.

Friedan, B. (1976) *The Feminine Mystique*, Harmondsworth: Penguin.

—— (1991) 'Can a feminist be beautiful?', *Allure*, March: 60, 64, 66.

Frow, J. (1984) 'Spectatorship', *Australian Journal of Communication*, 5 and 6, January–December: 21–38.

Gaines, J. and Herzog, C. (1990) *Fabrications: Costume and the Female Body*, New York and London: Routledge.

Garber, M. (1992) *Vested Interests: Cross-Dressing and Cultural Identity*, New York and London: Routledge.

Gerht, K. and Carter, K. (1990) 'Serving the international buyer: U.S. and Canadian shopping orientations in store and catalog environments', *American Review of Canadian Studies*, 20, 2: Summer: 219–33.

Geist, C. and Nachbar, J. (eds) *The Popular Culture Reader*, 3rd edn, Bowling Green, Ohio: Bowling Green University Popular Press.

Gell, A. (1977) 'Magic, perfume, dream . . . ', in I. Lewis (ed.), *Symbols and Sentiments*, London: Academic Press: 25–38.

Genders, R. (1972) *Perfume Through the Ages*, New York: G.P. Putnam's Sons.

Gentle, K. (1988) 'The new male: myth or reality', in J. Ash and L. Wright (eds), *Components of Dress*, London: Routledge: 98–9.

Gerrie, A. (1992) 'Romeo Gigli', *Clothes Show Magazine*, March: 36–9.

Goffman, E. (1965) 'Attitudes and rationalisations regarding body exposure', in M.E. Roach and J. Eicher (eds), *Dress, Adornment and the Social Order*, New York: John Wiley & Sons: 50–2.

Goldman, R. (1987) 'Marketing fragrances: advertising and the production of commodity signs', *Theory, Culture and Society*, 4, 4: 691–726.

—— (1992) *Reading Ads Socially*, London and New York: Routledge.

Goldstein, C. (1988a) 'Hongkong borders on a garment-making boom', *Far Eastern Economic Review*, 25 February: 70–2.

—— (1988b) 'South Koreans fashion new corporate identity', *Far Eastern Economic Review*, 25 February: 72–3.

Goodyer, P. (1992) 'Love, sex and the dieting woman', *Cleo*, March: 74–9.

Gorden, W., Infante, D. and Braun, A. (1985) 'Communicator style and fashion innovativeness', in M. Solomon (ed.), *The Psychology of Fashion*, Lexington, Mass.: Lexington Books: 161–76.

Grant, L. (1992) 'Can Calvin Klein escape', *Los Angeles Times Magazine*, 23 February: 16–22.

Griggers, C. (1990) 'A certain tension in the visual/cultural field: Helmut Newton, Deborah Turbeville, and the *Vogue* fashion layout', *Differences*, 2, 2: 76–104.

Hall, C. (1985) *The Forties in Vogue*, London: Octopus Books.

Hall-Duncan, N. (1979) *The History of Fashion Photography*, New York: Alpine Book Co. Inc.

Hamilton, A. (1992) 'Vintage Levi's fetch $19,000', *Australian*, 9 September: 12.

Hanson, K. (1990) 'Dressing down dressing up – the philosophic fear of fashion', *Hypatia*, 5, 2, Summer: 107–21.

Harrison, M. (1985) 'Introduction', in D. Bailey, *Shots of Style*, London: Victoria & Albert Museum: 13–55.

—— (1991) *Appearances: Fashion Photography Since 1945*, London: Jonathan Cape.

Hart, A. (1984) 'Men's dress', in N. Rothstein (ed.), *Four Hundred Years of Fashion*, London: Victoria & Albert Museum: 49–75.

Hart, J. (1985) 'What's wrong with fashion photography?', *Creative Camera*, 252, December: 27–9.

Hartman, R. (1980) *Birds of Paradise: An Intimate View of the New York Fashion World*, New York: Delta.

Haug, W. (1986) *Critique of Commodity Aesthetics*, Cambridge: Polity Press.

Hay, L. (1976) *Management and Design in the Women's Fashion Industry*, London: Design Council.

Healy, R. (1992) *Balenciaga: Masterpieces of Fashion Design*, Melbourne: National Gallery of Victoria.

Hesse-Biber, S. (1991) 'Women, weight and eating disorders', *Women's Studies International Forum*, 14, 3: 173–91.

Hoch, P. (1979) *White Hero, Black Beast*, London: Pluto Press.

Holland, N. (1992) 'Fashioning Cuba', in A. Parker, M. Russo, D. Sommer and P. Yaeger (eds), *Nationalisms and Sexualities*, New York and London: Routledge: 147–56.

Hollander, A. (1980) *Seeing Through Clothes*, New York: Avon Books.

Horin, A. (1983) 'What price corporate feminism?', *National Times*, 29 July–4 August: 8.

Howell, G. (1991) 'Shock, skill and signature stubble, designer Jean Paul Gaultier on show', *Vogue Australia*, August: 144–51; 166–2.

Huck, P. (1991) 'Speedo: the world's cossie', *Australian Financial Review*, 6 September: 36.

Hume, M. (1992) 'Girdles on top', *Elle* (UK), April: 144.

Imrie, T. (1984) 'Double page dream', *British Journal of Photography Annual*: 27–33.

—— (1986) 'Pure new wool: a photo campaign for the mid-80s', *British Journal of Photography Annual*: 8–11.

Isozaki, A. (1978) 'What are clothes? . . . A fundamental question', in Issey Miyake, *East Meets West*, Tokyo: Heibonsha: 54–6.

James, S. (1984) *The Princess of Wales Fashion Handbook*, London: Orbis Publishing.

Joel, A. (1984) *Best Dressed: 200 Years of Fashion in Australia*, Sydney: Collins.

Johnson, L. (1990) 'The patriarchal economies in the Australian textile industry', *Antipode*, 22, 1: 1–32.

Jones, L.-A. (1992) 'Naomi: supermodel, superstar', *Sunday Mail Magazine*, 26 July: 10–11.

Jones, T. (1992) 'Rei Kawakubo: Comme des Garçons', *i-D*, 104, May: 72–3.

Jordan, A. (1965) 'Healthy dress for men', in M.E. Roach and J. Eicher (eds), *Dress, Adornment and the Social Order*, New York: John Wiley & Sons: 302–7.

Keenan, B. (1977) *The Women We Wanted to Look Like*, London: Macmillan.

Kennett, F. (1975) *History of Perfume*, London: Harrap.

Khan, N. (1992) 'Asian women's dress: from Burqah to Bloggs – changing clothes for changing times', in J. Ash and E. Wilson (eds), *Chic Thrills*, London: Pandora Press: 61–74.

Kidwell, C. (1968) 'Women's bathing and swimming costume in the United States', *United States National Museum Bulletin 250, Paper 64*, Washington, DC: US Government Printing Office: 3–32.

—— (1989) 'Gender symbols or fashionable details?', in C. Kidwell and V. Steele (eds), *Men and Women: Dressing the Part*, Washington, DC: Smithsonian Institution Press: 124–43.

Kidwell, C. and Christman, M. (1974) *Suiting Everyone: The Democratisation of Clothing in America*, Washington, DC: Smithsonian Institution Press.

Kidwell, C. and Steele, V. (eds) (1989) *Men and Women: Dressing the Part*, Washington, DC: Smithsonian Institution Press.

Kirk, M. (1969) 'New Guinea festival of faces', *National Geographic Magazine*, 136 (1): 148–56.

Kohn, M. (1989) 'The best uniforms', in A. McRobbie (ed.), *Zoot Suits and Second-Hand Dresses*, Basingstoke, Hampshire: Macmillan: 141–9.

König, R. (1973) *The Restless Image*, London: Allen & Unwin.

Koren, L. (1984) *New Fashion Japan*, Tokyo and New York: Kodansha International.

Kroeber, A.L. (1919) 'On the principle of order in civilisation as exemplified by changes in fashion', *American Anthropologist*, 21: 235–63.

Kroker, A. and Kroker, M. (eds) (1987) *Body Invaders: Panic Sex in America*, New York: St Martins.

Kunzle, D. (1977) 'Dress reform as antifeminism: a response to Helene E. Robert's "The exquisite slave: the role of clothes in the making of the Victorian woman"', *Signs*, 2, 3: 570–9.

—— (1982) *Fashion and Fetishism*, Totowa, N.J.: Rowman & Littlefield.

Lang, K. and Lang, G. (1965) 'Fashion and fashion leadership', in M.E. Roach and J. Eicher (eds), *Dress, Adornment and the Social Order*, New York: John Wiley & Sons: 322–46.

Laver, J. (1968) *Dandies*, London: Weidenfeld & Nicolson.

—— (1985) *Costume and Fashion: A Concise History*, London: Thames & Hudson.

Lawson, V. (1990) 'Appearance money', *Sydney Morning Herald Good Weekend Magazine*, 31 March: 28–33.

Leach, E. (1958) 'Magical hair', *Royal Anthropological Institute of Great Britain and Ireland*, 88: 142–64.

Leach, W. (1984) 'Transformations in a culture of consumption: women and department stores 1890–1925', *Journal of American History*, 71, 2, September: 322–30.

Lees, C. (1988) 'Good looks, bigger bucks', *Bulletin*, 5 July: 124–5.

Lemire, B. (1990) 'The theft of clothes and popular consumerism in early modern England', *Journal of Social History*, 24, 2: 255–76.

Leopold, E. (1992) 'The manufacture of the fashion system', in J. Ash and E. Wilson (eds), *Chic Thrills*, London: Pandora Press: 101–17.

Lester, E. (1992) 'Buying the exotic "other": reading the "banana republic" mail order catalog', *Journal of Communication Inquiry*, 16, 2: 74–85.

Lévi-Strauss, C. (1969) 'The art of Asia and America', in *Structural Anthropology*, London: Allen Lane: 245–68.

—— (1973) *Totemism*, Harmondsworth: Penguin.

—— (1976) *Tristes Tropiques*, Harmondsworth: Penguin.

Lloyd, D. (1988) 'Assemblage and subculture: the casuals and their clothing', in J. Ash and L. Wright (eds), *Components of Dress*, London: Routledge: 100–6.

Lloyd, V. (1986) *The Art of Vogue Photographic Covers*, London: Octopus Books.

Logan, L. (1992) 'The geographical imagination of Frederic Remington: the invention of the cowboy west', *Journal of Historical Geography*, 18, 1: 75–90.

Lowe, E. and Lowe, J. (1985) 'Quantitative analysis of women's dress', in M. Solomon (ed.), *The Psychology of Fashion*, Lexington, Mass.: Lexington Books: 193–206.

Lynch, M. (1987) 'The body: thin is beautiful', *Arena*, 79: 128–45.

Lyons, J. (1992) 'Elle and the body politic', *Sydney Morning Herald Good Weekend Magazine*, 3 October: 10–21.

McCarthy, P. (1990) 'The single girl's best friend', *Sydney Morning Herald Good Weekend Magazine*, 5 May: 58–63.

McCracken, G. (1985) 'The trickle-down theory rehabilitated', in M. Solomon (ed.), *The Psychology of Fashion*, Lexington, Mass.: Lexington Books: 39–54.

—— (1990) *Culture and Consumption: New Approaches to the Symbolic Character of Consumer Goods and Activities*, Bloomington and Indianapolis: Indiana University Press.

McDowell, C. (1984) *McDowell's Directory of Twentieth Century Fashion*, London: Frederick Muller.

McLean, P. (1991) 'Perfume wars', *Sunday Mail Magazine*, 13 January: 2.

MacLeod, A. (1992) 'Hegemonic relations and gender resistance: the new veiling as accommodating protest in Cairo', *Signs*, 17, 3: 533–57.

McRobbie, A. (1984) 'Dance and social fantasy', in A. McRobbie and M. Nava (eds), *Gender and Generation*, London: Macmillan: 130–61.

—— (1989a) 'Second-hand dresses and the role of the ragmarket', in A. McRobbie (ed.), *Zoot Suits and Second-Hand Dresses*, Basingstoke, Hampshire: Macmillan: 23–49.

—— (1989b) (ed.) *Zoot Suits and Second-Hand Dresses*, Basingstoke, Hampshire: Macmillan.

McRobbie, A. and Nava, M. (eds) (1984) *Gender and Generation*, London: Macmillan.

Mansfield, S. (1992) 'We can always get what we want', *Advertiser*, 4 January: 2.

Martin, R. and Koda, H. (1990) *Splash! A History of Swimwear*, New York: Rizzoli.

Martyn, N. (1976) *The Look: Australian Women in their Fashion*, Australia: Cassell.

Matura, R. (1978) 'A manufacturer's view of fashion management life styles', in E. Richards and D. Rachmann (eds), *Market Information and Research in Fashion Management*, Chicago: American Marketing Association: 2–4.

Mauss, M. (1973) 'Techniques of the body', *Economy and Society*, 2, 1: 70–87.

—— (1979) *Sociology and Psychology*, London: RKP.

—— (1985) 'A category of the human mind: the notion of person; the notion of self', in M. Carrithers, S. Collins and S. Lukes (eds), *The Category of Person*, Cambridge: Cambridge University Press: 1–25.

Mayer, R. and Belk, R. (1985) 'Fashion and impression formation among children', in M. Soloman (ed.), *The Psychology of Fashion*, Lexington, Mass.: Lexington Books: 293–308.

Maynard, M. (1986) 'Fashion', catalogue for exhibition of fashion plates, 16 August–3 September, Brisbane: Cintra House Galleries.

Mazrui, A. (1970) 'The robes of rebellion', *Encounter*, 34, 2: 19–30.

Midgley, D. (1973) 'The seamless stocking saga', in G. Wills and D. Midgley (eds), *Fashion Marketing*, London: Allen & Unwin: 415–31.

Miller, T. (1990) 'Sport, media and masculinity', in D. Rowe and G. Lawrence (eds), *Sport and Leisure*, Sydney: Harcourt Brace Jovanovich: 74–95.

Millum, T. (1975) *Images of Women: Advertising in Women's Magazines*, London: Chatto & Windus.

Minchinton, W. (1982) 'Convention, fashion and consumption: aspects of British experience since 1750', in H. Baudet and H. van der Meulen (eds), *Consumer Behaviour and Economic Growth in the Modern Economy*, London: Croom Helm: 209–31.

Miyake, I. (1978) *East Meets West*, Tokyo: Heibonsha.

Moers, E. (1960) *The Dandy: Brummell to Beerbohm*, Lincoln and London: University of Nebraska Press.

Morgan, K. (1991) 'Women and the knife: cosmetic surgery and the colonization of women's bodies', *Hypatia*, 6, 3, Fall: 25–53.

Morgenson, G. (1991) 'How Mattel models a money magnet', *Business Review Weekly*, 1 February: 55–6.

Mort, F. (1988) 'Boys own? Masculinity, style and popular culture', in R. Chapman and J. Rutherford (eds), *Male Order*, London: Lawrence & Wishart: 193–224.

Moss, E. (1978) 'Adjusting fashion management to the new life style', in E. Richards and D. Rachman (eds), *Market Information and Research in Fashion Management*, Chicago: American Marketing Association: 34–40.

Mulvey, L. (1975) 'Visual pleasure and narrative cinema', *Screen*, 16, 3: 6–18.

Murray, D. and Deabler, H. (1957) 'Colors and mood-tones', *Journal of Applied Psychology*, 41, 5: 278–83.

Myers, K. (1987) 'Fashion 'n' passion', in R. Betterton (ed.), *Looking On: Images of Women in the Visual Arts*, London: Pandora: 58–65.

Myers, P. and Biocca, F. (1992) 'The elastic body image: the effect of television advertising and programming on body image distortions in young women', *Journal of Communication*, 42, 3: 108–33.

Nag, D. (1991) 'Fashion, gender and the Bengali middle class', *Public Culture*, 3, 2: 93–112.

Nava, M. (1991) 'Consumerism reconsidered: buying and power', *Cultural Studies*, 5, 2: 157–73.

Newton, S.M. (1974) *Health, Art and Reason. Dress Reformers of the 19th Century*, London: John Murray.

—— (1975) 'Fashions in fashion history', *Times Literary Supplement*, 21 March: 305.

Nicklin, L. (1984) 'How Japan captured Paris and Fifth Avenue', *Bulletin*, 15 May: 58–62.

—— (1990) 'The man who re-dressed the Australian man', *Bulletin*, 21 August: 46–7.

Norwood, S. (1987) 'Dressed for success', *Australian Accountant*, 57, 10, November: 35–8.

Nystrom, P. (1973) 'Character and directions of fashion movements', in G. Wills and D. Midgley (eds), *Fashion Marketing*, London: Allen & Unwin: 193–205.

Ogilvy, D. (1963) *Confessions of an Advertising Man*, London: Mayflower-Dell.

O'Hanlon, M. (1983) 'Handsome is as handsome does: display and betrayal in the Wahgi', *Oceania*, 53, 4: 317–33.

Paoletti, J. (1985) 'Ridicule and role models as factors in American men's fashion change 1880–1910', *Costume*, 29: 121–34.

Paoletti, J. and Kregloh, C. (1989) 'The children's department', in C. Kidwell and V. Steele (eds), *Men and Women: Dressing the Part*, Washington, DC: Smithsonian Institution Press: 22–41.

Partington, A. (1992) 'Popular fashion and working-class affluence', in J. Ash and E. Wilson (eds), *Chic Thrills*, London: Pandora Press: 145–61.

Penn, I. (1988) *Issey Miyake: Photographs by Irving Penn*, Boston: A New York Graphic Society Book.

Perkins, Z. and Woram, C. (1991/2) 'Say chic', *Studio Collections*, Spring/Summer: 34–7.

Perna, R. (1978) 'A national chain looks at fashion management', in E. Richards and D. Rachman (eds), *Market Information and Research in Fashion Management*, Chicago: American Advertising Association: 41–5.

Perrot, P. (1981) 'Suggestions for a different approach to the history of dress', *Diogenes*, 114: 157–76.

Perrottet, T. (1993) 'Inside Miss Universe Inc', *Sydney Morning Herald Good Weekend Magazine*, 9 January: 18.

Phizacklea, A. (1990) *Unpacking the Fashion Industry*, London: Routledge.

Polhemus, T. and Proctor, L. (1978) *Fashion and Anti-Fashion*, London: Thames & Hudson.

Pollard, J. (1963) *Swimming: Australian Style*, Melbourne: Lansdowne Press.

Pollock, G. (1977) 'What's wrong with images of women?', *Screen Education*, 24: 25–33.

Poole, R. (1973) 'Introduction', in C. Lévi-Strauss, *Totemism*, Harmondsworth: Penguin: 9–63.

Pooser, D. (1987) *Always in Style with Colour*, Crows Nest: Little Hills Press.

Probert, C. (1981) *Swimwear in Vogue since 1910*, New York: Condé Nast Publications.

Pumphrey, M. (1987) 'The flapper, the housewife and the making of modernity', *Cultural Studies*, 1, 2: 179–94.

—— (1989) 'Why do cowboys wear hats in the bath? Style politics for the older man', *Critical Quarterly*, 31, 3, Autumn: 78–100.

Quant, M. (1967) *Quant by Quant*, London: Pan Books.

—— (1986) *Quant on Make-up*, London: Century Hutchison Ltd.

Radner, H. (1989) '"This time's for me": Making up and feminine practice', *Cultural Studies*, 3, 3: 301–22.

Reekie, G. (1987) 'Sydney's big stores 1880–1930: gender and mass marketing', unpublished PhD thesis, University of Sydney.

—— (1991) 'Impulsive women: predictable men: psychological constructions of sexual difference in sales literature to 1930', *Australian Historical Studies*, 97, October: 359–77.

—— (1993) *Temptations: Sex, Selling and the Department Store*, Sydney: Allen and Unwin.

Richards, E. and Rachman, D. (eds) (1978) *Market Information and Research in Fashion Management*, Chicago: American Marketing Association.

Richardson, J. and Kroeber, A.L. (1940) 'Three centuries of women's dress fashions: a quantitative analysis', *Anthropological Records*, 5, 2: 235–63.

Richie, D. (1973) 'The Japanese art of tattooing', *Natural History*, December: 50–9.

Roach, M.E. and Eicher, J. (eds) (1965) *Dress, Adornment and the Social Order*, New York: John Wiley & Sons.

Roberts, H.E. (1977) 'The exquisite slave: the role of clothes in the making of the Victorian woman', *Signs*, 2, 3: 554–69.

Robinson, D. (1958) 'Fashion theory and product design', *Harvard Business Review*, 36, 6, November–December: 126–38.

—— (1961) 'The economics of fashion demand', *Quarterly Journal of Economics*, 75, 3, August: 376–98.

—— (1973) 'Fashion theory and product design', in G. Wills and D. Midgley (eds), *Fashion Marketing*, London: Allen & Unwin: 433–50.

—— (1975) 'Style changes: cyclical, inexorable and foreseeable', *Harvard Business Review*, 53, 6, November–December: 121–31.

—— (1976) 'Fashions in shaving and trimming of the beard: the men of the *Illustrated London News*, 1842–1972', *American Journal of Sociology*, 81, 5: 1133–41.

Robinson, G. (1983) 'Designer discounts: a boom for fashion', *National Times*, 15–21 July: 44.

Robinson, J. (1976) *The Golden Age of Style*, New York and London: Harcourt Brace Jovanovich.

—— (1986) 'Clothing', in *Made in Australia*, Sydney: William Heinemann Australia.

—— (n.d.) *The Fine Art of Fashion: An Illustrated History*, Kensington, NSW: Bay Books.

Roderick, I. (1992) 'Uniting the colours of Benetton: an ethnographic romance', Paper presented to the Symposium on Marginal Practice: Marginal Theory, Centre for Research on Culture and Society, Carleton University, Ottawa, Canada, 20–21 March.

Rook, D. (1985) 'Body cathexis and market segmentation', in M. Solomon (ed.), *The Psychology of Fashion*, Lexington, Mass.: Lexington Books: 233–42.

Rothstein, N. (ed.) (1984) *Four Hundred Years of Fashion*, London: Victoria & Albert Museum.

Rubinstein, H. (1972) *My Life for Beauty*, New York: Paperback Library.

Rubinstein, R. (1985) 'Color, circumcision, tattoos, and scars', in M. Solomon (ed.), *The Psychology of Fashion*, Lexington, Mass.: Lexington Books: 243–54.

Rudolph, B. (1991) 'The supermodels', *Time*, 6, 37, 16 September: 70–6.

Ruehl, P. (1988) 'Advertising goes for new improved sexism', *Australian Financial Review*, 20, September: 1, 8.

Rutherford, J. (1988) 'Who's that man?', in R. Chapman and J. Rutherford (eds), *Male Order*, London: Lawrence & Wishart: 21–67.

Rutt, R. (1990) 'The Englishman's swimwear', *Costume*, 24: 69–84.

Safe, M. (1990) 'Model children', *Sydney Morning Herald Good Weekend Magazine*, 16–17 June: 20–7.

Sahlins, M. (1976) *Culture and Practical Reason*, Chicago and London: The University of Chicago Press.

Saint Laurent, Y. (1983) *Yves Saint Laurent*, New York: The Metropolitan Museum of Art.

Saisselin, R. (1959–60) 'From Baudelaire to Christian Dior: the poetics of fashion', *Journal of Aesthetics and Art Criticism*, 18, 1, September: 109–15.

Sanders, J. (1992) 'Dress and textiles', in J. Broadbent and J. Hughes (eds), *The Age of Macquarie*, Melbourne: Melbourne University Press: 143–56.

Sapir, E. (1931) 'Fashion', *Encyclopaedia of the Social Sciences*, 5: 139–44.

Sawchuk, K. (1987) 'A tale of inscription/fashion statements', in A. Kroker and M. Kroker (eds), *Body Invaders: Panic Sex in America*, New York: St Martins: 61–77.

Scheuring, D. (1989) 'Heavy duty denim: "quality never dates"', in A. McRobbie (ed.), *Zoot Suits and Second-Hand Dresses*, Basingstoke, Hampshire: Macmillan: 225–36.

Schneider, J. (1987) 'The anthropology of cloth', *Annual Review of Anthropology*, 16: 409–48.

Schreier, B. (1989) 'Sporting wear', in C. Kidwell and V. Steele (eds), *Men and Women: Dressing the Part*, Washington, DC: Smithsonian Institution Press: 92–123.

Seebohm, C. (1982) *The Man who was 'Vogue'*, London: Weidenfeld & Nicolson.

Seidler, V. (1989) *Rediscovering Masculinity*, London: Routledge.

Sheehan, P. (1986) 'Why were we born so beautiful?', *Sydney Morning Herald Good Weekend Magazine*, 29 November: 62–5.

Sheridan, S. (ed.) (1988) *Grafts: Feminist Cultural Criticism*, London: Verso.

Sherrill, M. (1992) 'The once and future model', *Allure*, June: 88–9, 114.

Shields, V.R. (1990) 'Advertising visual images: gendered ways of seeing and looking', *Journal of Communication Inquiry*, 14, 2, Summer: 25–39.

Shorter, E. (1982) 'The architecture of the body', in *The History of Women's Bodies*, London: Allen Lane: 17–31.

Shrimpton, J. (1965) *The Truth About Modelling*, New York: Bantam Books.

—— (1990) *Jean Shrimpton: An autobiography*, London: Ebury Press.

Sillitoe, P. (1988) 'From head-dresses to head-messages: the art of self-decoration in the highlands of Papua New Guinea', *Man*, 23, 2, June: 298–318.

Silmon, P. (1986) *Bikini*, London: Virgin Books.

Silverman, K. (1986) 'Fragments of a fashionable discourse', in T. Modleski (ed.), *Studies in Entertainment*, Bloomington and Indianapolis: Indiana University Press: 139–52.

Simmel, G. (1973) 'Fashion', in G. Wills and D. Midgley (eds), *Fashion Marketing*, London: Allen & Unwin: 171–91.

Simmonds, D. (1987) 'Diana and Sarah: images of ourselves', *Australian Left Review*, 99, Autumn: 13–18.

Sinclair, J. (1973) *Wigmen of Papua*, Milton: Jacaranda Press.

Soden, D. (1991) 'Dickinson seeks bargains in print', *B & T*, 19 April: 7, 33.

Soh, C-H. (1992) 'Skirts, trousers, or *hanbok*? The politics of image making among Korean women legislators', *Women's Studies International Forum*, 15, 3: 375–84.

Soloman, M. (ed.) (1985) *The Psychology of Fashion*, Lexington, Mass.: Lexington Books.

Sontag, S. (1978) 'The Avedon eye', *Vogue* (UK), December: 174–7.

Spencer, N. (1992) 'Menswear in the 1980s', in J. Ash and E. Wilson (eds), *Chic Thrills*, London: Pandora Press: 40–8.

Squiers, C. (1980) 'Slouch, stretch, smile and leap', *Artforum*, November: 46–54.

Squires, W. (1991) 'Model mafia', *Mode*, September: 72–6.

Stead, K. (1991) 'Heists of fashion', *Australian Magazine*, 22–3 June: 34–41.

—— (n.d.) 'Women of the cloth', *Sydney Morning Herald Good Weekend Magazine*, 50–3.

Steele, V. (1985a) *Fashion and Eroticism: Ideals of Feminine Beauty from the Victorian Era to the Jazz Age*, New York: Oxford University Press.

—— (1985b) 'The social and political significance of Macaroni fashion', *Costume*, 19: 94–109.

—— (1988) *Paris Fashion*, Oxford: Oxford University Press.

—— (1989a) 'Appearance and identity', in C. Kidwell and V. Steele (eds), *Men and Women: Dressing the Part*, Washington, DC: Smithsonian Institution Press: 6–21.

—— (1989b) 'Clothing and sexuality', in C. Kidwell and V. Steele (eds), *Men and Women: Dressing the Part*, Washington, DC: Smithsonian Institution Press: 42–63.

—— (1989c) 'Dressing for work', in C. Kidwell and V. Steele (eds), *Men and Women: Dressing the Part*, Washington, DC: Smithsonian Institution Press: 64–91.

—— (1991) *Women of Fashion*, New York: Rizzoli.

—— (1992) 'Chanel in context', in J. Ash and E. Wilson (eds), *Chic Thrills*, London: Pandora Press: 118–26.

Stephen, A. (1983) 'Mass produced photography in Australia during the inter-war years', *Art Network*, 9, Autumn: 40.

Storace, P. (1991) 'Man talk', *Allure*, November: 42.

Strathern, A. (1987) 'Dress, decoration, and art in New Guinea', in M. Kirk, *Man as Art: New Guinea Body Decoration*, London: Thames & Hudson: 15–36.

Strathern, M. (1979) 'The self in self-decoration', *Oceania*, 48: 241–57.

Sturman, S. (1978) 'Information systems and Warner's slimwear', in E. Richards and D. Rachman (eds), *Market Information and Research in Fashion Management*, Chicago: American Marketing Association: 18–22.

Symons, S. (1987) 'The Great Travelling YSL Roadshow', *Sydney Morning Herald Good Weekend Magazine*, 16 May: 16–21.

Synnott, A. (1990) 'Truth and goodness, mirrors and masks. Part II: a sociology of beauty and the face', *British Journal of Sociology*, 41, 1: 55–76.

Tausk, P. (1973) 'Mutual influences between photography and painting', *British Journal of Photography Annual*: 148–61.

Taylor, A.L. (1983) 'Rough times in the rag trade', *Time*, 29 August: 42–4.

Taylor, L. (1983) *Mourning Dress: A Costume and Social History*, London: George Allen & Unwin.

—— (1992) 'Paris couture, 1940–1944', in J. Ash and E. Wilson (eds), *Chic Thrills*, London: Pandora Press: 127–44.

Taylor Fleming, A. (1991) 'Living dolls', *Allure*, March: 128–33.

Tolman, R. (1969) *Beautician's Guide to Beauty, Charm, Poise*, Bronx, N.Y.: Milady Publishing Corporation.

Tomlinson, A. (ed.) (1990) *Consumption, Identity and Style*, London: Routledge.

Tredre, R. (1992a) 'Fashion industry poised to show who wears the trousers', *Independent*, 1 April: 8.

—— (1992b) 'See, it can be cool to slouch', *Independent*, 9 April: 17.

Triggs, T. (1992) 'Framing masculinity. Herb Ritts, Bruce Weber and the Body Perfect', in J. Ash and E. Wilson (eds), *Chic Thrills*, London: Pandora Press: 25–9.

Tulloch, C. (1992) 'Rebel without a pause: black street style and black designers', in J. Ash and E. Wilson (eds), *Chic Thrills*, London: Pandora Press: 84–98.

Turner, B. (1984) *The Body and Society*, Oxford: Basil Blackwell.

—— (1990) 'The talking disease: Hilda Bruch and anorexia nervosa', *Australian and New Zealand Journal of Sociology*, 26, 2: 157–69.

Turner, T. (1969) 'Tchikrin: a Central Brazilian tribe and its symbolic language of bodily adornment', *Natural History*, October: 50–70.

Twiggy (1975) *Twiggy: An Autobiography*, London: Hart-Davis, MacGibbon.

Ucko, P. (1969) 'Penis sheaths: a comparative study', *Proceedings of the Royal Anthropological Institute of Great Britain and Ireland*: 27–68.

United Airlines (1992) 'Duty Free Catalogue'.

Upton, K. (1989) 'Scented journey', *Vogue* (Australia), November: 150–1; 204, 206.

Veblen, T. (1970) *The Theory of the Leisure Class*, London: Allen & Unwin.

Venables, D.R. and Clifford, R.E. (1973) 'Academic dress', in M. Douglas (ed.), *Rules and Meanings*, Harmondsworth: Penguin:

Walkerdine, V. (1984) 'Some day my prince will come', in A. McRobbie and M. Nava (eds), *Gender and Generation*, London: Macmillan: 162–84.

Walsh, M. (1979) 'The democratization of fashion: the emergence of the women's dress pattern industry', *Journal of American History*, 66, 2, September: 299–313.

Wark, McK. (1991) 'Fashioning the future: fashion, clothing, and the manufacturing of post-Fordist culture', *Cultural Studies*, 5, 1: 61–76.

Warneminde, M. (1991) 'Fakes: the futile fight', *Bulletin*, 8 October: 36–41.

Warner, P. (1988) 'Public and private: men's influence on American women's dress for sport and physical education', *Dress: The Journal of the American Costume Society*, 14: 48–55.

Wass, B. (1979) 'Yoruba dress in five generations of a Lagos family', in J. Cordwell and R. Schwarz (eds), *The Fabrics of Culture*, The Hague, Paris, New York: Mouton: 331–48.

Weibel, K. (1977) *Mirror Mirror: Images of Women Reflected in Popular Culture*, New York: Anchor Books.

Wells, L. (1991) 'Barbie backlash', *Allure*, November: 14.

Wexner, L. (1954) 'The degree to which colors (hues) are associated with mood-tones', *Journal of Applied Psychology*, 38, 6: 432–35.

White, C.L. (1970) *Women's Magazines 1693–1968*, London: Michael Joseph.

White, P. (1973) *Poiret*, London: Studio Vista.

—— (1986) *Elsa Schiaparelli: Empress of Paris Fashion*, London: Aurum Press.

Wilde, W.H. (1988) *Courage a Grace*, Melbourne: Melbourne University Press.

Williams, D. (1989) '90 years of Aussie cossies', *Sunday Mail Magazine*, 29 January: 42–3.

Williams, R. (1982) *Dream Worlds: Mass Consumption in Late Nineteenth-Century France*, Berkeley: University of California Press.

Williams, S. (1990) 'Non-fluff, glossy, how-to – and more and more', *Bulletin*, 10 April: 84–6.

Wills, G. and Midgley, D. (eds) (1973) *Fashion Marketing*, London: Allen & Unwin.

Wilson, E. (1985) *Adorned in Dreams: Fashion and Modernity*, London: Virago.

—— (1992) 'Fashion and the postmodern body', in J. Ash and E. Wilson (eds), *Chic Thrills*, London: Pandora Press: 3–16.

Windschuttle, E. (1980) 'The new science of etiquette', *The Push*, 7: 58–80.

Winship, J. (1978) 'A woman's world: "woman" – an ideology of femininity', in Women's Studies Group, *Women Take Issue*, London: Hutchinson: 133–54.

—— (1987) *Inside Women's Magazines*, London: Pandora Press.

—— (1991) 'The impossibility of *Best*: enterprise meets domesticity in the practical women's magazine of the 1980s', *Cultural Studies*, 5, 2, May: 131–56.

Wolf, N. (1991) *The Beauty Myth*, London: Vintage.

Women's Studies Group (1978) *Women Take Issue*, London: Hutchinson.

Woolson, A. (ed.) (1974) *Dress-Reform*, New York: Arno Press.

Wright, T. (1922) *The Romance of the Shoe* (Being the History of Shoemaking), London: C.J. Farncombe & Sons.

Wyndham, S. (1990) 'The business of being Elle', *Australian Magazine*, 14–15 April: 20–6.

Yaeger Kaplan, A. (1987) 'Taste wars: American professions of French culture', *Yale French Studies*, 73: 156–72.

Yarwood, D. (1982) *The Encyclopedia of World Costume*, New York: Charles Scribner & Sons.

Yeatman, A. (1990) *Bureaucrats, Technocrats, Femocrats*, Sydney, Wellington, London, Boston: Allen & Unwin.

Name index

Subject index

also fashion catalogues
designers 7, 13, 56, 58–9, 60–1, 74, 97,
108, 165, 167, 192,195, 211, 213, 215,
223; women 61; *see also* elite fashion;
haute couture
dieting 65–9, 80, 84–5, 87, 118, 158; *see
also* anorexia nervosa; bulimia nervosa

eighteenth-century dress 12, 47–9, 181,
195, 205
elite fashion 15, 211, 221, 225
ethnic influences in fashion 36–43
etiquette 11, 55, 62–4, 115–17, 161, 176,
180; guides 47–55; for men 180, 186, 188
European: culture 154, 156, 158, 164,
176, 178–85, 189; dress 157, 190, 195;
fashion 3, 17; 'looks' 59–60; *see also*
Western dress; Western fashion
everyday fashion 59, 210–12, 213, 225
exoticism, in fashion 17–43, 155, 162,
169, 223

fabrics: made from artificial fibres 129,
131, 141, 147, 189; knitted 119, 141,
146; linen 119; lycra 129, 141; rayon
129, 141; silk 119, 129, 131, 200; used
in swimwear 138, 139, 141, 143–4,
147, 149
fashion: definitions of 2, 5–6; catalogues 74,
77, 144, 189, 207–9; custom 9; editors
59–60, 92, 97, 100, 108; failures 14;
systems of 5, 13, 16, 17, 43, 44–7
fashion industry 74, 100, 108, 194, 200,
208, 209, 210, 217; counterfeiting 213
fashion models 70, 73–91, 131; and
catwalk (runway) modelling 79–80;
demoiselles de magasin 76–7;
exclusive contracts 89–90; male 133,
203; *see also* photographic modelling;
supermodels
female: being 44–69; pleasure 9, 112,
114; role models 70–91
feminine, being 44–69
femininity 13, 32, 35, 44, 70–91, 157–8,
161, 162–3, 164, 290–10, 219, 221;
techniques of 44–69, 92, 101–14, 115–18
feminism: and career dressing 30; and
corsetry 125; feminist critiques of fashion
53–5, 109, 111–14, 116; and 'femocrat'
dressing 11; and masculinity 197
folk dress/costume 36–8

gendered consumption 70–91, 127, 192,
194, 199, 209
Gibson Girl 73–4, 76, 123, 165, 189

habitus: and body 23, 76, 136, 209; and
body decoration 154, 156, 157, 162,
164, 165, 168, 223, 225; and culture
155; definition of 4, 9; and fashion
10–15, 58, 64, 66, 69
hanbok 29
haute couture 41, 59, 105, 210, 211, 213,
223; *see also* elite fashion
high street fashion 13–14, 60, 162, 213
Hollywood 7, 15, 74–5, 101, 146, 148,
151, 160, 161, 209, 215
homosexuality 179, 191

India: dress in 28, 30–6; Indian fashion
38–9
Islamic cultures: dress in 29; use of veil in
29

Japan: fashion designers 40–1; use of
cosmetics 156; *see also* tattooing in
Japan
jeans 194–6, 215, 217, 219; Levi jeans
194–5, 215

Kenya 28
Korea, dress in 29–30, 39, 221, 223
kurtas 35, 38

lingerie 12, 127, 129, 146, 151

Macaronis 182–3
magazines: covers 18, 100; fashion 9, 98,
111, 144, 192–3, 206; in India 35–6;
women's 9, 47–55, 209
make-up *see* cosmetics
male fashion 13, 44–5, 115–16, 176–203;
dress reform 189, 190; history of 176,
178; men's underwear 131–6; neckties
185, 188, 189, 190, 203, 221; and
public status 179; shaving 178; shorts
189–90; skirt for men 200, 203; suits
181, 185, 186–8 189–92, 203, 217;
work clothes 186, 192, 197
masculinity 13, 91, 101, 114, 131–6,
172–3, 176–203; changing ideas of
gender 178; male bodies 131; male
sexuality 114, 131–6, 176, 192, 195